# Adobe® Acrobat® 8
## in the Office

DONNA L. BAKER

Adobe

**Adobe® Acrobat® 8 in the Office**
Donna L. Baker

This Adobe Press book is published by Peachpit.

**Peachpit**
1249 Eighth Street
Berkeley, CA 94710
510/524-2178, 510/524-2221 (fax)
www.adobepress.com

Peachpit Press is a division of Pearson Education.
For the latest on Adobe Press books, go to www.adobepress.com.

To report errors, please send a note to errata@peachpit.com.

Copyright © 2007 by Donna L. Baker

Project Editor: Karyn Johnson
Developmental Editor: Anne Marie Walker
Production Editor: Hilal Sala
Technical Editors: Tom Carson, Stephen Bird
Compositor: Danielle Foster
Proofreader: Kim Carlson
Indexer: Jack Lewis, j & j indexing
Interior designers: Charlene Charles-Will, Karen Kemp
Cover Design: Charlene Charles-Will

ISBN 0-321-47080-X

9 8 7 6 5 4 3 2 1

Printed and bound in the United States of America

*For Ernie and for Janis—*
*two of the strongest people I know*

# Acknowledgments

Thanks to Terry for being the profoundly patient man that he is. Thanks to my girl Erin for her ongoing encouragement. Thanks to Daisy and Abby for keeping me company and for inspiring project heroines. Thanks to Deena for keeping me youthful, and to Tom Waits for keeping me soulful.

Kudos to the Peachpit team. This book is a glowing testament to what they can do in spite of my best efforts to throw serious wrenches—multiple fractures and a laptop dying an excruciating death on the road—into the works. Many thanks to Anne Marie Walker, my star developmental editor and source of amusing tidbits; Karyn Johnson, project editor and keeper of the path; my production editor, Hilal Sala; and Becky Morgan, my biggest fan and supporter.

I'd like to thank Stephen Bird, a Canadian lawyer I met through our mutual exploration of the PDF world. Stephen graciously agreed to tech edit my legal project to ensure it was feasible and logical. I've enjoyed working with you.

Finally, I owe a special thanks to my pal and frequent collaborator, Tom Carson, who served as tech editor for this book. It's been a great project. What should we do next?

I applaud you all mentally. I'd stand up and applaud you all, but would probably fall off my crutches and break something else!

# Contents

# 3 Communicating with Comments 55

# 7 Assembling a Library 157

## 8  Communicating with Technical Drawings          181

# 9   Packaging and Preparing Legal Documents   211

# 10   Streamlining Form Development and Data Management   237

## 11 Building a Powerful Interactive Document   271

# 12 Secure Reviewing and Reporting 301

# Introduction

Ask anybody who interacts with computers and documents to describe a PDF (Portable Document Format) file. For the most part, you'll receive responses describing a format used for creating documents that look like the original, print with the layout of the original, and use the same text and images as the original. While the response is correct, it barely brushes the surface.

Do any of these situations sound familiar?

- You collaborate closely with a group of people on projects that necessitate meeting every day or so. You crowd into someone's office or cubicle, stand around his or her computer or your sketches, and try to get comfortable as you work.

- You need to send material to court presented in its native appearance, which includes redacted content, but you'd like to be able to access the contents readily.

- You're a designer and have plans you want to discuss with a client during preliminary development of the project. You want to point out several issues of importance but don't at this stage need a laundry list of detail.

- You'd like to increase your company's reach into a new market and hope to use a simple form to gather basic demographic information about your market that can be quickly collated and analyzed.

- You need to make new presentations and other business materials. You have plenty of source materials available—all that's missing is a way to unify the content and make it appear cohesive.

It may come as a surprise to learn that all these scenarios can be managed in Acrobat. You just need to know how to find them and how to use them.

# Is This Book for You?

I wrote this book from the perspective of a business person. Each project contains a scenario to give you a background of the environment and situations in which Acrobat can be used to solve a particular dilemma or produce a specific type of output. If you have issues with document control and management, this book definitely is for you. You are sure to find something that piques your interest or asks and answers the same questions you may ask yourself every day.

I have not written the book for a computer novice. I make assumptions throughout that you have experience with the software you are using in combination with Acrobat 8 Professional.

Some projects use material created in various source programs, ranging from Microsoft Word to Visio to Photoshop. You don't need the applications to follow along with the projects. On the book's companion Web site at www.donnabaker.ca/downloads.html, you'll find copies of the source files as well as PDF versions. The book assumes you are using Acrobat 8 Professional to build the projects, but anyone with Adobe Reader 7 or 8, or Acrobat versions 6–8 will be able to view and use the projects once they are created.

# Goals of This Book

Hundreds of millions of copies of Adobe Reader are in use across the planet—that is how many people could potentially see your work. With some of the new features introduced in Acrobat 8 Professional, not only can all those people see your work, but they can now interact with it as well. Acrobat 8 Professional allows you to enable a document for use in Adobe Reader 7 or 8 so users can add comments and markups to a document, digitally sign the file, and fill out and save forms. If you've ever considered the ways in which you and your colleagues usually interact with a PDF file, you'll quickly see how far-reaching the enabled documents have become.

Simply because it is so functional in such a broad range of areas, Acrobat can be very intimidating. And when you have a deadline that's fast approaching, it's even more daunting a task to figure out how Acrobat can best serve your needs.

# Using the Guide

*Adobe Acrobat 8 in the Office* is a guide to using Acrobat in your office, workplace, or home office, just as its title says. You'll find a variety of case studies and scenarios that may match your own to varying degrees. It isn't likely you'll find your exact scenario, but you'll find processes and tasks that parallel those on your to-do list. The projects show you how to make your workday more productive.

The beauty of a program like Acrobat is its cornucopia of functions and features. Not everyone has the time or the inclination to become a power user and effectively harness all those functions and features. That's where I come in. The projects identify problems, provide a task list, and then show you how a solution can be achieved using Acrobat. I encourage you to take these lessons and concepts and apply them to your own circumstances.

The scope of the book is to show you how to apply Acrobat, not how to perform common tasks like saving a document, so you won't find instructions for working in source programs. You will find information on preparing documents in other programs as they relate to use in Acrobat.

## Introducing the Experts

In order to make the book as logical and usable as possible, every effort was made to incorporate practical, feasible, and productive workflows. Two professionals from different disciplines assisted in making the projects authentic.

### Tom Carson

Tom has over 25 years of experience as a civil/environmental professional engineer. Since 1999 he has worked with Acrobat in a variety of industries, as well as all levels of government. He is currently applying Acrobat to creative learning processes in K–12 and higher education. Tom has been an ACE (Adobe Certified Expert) for Acrobat since version 4 of the program. Tom and I coauthored *Adobe Acrobat and PDF for Architecture, Engineering and Construction* (Springer, 2005) and *Adobe Acrobat 6: The Professional User's Guide* (Apress, 2004).

### Stephen Bird

Stephen Bird has been a lawyer since 1974. He joined the Lanark, Leeds & Grenville Legal Clinic in 1990 and is a member of Legal Aid Ontario's IT Advisory Committee. Since December 1993 Stephen has published more than 100 technology articles for *The Lawyer's PC* and *The Perfect Lawyer*. He is a former editor of the *CSALT Review* and a former director of the Canadian Society for the Advancement of Legal Technology. He has presented papers at Technology for Lawyers conferences and, for a change of pace, he coauthored *Recreation and the Law* (Carswell, 1993, 1997).

## How to Use This Book

This book isn't a manual, and while the scenarios can be amusing at times, it isn't a novel to be read from cover to cover. Instead, it looks at a range of scenarios that you might face in your workplace and shows you how you can use Acrobat to help solve many common workflow and document management problems.

Chapter 1, "Getting Your Bearings," describes how the program works from a functional standpoint. In this chapter, you'll see how the Acrobat program is structured and how to manipulate its features. The chapter is also designed to give you terms of reference: Acrobat has many panels, dialogs, and tools that can be used in combination or chosen based on how you like to work. The book's chapters refer to the program features but don't offer specific details on how to access them. If you are interested in working with one of Acrobat's toolbars, such as Advanced Editing, you have to know where to access the tools. Chapter 1 tells you where to find them.

A number of common Acrobat processes are used in multiple chapters, simply because they are so prevalent in Acrobat workflows. In some cases, a process is a major focus of the chapter, such as the PDF Package produced in Chapter 9, "Packaging and Preparing Legal Documents." In other projects, combining the information into a package is secondary to the work accomplished with the material after it is put in the package.

## Conventions Used in This Book

As you learn to work in Acrobat, consider how you can apply your usual work habits in the program. You are sure to find your preferred way of working, whether your preference is using shortcut menus, toolbars, or the graphic designers' mouse-click, right-hand/keystrokes, left-hand method.

I generally reference tools on toolbars and shortcut menus in the projects to make it easy to follow along, in cases where a command is only available from a menu that is included as well. Although the screen shots show the Windows version of Acrobat, the commands throughout the book are given for both Windows and Macintosh.

Here's an example of how instructions are presented in the book. Suppose you are reading about cropping a page. You can access the same command in these ways:

- Right-click (Windows)/Control-click (Macintosh) the page in the Pages panel to display the shortcut menu, and choose Crop Pages.

- Click the Options button in the Pages panel to display the menu, and choose Crop Pages.

- Choose Document > Crop Pages from the main program menu.

- Click the Crop tool on the Advanced Editing toolbar.

- Press the "C" key on the keyboard to activate the Crop tool if the single key accelerator preference is set in the General section of the Preferences dialog.

Although all these methods work equally well, describing them all for each operation throughout the book is repetitious and boring to read. When you see my description for accessing a command, usually a shortcut menu and the toolbar, substitute your favored method.

## Online Content

The chapters in this book are project based. The source material for all projects is available from the *Adobe Acrobat 8 in the Office* Web page located at www.donnabaker.ca/downloads. html.

Each chapter's projects come in multiple forms. You'll find the raw documents and the completed PDF projects on the Web site. There are usually interim PDF files, and I have provided many ancillary files, such as source images, and source Word, Excel, or other files.

 **DOWNLOAD** The files available for download are indicated in the text with an icon in the margin.

For example, in the Chapter04 folder you will find two JPG images, named Vim_coverA. jpg and Vim_coverB.jpg, which are used to build the project's PDF file. The PDF file constructed in Acrobat is named according to the chapter's project, for instance, Vim_ covers.pdf.

All chapters include project files listed prior to where they are first used in the project. However, it isn't necessary to download and work with the files for the projects to be useful. They are there to help you visualize the project details and assist you with creating the sample. Additionally, most chapters include bonus material on the Web site that provides complementary information on topics described in the chapter, or further information on the case studies.

Now, let's look at all those great Acrobat features you've heard about.

# Getting Your Bearings

1

Adobe Acrobat 8 Professional is a rare piece of genuinely multipurpose software that is many things to many people, making it difficult to define its use in a couple of words. Adobe describes Acrobat as a program designed to "Provide the essential applications and services that help knowledge workers communicate and collaborate with confidence."

That's a loaded statement if I have ever read one! As you read through the projects in this book, you'll see how the different workflows, processes, and features of Acrobat 8 Professional achieve different aspects of the program's functional statement. My goal isn't to serve as a spokesperson for Adobe but as a guide to help you understand how different aspects of Acrobat 8 output and functionality come together.

You can use Acrobat 8 Professional for combining different types of files into a PDF file and unifying it with consistent headers and backgrounds (providing a service for workers.) You can also use Acrobat to distribute a measured drawing that users working with Adobe Reader 8 can mark up and measure (knowledge worker communication) or for designing an e-mail or Web folder based method of exchanging reviewing comments (knowledge worker collaboration.)

In this chapter, we'll take a quick tour of the program and look at some of its features and tools. If you're interested in customizing the interface to make your work in Acrobat more efficient, tips that help you do so appear throughout the book.

# Introducing Acrobat 8 Professional

Adobe Acrobat 7 introduced some terrific new features for organizing and managing PDF files. For the first time, users had the ability to enable a PDF file to use commenting and markup tools in Adobe Reader, effectively opening up one of Acrobat's strongest features to millions more users. The trend toward greater functionality continues with Acrobat 8.

Here are some of the new feature highlights of Acrobat 8 Professional:

- The Getting Started with Adobe Acrobat 8 Professional window opens over the program window, displaying an overview of program functionality and links to program features and Help files.

- Use a wizard to set up a shared review without requiring server administrator support. The review's comments are stored on a server folder and participants receive comments automatically.

- Collaborate in real time using Acrobat Connect for personal Web conferencing.

- Enable Adobe Reader 8 users to collaborate on documents, including reviewing with complete commenting and markup tools, filling in and saving PDF forms locally, and digitally signing PDF documents.

- Create a PDF/A compliant document, add metadata, and optimize the file directly from a scanner; create PDF/A and other standards-compliant documents using the PDFMaker.

- Organize the program interface by configuring and using custom toolbars; move and position secondary windows and panes.

- Create, locate, and control security policies through the Managing Security Policies window with the assistance of wizards.

- Permanently delete sensitive text or image content with redaction tools.

- Use a forms wizard to recognize and automatically add fields to a document.

- Compile a number of PDF files into a single package including a navigation interface without combining them into a single file.

- Open a blank PDF document or add a blank page to a PDF document!

## Acrobat Versions

Acrobat comes in several versions, each useful for working with documents in different ways or in different situations. This book concentrates on Acrobat 8 Professional. Because there are differences among the features available in the various versions of the program, some of the most important features and which versions of the program they apply to are listed in **Table 1.1**. The table includes Acrobat Elements, which is a specialized version of the program for enterprise environments; Adobe Reader 8; and Acrobat 8 Standard and Professional versions.

**NOTE** Acrobat 7 3D is another product in the Acrobat family, although a version 8 is not available. The 3D product contains all the features of Acrobat 7 Professional as well as a number of other tools designed for converting, inserting, configuring, using, and distributing embedded 3D content.

**Table 1.1** Acrobat Versions and Their Features

| | ADOBE READER 8 | ACROBAT ELEMENTS | ACROBAT 8 STANDARD | ACROBAT 8 PROFESSIONAL |
|---|---|---|---|---|
| View, search, and print PDF files | X | X | X | X |
| Collaborate online in real time and share documents using Start Meeting | X | X | X | X |
| Automatically hide program tools and menus to view the document only in the Reading view | X | X | X | X |
| Combine PDF files as either a single file or as a package containing a number of files | | | X | X |
| Search within a PDF document or folder, look for specific components on a page, search subdocuments in PDF Package, search attached PDF files | X | X | X | X |
| Add, remove, save, customize headers, footers, watermarks, and backgrounds | | | X | X |
| Inspect PDF files for attributes ranging from metadata to hidden content and remove any or all attributes | | | X | X |
| Others aside from review initiator can serve as proxy for users outside a firewall in a shared review | | | X | X |
| Form creation wizard uses a template or existing documents in a number of formats, uses auto field recognition process, adds custom content | | | | X (Windows) |

**Table 1.1** *continued*

|  | ADOBE READER 8 | ACROBAT 8 ELEMENTS | ACROBAT 8 STANDARD | ACROBAT 8 PROFESSIONAL |
|---|---|---|---|---|
| Enable Adobe Reader 8 users to work with Commenting tools |  |  |  | X |
| Create PDF documents from all applications that print |  | X | X | X |
| Combine source documents into a PDF document |  |  | X | X |
| Use content from Microsoft Office programs, including Word, Excel, PowerPoint, Outlook, Internet Explorer, Access, and Publisher (Windows) |  |  | X | X |
| Manage document reviews |  |  | X | X |
| Use security such as passwords and certificates |  | X | X | X |
| Use content from AutoCAD, Microsoft Visio, and Microsoft Project, including layers and object data (Windows) |  |  |  | X |
| Preflight high-end print jobs |  |  |  | X |

# Starting at the Beginning

When was the last time you opened a new piece of software that you'd never used before, or opened a new version of a program you've used for some time after it had been through a major redevelopment? Although you are sure to recognize some of the features and labels immediately, the experience can be more than a little intimidating.

## I Need to Do...

To help you figure out what Acrobat 8 Professional does and how to get your job done, the program launches with the Getting Started with Adobe Acrobat 8 Professional dialog (**Figure 1.1**). This clear, simple-to-use interface is your introductory guide to the program.

Click a button to open an information dialog with
links and information on important features.

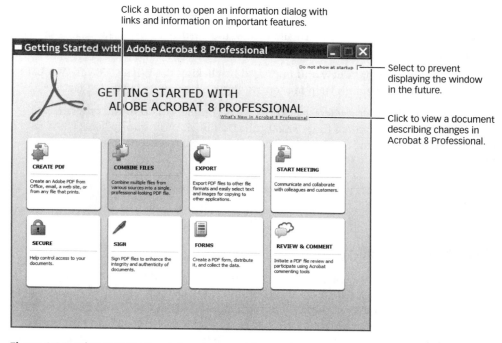

Select to prevent
displaying the window
in the future.

Click to view a document
describing changes in
Acrobat 8 Professional.

**Figure 1.1** Acrobat 8 Professional shows you workflow options when you first open the program.

The primary workflows to follow in Acrobat 8 Professional are represented by a series of eight buttons in the Getting Started with Adobe Acrobat 8 Professional dialog. Each button defines a type of Acrobat function and representative icon as well as a caption explaining what the category does. The options are the following:

- **Create PDF.** Create an Adobe PDF from Office, e-mail, a Web site, or from any file that prints.

- **Combine Files.** Combine multiple files from various sources into a single, professional-looking PDF file.

- **Export.** Export PDF files to other file formats and easily select text and images for copying to other applications.

- **Start Meeting.** Communicate and collaborate with colleagues and customers.

- **Secure.** Help control access to your documents.

- **Sign.** Sign PDF files to enhance the integrity and authenticity of documents.

- **Forms.** Create a PDF form, distribute it, and collect the data.

- **Review & Comment.** Initiate a PDF file review and participate using Acrobat commenting tools.

Be sure to check out what's new and improved by clicking the What's New in Acrobat 8 link. A page in the program's Help files opens, describing new or expanded features.

When you reach the point where you know what you plan to do in the program and where to find the appropriate tools, select the "Do not show at startup" check box at the upper right of the Getting Started with Adobe Acrobat 8 Professional dialog to suppress the window in the future.

> **NOTE** You can view the window again by choosing Help > Getting Started with Adobe Acrobat 8 Professional.

## Finding Your Way

Whether you're new to the program or just getting up to speed with the new version, I encourage you to check out where each button on the Getting Started with Adobe Acrobat 8 Professional dialog leads. The information is well designed and gives you insight into both how the program can meet your work requirements and new types of activities you may not have imagined you could do in Acrobat. For example, clicking the Create PDF button opens the dialog shown in **Figure 1.2**. On the dialog you find:

- Highlights of features and activities for that section of the Acrobat program's functionality.

- Categorized groups of activities, like those shown in the figure that include creating PDF files in Acrobat, creating PDF files from other applications, and using the Adobe PDF Printer.

- Task links 🔘 to click, such as Create PDF from a File, to open its corresponding program dialog.

- Info links 🔘 to click, such as Learn How to Create PDFs from Other Applications, to open the information page in the Acrobat Help files.

Once you have read through the information or found the task you need, click Home in the upper-left corner to return to the Getting Started with Adobe Acrobat 8 Professional dialog. If you like, select the "Do not show at startup" check box at the upper right to suppress the Getting Started dialog in future work sessions.

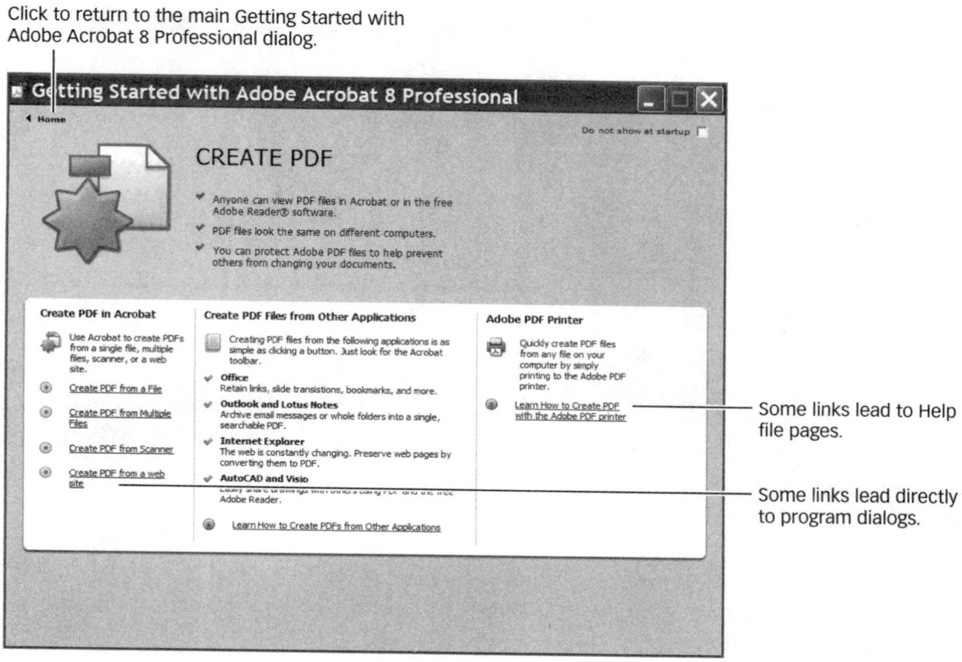

Click to return to the main Getting Started with
Adobe Acrobat 8 Professional dialog.

**Figure 1.2** Each task area's dialog lists information and program features.

# The Interface

Like most programs, Acrobat Professional has an interface composed of menus, toolbars, and a variety of work areas or panels (**Figure 1.3**). You can access many features and functions through the interface in a number of different ways or by using the shortcut keystroke combinations. Whichever method you choose really depends on what you feel comfortable with and how you like to work.

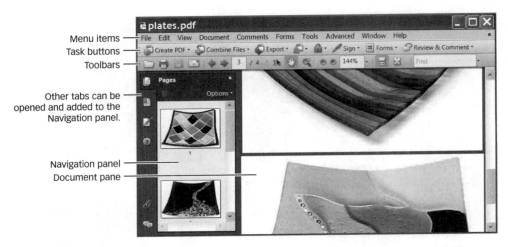

**Figure 1.3** Acrobat 8 Professional's interface is made up of several components arranged in the program window.

It's important to take some time to learn about the features and understand how the program works for two main reasons:

■ Knowing the features available lets you incorporate more of them into your workflow.

■ You will work faster and smarter when you learn to use the program and customize it to meet your needs.

## The Program Window

When you open Acrobat 8, take a few minutes to tour the program. Open the Navigation panels, click the Task buttons, and check out the toolbars' contents. You're bound to find something that is sure to boost your productivity! When you come across a feature of interest, be sure to experiment with it.

Acrobat's program window consists of several sections. You see menus and toolbars across the top, which contain tool icons and pull-down lists and menus. The remainder of the program window shows your document and a series of Navigation panels. The main menu displays across the top of the program and contains many common menu item headings such as File and Edit, along with Acrobat-specific headings, like Document and Comments (**Figure 1.4**). Many of the menu items are also available on Acrobat's toolbars. The name of the open, active document is shown at the top of the program window.

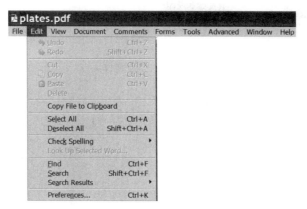

**Figure 1.4** Select program functions from the Main menu.

## Toolbars and Task Buttons

Acrobat contains a collection of toolbars available by choosing View > Toolbars. Most of the tools are also available by choosing Tools on the main menu (**Figure 1.5**).

**Figure 1.5** Tools are listed on the main menu as well as shown on toolbars.

You can spend a lot of time opening and closing toolbars using the menu. Save a couple of mouse clicks by working in the toolbar well, the area at the top of the program window that displays the toolbars. Right-click (Windows)/Control-click (Macintosh) in a blank space in the toolbar area to display the same options as those available by choosing View > Toolbars (**Figure 1.6**).

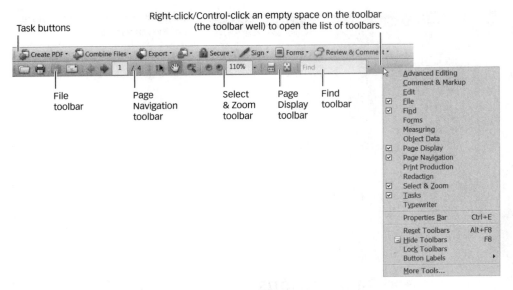

**Figure 1.6** All the toolbars and display options are available from the toolbar well.

To identify a tool or toolbar name quickly, move your pointer over the vertical hatched lines at the left of a toolbar to display its name in a tooltip or pause your pointer over a tool to show its name there (**Figure 1.7**).

**Figure 1.7** If you are unsure about a tool's or toolbar's name, you can display it in a tooltip by rolling the pointer over the icon.

While you are learning to work with Acrobat, you can show the labels next to the tool icons, but you may want to hide them when you become more proficient in order to maximize working space. To do this, choose View > Toolbars > Button Labels, and then select the Default, All, or No button label options.

> **NOTE** If you add multiple toolbars to the toolbar area or resize the program window to a smaller size, the labels are collapsed regardless of whether you choose the Default or All button label choices.

## Sorting your tools

Acrobat 8 introduces a terrific way to keep you organized in the program. For the first time you can add and remove tools from the different toolbars, allowing you to customize the interface according to the project you are working with and your usual work habits.

> **NOTE** You can't change the order of the tools on the toolbar, nor can you combine tools from several toolbars.

For example, the File toolbar contains four tools as the default view, but maybe you never use the Open and Save icons (**Figure 1.8**). However, you regularly use the Organizer and Attach File from Web page commands, which are not displayed on the toolbar.

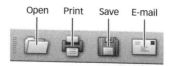

Figure 1.8 The default tools shown on a toolbar may or may not meet your needs.

## TOOLS FOR YOUR TYPE

You can organize Acrobat's toolbars the same way in which you organize your physical desk. Which group do you belong to?

- **Neatniks.** Lock the toolbars if you are the type of person who needs everything placed just so in order to function. You can customize the tool layout, and once the program is arranged to your satisfaction, choose View > Toolbars > Lock Toolbars (or select the command from the toolbar well's shortcut menu). The separator bars between the individual toolbars disappear. You can't lock floating toolbars—those you have pulled off the toolbar area—nor can you add them to a locked toolbar.

- **Some tidiness necessary.** Some people like things surrounding them during the workday and then like everything back in its place before they go home. Choose View > Toolbars > Default to reset the toolbar arrangement to the program default.

- **The rest of us.** I'm sure I'm not alone as a person who usually leaves things as they are when I quit work for the day. Often, seeing what I was working with the day before triggers my to-do list. The same can be said of toolbars. When you close and reopen Acrobat, the arrangement of toolbars and Task buttons remains as you last set them.

Follow these steps to customize the toolbar:

1. Choose View > Toolbars > More Tools, select the command from the toolbar well's shortcut menu, or choose Tools > Customize Toolbars to open the More Tools dialog.

2. Locate the toolbar list you'd like to customize.

3. Select tools to include and clear tools to exclude from the toolbar (**Figure 1.9**).

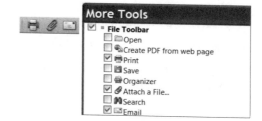

Figure 1.9 Add or remove tools from the toolbar

4. Click OK to close the dialog and make the changes in the toolbar. The newly config-ured toolbar is also shown in Figure 1.9 (left).

## Task buttons

Each Task button contains a set of commands for performing a particular function, such as creating a PDF file or commenting on a document (**Figure 1.10**). They are differ-ent from toolbars in that they contain related commands instead of related tools. Open a Task button by choosing View > Toolbars > Tasks and selecting the appropriate Task button. Display the Task button's bar by choosing View > Toolbars > Tasks.

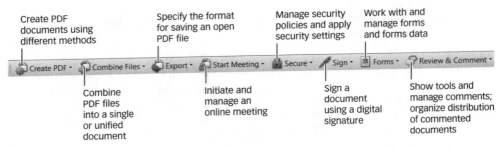

**Figure 1.10** Each Task button contains a group of related commands for performing a specific type of task.

Acrobat 8 contains a set of eight Task buttons:

- **Create PDF.** Use the commands for generating PDF documents using different methods, such as documents or scans.

- **Combine Files.** Choose commands for combining two or more PDF files, or building a PDF Package.

- **Export.** Select commands for exporting the active PDF document in one of many file formats.

- **Start Meeting.** Get an online collaboration in real time underway using these commands.

- **Secure.** Choose commands for using and managing security policies.

- **Sign.** Use the commands to add secure signatures to a document.

- **Forms.** Use the commands for creating and editing forms as well as other forms-related tasks.

- **Review & Comment.** Choose commands for things like showing the different Commenting toolbars and managing comments. Look for commands for managing a review cycle, such as starting a new review or opening the Tracker, a window used for managing reviews.

Click the Task button's down arrow to display its menu (**Figure 1.11**). Each Task button also includes a command to open its corresponding How To panel, which contains information on using the commands.

> **NOTE** Read about the How To panel in the section "Help Is Close at Hand" later in the chapter.

**Figure 1.11** The Secure Task button offers a number of ways to apply and manage document security in Acrobat.

## Navigation Panels

As soon as you open a file in Acrobat a column of icons displays at the left side of the program window. Click one of the default set of six icons to open a tabbed panel called a Navigation panel (**Figure 1.12**).

Use the different tab views to manage and control your document's content. The set of default icons, shown in Figure 1.12 from top to bottom, include:

- **Pages.** Go to specific pages by selecting page thumbnail images.

- **Bookmarks.** Go to different areas of the document or perform specific actions using bookmark links.

- **Signatures.** Read and verify signatures added to the document.

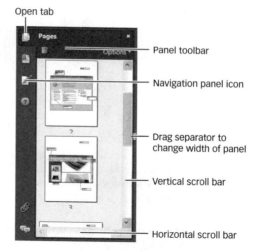

**Figure 1.12** The Navigation panel is docked to the left side of the program window.

- **How To.** Find and follow step-by-step instructions for performing different program tasks.

- **Attachments.** View a list of files attached to the active PDF document.

- **Comments.** View, reply, sort, and manage a list of comments applied to the active PDF document.

All panels open vertically at the left of the program window, except the bottom two Navigation tabs showing the Attachments and Commenting panels that open horizontally at the bottom of the program window.

There are many more Navigation tabs than those included in the default configuration. Follow these steps to add another tab to the panels:

**1.** Choose View > Navigation Panels and select other items from the menu (**Figure 1.13**).

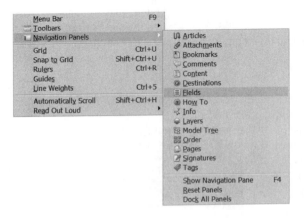

**Figure 1.13** Acrobat 8 Professional contains an extensive list of Navigation panel options.

**TIP** Save a couple of mouse clicks: Right-click/Control-click in the area of the icons displayed on the Navigation panel to open the menu shown in Figure 1.13.

**Figure 1.14** Selecting a new Navigation panel opens a tabbed dialog.

**2.** The newly selected Navigation items aren't automatically added to the column of icons in the Navigation panel. Instead, they are arranged in a preconfigured collection of tabbed dialogs. Select the tab you want to add to the panels (**Figure 1.14**).

**3.** Drag the tab for the panel you want to add from the dialog to the Navigation panel's area and release. The additional icon is now docked with other icons, and its tab is open (**Figure 1.15**).

**Figure 1.15** Drag the tab from the dialog to dock it with the other Navigation panel icons.

# Moving Through a Document

Earlier versions of Acrobat included a status bar running along the bottom of the program window to show layout and navigation tools. Acrobat 8 uses the Page Navigation and Page Display toolbars docked at the top of the program window to manage layout and navigation.

The default toolbar options are limited to the most commonly used tools (**Figure 1.16**). Access additional tools from the More Tools dialog by choosing View > Toolbars > More Tools.

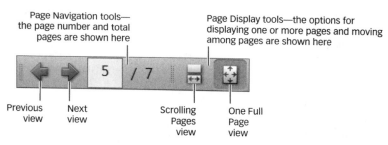

Page Navigation tools—
the page number and total
pages are shown here

Page Display tools—the options for
displaying one or more pages and moving
among pages are shown here

Previous view    Next view    Scrolling Pages view    One Full Page view

**Figure 1.16** Move through a document using the Page Navigation or the Page Display tools; change the viewing layout depending on the structure of your document.

The Page Navigation tools show the number of the visible page and the total page count as well as Previous and Next buttons to view the previous and next pages. The Page Display toolbar lets you choose between a continuous page view that you scroll and a single page view that shows one page at a time and isn't affected by scrolling. In Figure 1.16, the layout view is One Full Page (the One Full Page icon is highlighted).

# Opening and Saving Documents

One of the coolest things happened in Acrobat 8: Until this version, you couldn't add blank pages to an open document or open a new blank PDF file. We used all sorts of interesting workarounds like deleting content from an existing page or saving dummy PDF files having just a blank page to use as needed.

You still won't find a "New" command in the File menu, but choose File > Create PDF > From Blank Page to access the snazzy new feature (**Figure 1.17**). The other creation options include creating a PDF from a file, from multiple files, from a scanner, or from a Web page. You can also create a PDF from a clipboard image, which is a selected area of the document pane that is copied to the system clipboard.

**Figure 1.17** Generate a PDF file in one of several ways.

The only type of document that opens instantly in Acrobat is a PDF, but Acrobat can *convert* many types of documents automatically when you open them by choosing File > Open. For example, if you open a Microsoft Word document in Acrobat 8, it goes through an automatic conversion process before the file is displayed as a PDF. You can also use the Create PDF Task button's commands for creating a PDF in a variety of ways.

> **NOTE** For the most part, the conversion process requires that your system have the program that generated the source files installed. Acrobat 8 Professional converts the native AutoCAD .dwg format as well as InDesign .indd format to PDF without having the program installed.

You can save a PDF document in the usual way—that is, by using the Save command on the File menu or toolbar. Click the Export Task button to open its menu and choose a format from the menu or click More Formats to open a submenu (**Figure 1.18**). Once you make a selection, the Save As dialog opens. Name and save the file; you can click the Settings button to configure most types of files.

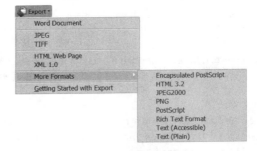

**Figure 1.18** Save a PDF file in several file formats.

# Help Is Close at Hand

Check out the offerings in the How To panel when you are first learning about Acrobat or learning how to use a new feature. The How To panel picks up where the Getting Started with Adobe Acrobat 8 Professional dialog leaves off.

Click the How To icon 🔣 on the Navigation panel to open the tab (**Figure 1.19**). The panel lists common tasks and contains information groupings on special topics such as print production or working with forms. Select a topic to display a list of common tasks or functions associated with that topic.

You can also revisit the How To contents by selecting Help > How To and choosing a topic title.

If you don't find what you are looking for in the How To panel, more help is just a click away! Use Acrobat's main Help feature to find in-depth information that goes beyond the step-by-step instructions on basic program functions. Click the Complete Acrobat 8.0 Help icon on the How To panel or Choose Help > Complete Acrobat 8.0 Help, or press the F1 key. The Adobe Help Viewer opens in a separate window.

You can access information in three ways with Acrobat's Help feature—by Contents, Index, or Search. Use the option that suits how you work and your Acrobat knowledge level:

■ **Contents.** If you are a very systematic person, you may find the default view in the Adobe Help Viewer the most useful. The Adobe Help Viewer opens to the Contents listing by default where topics are arranged in a hierarchy from broadest to most specific topics (**Figure 1.20**).

**Figure 1.19** Click one of the main topic areas in the How To window to open a list of topics.

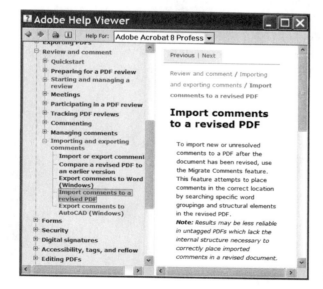

**Figure 1.20** The Contents tab is an easy way to find information if you are familiar with Acrobat.

■ **Index.** If you aren't sure what you are looking for, select a number or letter to show a list of terms on the Index tab. You may find a term that triggers a mental connection to the precise topic you need.

- **Search**. Use the Search tab if you are familiar with the program and want to find a specific topic. Type the search term in the "Find pages containing" field, and then click Search. Topics containing your search term are listed in the pane at the left of the Help window. Click a topic to display the content in the main pane; each instance of the search term is highlighted. If the highlighting is distracting, click the main pane of the Help window to deselect the highlights.

  **TIP** Instead of closing the Help window, minimize it; when you reopen it, the last content displayed is visible. Since the Help files are in a separate window from the program, you can arrange both Acrobat and the Help files on your desktop for ease of use.

## Making Your Exit

We have come to the end of the tour, as well as the end of this chapter. Close Acrobat as you would any program. When you reopen the program, the toolbars are arranged as you last left them. The Navigation panel, on the other hand, may or may not be displayed in the same way. Acrobat allows you to specify how you want its navigation features to display when a file is opened. For example, along with the document, you can show one of the Bookmarks, Pages, or the Attachments panel. Settings are not constant; that is, you decide how the navigation features are displayed on a file-by-file basis.

Now that you've seen how some of the tools and features work in Acrobat 8 Professional, you're ready to dive in and have some fun. The projects in this book show you how to use this extraordinary program to make your work and life a whole lot easier!

# Building a Cohesive Document

**2**

We often find ourselves overwhelmed by the number of programs and file formats we're inundated with on a daily basis. Suppose you want to view a Microsoft Word document, Excel spreadsheet, and PowerPoint presentation as one document. You could cut and paste content from one program to another, but wouldn't it be nice to use each document's structure? Or what if you needed to e-mail a document composed of Web pages from your company's Web site, a table from your coworker's PowerPoint presentation, and sample book pages that were saved in InDesign?

One of Acrobat's biggest contributions to creating order in the office is its ability to create a single document from a variety of sources. In this project, you'll learn how to merge a PowerPoint presentation, a Word document, an Excel spreadsheet, content from a Web page, and other sources into a single PDF document.

Combining the material into a cohesive PDF document is a time-saver and prevents you from having to repurpose the material manually. You'll use a number of Acrobat's unifying features, such as removing imported headers and footers and using Acrobat replacements throughout the document, setting consistent page sizes, and inserting page numbering to make the document's appearance uniform.

Download the project files and several iterations of the combined files from the book's Web site at www.donnabaker.ca/downloads.html to try out the project yourself.

 **DOWNLOAD** Along with project files, you'll find two bonus elements in the chapter's folder on the Web site—"Setting up a Slideshow," named **ch02_bonus1.pdf**, and "Converting an Advertisement in InDesign to PDF," named **ch02_bonus2.pdf**.

# Doggone It!

Joe and Jim Percy are twin brothers. Their tenacity, drive, and knowledge of pet owners and their needs have been instrumental in the development of their business, Doggone It!, which sells a spray cleaner specifically designed to remove pet stains from virtually any surface.

Their business has grown substantially, and they are ready to take it to the next level. They have sourced and licensed complementary products to sell under the Doggone It! brand, including shampoos, fur and skin treatment products, and other doggie grooming necessities.

Product expansion comes at a price, and the business is ripe for investors. At a closing event for a trade show they run into a woman who parlayed her fashion savvy and little pooches into a multimillion dollar online and retail business.

Jen Walford wants to talk to them about investing, but there's not much time. Both the twins and Ms. Walford have planes to catch in the morning; Jen's given them a chance to pitch to her over breakfast.

Joe and Jim may be big on ambition, but they are definitely short on time. The brothers need to pull together an information package from several sources that looks polished.

# Steps Involved in This Project

The logical solution for the Percy brothers is to work in Acrobat. With Acrobat, they can produce a document that will meet their requirements in the short amount of time they have (**Figure 2.1**).

To create their presentation, Joe and Jim need to do the following:

- Specify the slides they want to use from their PowerPoint presentation and convert them to PDF.

- Convert pages from their Web site, including customer testimonials extracted from a page.

- Create a merged PDF that includes the converted documents as well as several other documents that they decide they need to round out the presentation. The other documents include pages from two Word documents, an image, and an Excel spreadsheet.

- Reorder the document's pages and configure bookmarks.

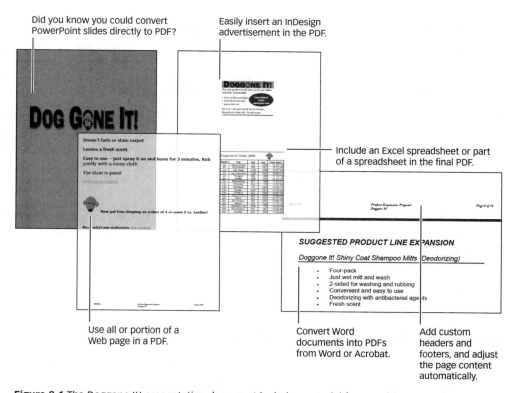

Did you know you could convert PowerPoint slides directly to PDF?

Easily insert an InDesign advertisement in the PDF.

Include an Excel spreadsheet or part of a spreadsheet in the final PDF.

Use all or portion of a Web page in a PDF.

Convert Word documents into PDFs from Word or Acrobat.

Add custom headers and footers, and adjust the page content automatically.

**Figure 2.1** The Doggone It! presentation document includes material from a wide range of programs.

- Remove Word, Excel, and Web page headers/footers created by PDFMaker 8.
- Adjust the sizes and reposition content on some of the pages.
- Extract a portion of the spreadsheet using the Snapshot tool and create a separate PDF document, which will then be used to replace the full spreadsheet page in the main document.
- Create and apply Header/Footer for file and save the settings.
- Shrink page content so headers/footers don't obscure page content.

To start their document package Joe and Jim decide to use some of the best slides from their trade show PowerPoint presentation and convert them to PDF.

# Creating a PDF from a PowerPoint Presentation

Joe and Jim use a PowerPoint presentation running in a loop as part of their trade show booth display. They could work from within either PowerPoint or Acrobat to convert the presentation. They want to use two of the presentation's slides in the package, which can be defined in the PDFMaker.

When you install Acrobat 8, the program also installs menus and toolbars in Microsoft Office programs. These plug-ins, called PDFMakers, have some settings particular to the type of program they are installed into, as well as collections of common settings shared by Acrobat and two components Acrobat 8 installs on your system—the Adobe PDF printer and Acrobat Distiller.

The Adobe PDF printer is a printer driver that is installed on your system like a physical printer or print settings such as fax printing. When you open a program's Print menu, you'll find the Adobe PDF printer on the list along with your other printers and print options. Acrobat Distiller is a separate program that is installed on your system and is used for converting files such as illustrations to PDF format.

## Preparing the Presentation for Conversion

The trade show presentation contains five slides, but Joe and Jim want to use only the first two slides as a PDF document. You can't select pages/slides to convert as you might for a printer, but you can hide the other slides in PowerPoint before converting the file.

 **DOWNLOAD** the original PowerPoint presentation named **doggoneit.ppt** if you want to experiment with selecting and converting PowerPoint slides. Download **doggoneit_ ppt.pdf** to see the converted presentation.

Follow these steps to hide slides in the presentation:

1. In either the Normal view or the Slide Sorter view, select the slides you want to hide. Slides 3, 4, and 5 in the sample project need to be hidden.

2. Choose Slide Show > Hide Slide or right-click/Control-click the selected slides and choose Hide Slide.

3. You see the slides' numbers display a strikethrough, indicating they are hidden (**Figure 2.2**).

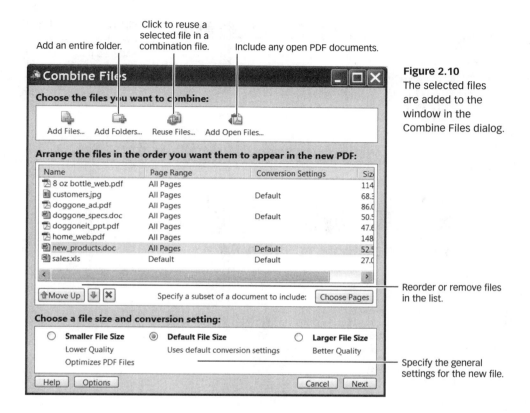

Add an entire folder.

Click to reuse a selected file in a combination file.

Include any open PDF documents.

**Figure 2.10**
The selected files are added to the window in the Combine Files dialog.

Reorder or remove files in the list.

Specify the general settings for the new file.

**4.** To modify the order of the content, click a file and then click Remove (to delete it from the list) or click the Move Up or down arrow button to adjust the selected document's order. In the sample project, Joe and Jim decide to leave the files in their original order—sorted by file type—and will adjust them later in the Pages panel.

## Specifying Pages to Include

Joe and Jim now need to specify the pages to include from one of the project files.

Only one page of the new_products.doc file is needed in the project. Follow these steps to specify content to include in the PDF document:

**1.** Select the new_products.doc file in the Combine Files dialog and click Choose Pages. The Preview and Select Page Range dialog opens (**Figure 2.11**).

**Figure 2.11** Specify the pages to use when adding a portion of a file.

2. Click the Pages radio button to activate the field and then type 1 to specify the page number to include in the project.

3. Click OK to close the dialog and return to the Combine Files dialog. The new_products. doc listing in the dialog now shows the selected page number in the Page Range column.

4. Click Next.

The Percys next modify a navigation feature and then create the new document.

## Specifying the File Type

In the dialog, choose the type of combined file you want to create. You can either merge all the separate documents into one or combine them into a package with a file linking the component pages. The "Merge files into a single PDF" option is the default and is the type chosen for this project (**Figure 2.12**).

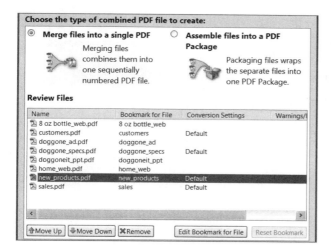

**Figure 2.12** Define whether the files are combined into a single file or into a collection.

# Renaming Assigned Bookmarks

In Figure 2.12, notice that all the files are now listed as a PDF file type and the file name is also listed as the bookmark. Bookmarks are a simple way of navigating in a PDF file. When combining the documents, each document is assigned a minimum of one bookmark to identify it as a component of the larger document. In some cases, such as Web pages and Word documents, additional bookmarks are added, as you'll see in the upcoming "Tweaking the Bookmarks" section.

For now, the brothers want to assign more descriptive bookmarks to keep track of the contents. The renamed bookmarks are listed in **Table 2.1**. Follow these steps to modify bookmark names:

1.  Click the name of the bookmark to select it, and then click Edit Bookmark for File to open a small dialog (**Figure 2.13**).

2.  Type a new name for the bookmark and click OK to close the dialog and change the bookmark's name in the Combine Files dialog.

3.  Select subsequent bookmarks and rename them.

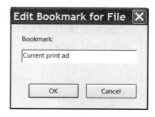

**Figure 2.13** Rename the bookmarks associated with the files' components.

**Table 2.1** Renamed File Bookmarks

| ORIGINAL BOOKMARK | NEW NAME |
|---|---|
| 8 oz bottle_web | Online product listing |
| customers | Customer comments |
| doggone_ad | Current print ad |
| doggone_specs | MSDS example |
| doggoneit_ppt | Welcome! |
| home_web | Web site homepage |
| new_products | New products |
| sales | Sales Q1 2006 |

The bookmarks can be modified in the Combine Files dialog or in Acrobat. Jim and Joe will tweak the rest of the bookmarks list in Acrobat, as soon as they create the merged file.

## Generating the Finished Document

When all the choices have been made in the wizard, it's finally time to produce the finished document. Acrobat follows through the list of files and merges the PDF pages into a single document, including those the program first converts from another file type.

Follow these steps to convert and merge the separate files:

1. Click Create to close the dialog and start the document processing. The files that are already PDF documents don't need processing. You see a number of progress bars as the files are processed. Acrobat notifies you when the files have finished processing (**Figure 2.14**). Click the left and right arrows below the preview thumbnail to check out the pages in the project.

Conversion status          Number of processed files

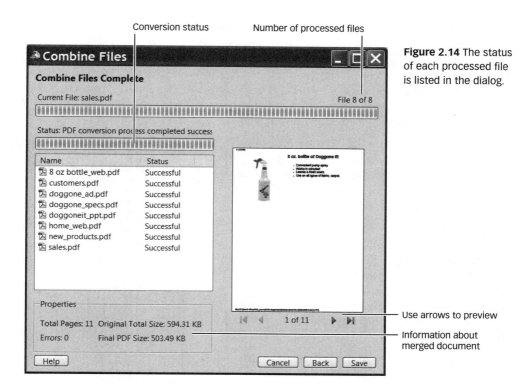

**Figure 2.14** The status of each processed file is listed in the dialog.

Use arrows to preview

Information about merged document

2. Click Save to open the Save As dialog. Acrobat names the combined document Binder1.pdf and stores it in the source files' folder by default.

3. If you prefer, rename the file and choose a different storage location. The project file is named combo01.pdf. Click Save to close the dialog and open the document in Acrobat.

Finally, it's time for Joe and Jim to get into the document and see what they have to work with.

# Tweaking the Bookmarks

Bookmarks are navigational links listed in the Bookmarks panel that display page content in the Document pane when clicked. Jim and Joe want to simplify their bookmarks considerably and reorder the content in the document.

 **DOWNLOAD** If you would like to start from this point in the project, download **combo01.pdf** from the book's Web site. To see how the project looks after modifying bookmarks, download **combo02.pdf**.

To view the document's bookmarks, follow these steps:

1. Click the Bookmarks icon 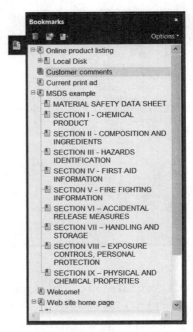 in the Navigation panel to open it.

2. If there are bookmarks with long names, as in this project, click the Options button at the top of the Bookmarks panel and choose Wrap Long Bookmarks from the pull-down menu. Bookmarks whose character length exceeds the width of the panel are automatically wrapped to the next line so you can read the names clearly.

3. Click the expand icons to the left of some of the bookmarks to open their hierarchies (**Figure 2.15**). If you prefer, select the bookmark and click "Expand current bookmark" on the Bookmarks panel's toolbar.

Acrobat converts files to PDF using the settings selected in your source programs. For example, the headings in the Word document are converted to bookmarks, and the network path and Web page name are converted to separate bookmarks during the Web page conversion. Although the Bookmarks list might look complicated and confusing, it doesn't have to be.

Here's the approach Joe and Jim take to clean up the disorder and get their navigation on track:

1. Delete any bookmarks you don't want to use.

2. Test the view of the bookmarks by clicking them and seeing the page layout in the Document pane. When you click a bookmark, you should see the page showing the start of the section in the Document pane.

3. Change the order of the bookmarks to match the document's page order.

4. Add new bookmarks if necessary.

5. Rename the remaining bookmarks.

6. Retest and reorder the bookmarks as necessary.

**Figure 2.15** Open and display the document's bookmarks. There are a lot of them!

# Weeding Out Bookmarks

Naming the assigned bookmark for each document before merging the files saves a big step and helps the brothers orient themselves in the Bookmarks panel, but there are quite a few bookmarks added during file conversions to remove.

Your approach to the culling may differ, but keep these points in mind:

- To delete a bookmark, click it to select it in the Bookmarks panel and press Delete. Shift-click to select a contiguous selection of bookmarks, or select more than one bookmark at a time by holding the Ctrl/Command key and clicking the bookmarks (**Figure 2.16**).

- Remove all the bookmarks except for those that match the set of bookmarks assigned and configured in the Combine Files dialog as listed in Table 2.1.

- Selecting a parent bookmark will delete its child or nested bookmarks as well. For example, in Figure 2.16, the bookmark named "Online product listing" has a child bookmark named "Local Disk," which in turn has a child bookmark named "8 oz bottle." Selecting and deleting the "Local Disk" bookmark also deletes its nested bookmark "8 oz bottle."

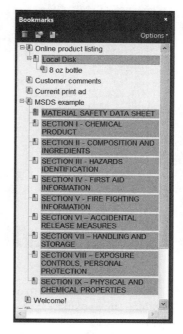

**Figure 2.16** Select the bookmarks to remove from the list.

# Ordering and Testing

When the list of bookmarks is substantially shorter, checking the bookmarks and setting their order is a breeze.

One by one, click through the bookmarks and see how their content looks in the Document pane. Depending on the size of the program window, the pages may or may not fill the Document pane (**Figure 2.17**). The bookmarks in the project show the same magnification; that is, the zoom is set at the same value so the content displays uniformly.

At the start of the project, the component files were added to the Combine Files dialog in their default order, sorted by file type. As you look through the pages, you will see that they are not in a logical order by any means.

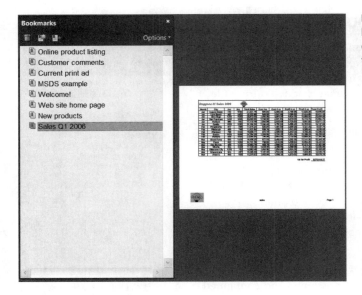

**Figure 2.17** Test the bookmarks' displays by clicking them one by one in the Bookmarks panel.

Like deleting extra bookmarks, the approach you take to organize the bookmarks can vary. There are a couple of ways to reorder the list: one requires precise mouse control, the other doesn't. Here's how:

- **For the mouse-savvy.** Click the bookmark to be moved, and drag upward or downward. You see a small black arrow and a horizontal line indicating where the bookmark is dropped when the mouse is released (**Figure 2.18**). Don't drag the bookmarks left or right or you'll reset them as nested or parent bookmarks.

- **For the rest of us.** Click the bookmark you need to move, and choose Options > Cut from the Bookmarks panel's Option menu to cut the bookmark from the list. Then click the bookmark above the location where you want to move the cut bookmark and choose Options > Paste after Selected Bookmark to paste it into its new location.

  **TIP** Use the shortcut keys Ctrl/Control-X to cut and Ctrl/Control-V to paste the bookmarks if you prefer.

The finished list of bookmarks is shown in **Figure 2.19**.

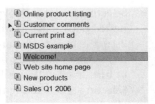

**Figure 2.18** Reorder the bookmarks in their list by dragging in the panel.

**Figure 2.19** The finished set of bookmarks is listed in a logical presentation order.

Joe and Jim decide it's a good idea to save the document at this point to preserve their changes. The project file is saved as combo02.pdf. Next up, the twins take a look at the document's pages.

# Reordering the Pages

The bookmarks are correct in their list, but that doesn't mean the document's pages are ordered correctly. Take a look at **Figure 2.20**: You see the Welcome page is the first bookmark in the list, and you'd assume that should be page 1 in the document as well, right? Not so. The page number shown in the Page Navigation toolbar indicates the Welcome page is page 6 of 11 pages. To reorder the pages Jim and Joe turn to the Pages panel.

 **DOWNLOAD** If you would like to start from this point in the project, download **combo02.pdf** from the book's Web site. To see how the project looks after modifying the page order, download **combo03.pdf**.

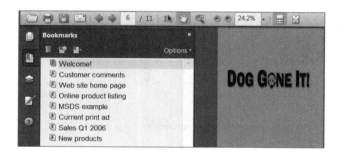

**Figure 2.20** The first bookmark in the list doesn't correspond to the first page in the document.

Click the Pages icon to open the tab displaying the Pages panel (**Figure 2.21, next page**). Notice the pages are listed as thumbnail images with a number below them. Note the following also:

- The pages are different sizes.

- The spreadsheet page has a different orientation.

- Some content on some pages isn't centered.

The boxed area on the thumbnail defines what is seen on the Document pane.

Some content on some pages isn't centered.

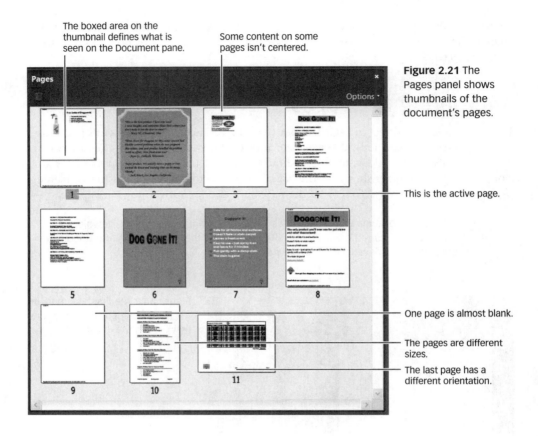

**Figure 2.21** The Pages panel shows thumbnails of the document's pages.

This is the active page.

One page is almost blank.

The pages are different sizes.

The last page has a different orientation.

- One page from the converted Web site is blank except for the page footer.

- The area of page 1 that is surrounded by a box (red in the program) indicates what portion of the page is shown in the Document pane.

- The selected page's thumbnail and number are highlighted.

The first task is to order the pages to match the order of the bookmarks.

> **TIP** Before modifying the sequence in the Pages panel, drag the right border of the panel to the right to increase the size of the panel until you can see all of the thumbnails. If you are having difficulty seeing the content of the thumbnails, click the Options button at the top of the Pages panel and choose Enlarge Page Thumbnails. You can choose the command repeatedly until you can see the thumbnails clearly.

Depending on how familiar you are with the document pages, you can work exclusively from the Pages panel or move back and forth between the Pages and Bookmarks panels, or both, by following these steps:

1.  Click the Bookmarks panel and select the first bookmark. Notice that the page number shown in the Page Navigation toolbar indicates the Welcome page is page 6 of 11 pages, shown earlier in Figure 2.20.

2.  Click the Pages tab to display the Pages panel and the thumbnail images. Page 6 is highlighted on the panel.

3.  Press Ctrl/Control and click page 7 to select it as well.

4.  Drag the two pages up and left, and then release the mouse when you see a vertical line at the upper left position of the thumbnails (**Figure 2.22**).

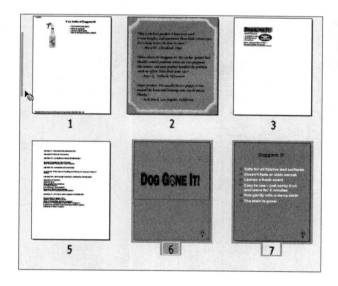

**Figure 2.22** Rearrange the page order in the Pages panel by dragging thumbnails to a new location.

5.  Click the Bookmarks tab to show the Bookmarks panel again and check where the Welcome page and its second blank page are located. The bookmark is at page 1 as it should be.

6.  Back on the Pages panel, click the thumbnail for page 4—the ad listing customer opinions of the product—and drag it to the page 3 position.

7. See the empty page (**Figure 2.23**)? Select the blank page's thumbnail on the Pages panel and press Delete 🗑 at the top of the Pages panel. A message asks if you are sure you want to delete the page. Click OK to close the dialog and delete the page.

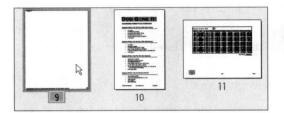

**Figure 2.23** This page was converted as a second page from the Doggone It! Web site's homepage and has no content except for the header.

8. Continue moving and adjusting locations for the pages until the order matches that shown in **Figure 2.24** and listed in **Table 2.2**.

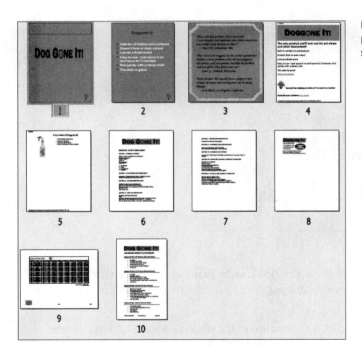

**Figure 2.24** The amended page order matches the sequence of bookmarks.

9. Save the file to preserve the edits. The project file is named combo03.pdf.

Flipping through the document pages shows the correct order, but Joe and Jim also notice there are some problems like extra content or content not centered on the page. They'll take care of these details next.

**Table 2.2** Final Page Order

| PAGE | DESCRIPTION |
| --- | --- |
| 1 | Doggone It! presentation page |
| 2 | Second page from presentation |
| 3 | Customer testimonial |
| 4 | Web site first page |
| 5 | Product sample page from Web site |
| 6 | MSDS (Material Safety Data Sheet) first page |
| 7 | MSDS second page |
| 8 | Print advertisement |
| 9 | Sales spreadsheet |
| 10 | New product list |

# Tweaking Page Content

Now that the pages are in order the brothers can fine-tune the page content. Some of the documents that make up the combo file were created using default settings from their respective source programs that included extra elements like headers and footers. Other pages contain a big splashy logo, which is fine when the file is a single document, but can be distracting when viewed in a merged file like the Percys are working with.

 **DOWNLOAD** If you have been working through the project, continue with your own file. If you prefer, download the file **combo03.pdf** from the book's Web site to start from this point. An iteration of the project file, named **combo04.pdf**, includes the page edits described in this section.

After looking through the pages carefully, Joe and Jim decide to make three changes:

1. Delete extra page content, such as the headers and footers and too-large logos.

2. Reposition some of the page content, like the print ad and the sample product page from the Web site.

3. Resize some content, such as the logo on the first page of the document.

# Deleting Extra Page Content

The plan is to use Acrobat's header and footer features to unify the document's appearance. The brothers can't add the new footers until the preexisting ones are removed. They also need to remove a few extra elements from the pages.

Follow these steps to delete extra content from a page:

1. Right-click/Control-click the toolbar well to open the list of toolbars and choose Advanced Editing. Drag the toolbar to dock it with the other toolbars at the top of the program window.

2. Display page 1 of the document in the Document pane. The first item to remove is the dog logo at the bottom right of the page.

3. Click the TouchUp Object tool ![icon] on the Advanced Editing toolbar.

4. Click the logo with the tool to show a bounding box surrounding the object (**Figure 2.25**).

5. Press Delete to remove the object from the page.

**Figure 2.25** The TouchUp Object tool lets you select items on the page for editing.

6. Continue through each page of the document, selecting and deleting content as follows:

   - **Page 2**. Remove the logo at the bottom right of the page.

   - **Pages 4 and 5**. Remove the header and footer from the top and bottom of the converted Web pages.

   - **Page 6**. Remove the Doggone It! logo from the top of the page.

   - **Page 9**. Remove the footer from the page. Ctrl-click/Control-click to select all three elements of the footer at once (**Figure 2.26**).

**Figure 2.26** Select multiple objects for deletion at the same time.

   - **Page 10**. Delete the logo at the top of the page and the footer at the bottom of the page.

7. Save the file to preserve the edits.

Both the product page from the Web site on page 5 and the print advertisement on page 8 should be centered on the page. Joe and Jim will use an Advanced Editing tool and some simple tricks and commands to place the content correctly on the page.

## Repositioning Objects on the Page

To modify the position of the example product Web page's content on the page, Joe and Jim again go to the Advanced Editing toolbar.

Follow these steps to move the content to the page's center:

**1.** Click the page's thumbnail to select it in the Pages panel. The product page is page 5.

**2.** Click One Full Page 🔲 on the Page Navigation toolbar to show the full page in the Document pane.

**3.** Click the TouchUp Object tool 📝 on the Advanced Editing toolbar.

**4.** Drag a marquee around the page's content on the Document pane and release the mouse. Each object on the page is identified by a bounding box (**Figure 2.27**).

Figure 2.27 Drag a marquee to select all objects within its boundaries.

**5.** Press Ctrl-X/Command-X to delete the selected objects.

**6.** Press Ctrl-V/Command-V to paste the content back on the page. Acrobat automatically places it at the center of the page.

Nice trick! Repeat the process with the advertisement on page 9.

To perfect the layouts on the other pages, such as those where the page logos were removed, drag a marquee around the page content with the TouchUp Object tool and drag to the desired location, or nudge the content using the arrow keys. You can use the grid and guides for precise positioning (**Figure 2.28**). Check out how to use the grid and guides in Chapter 4.

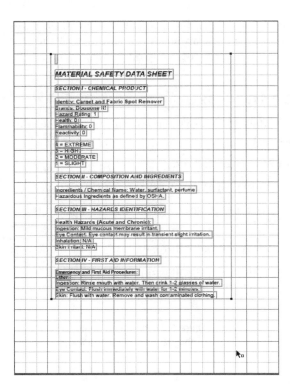

**Figure 2.28** Use the placement grid and guides to nudge content into place.

### IMAGE TROUBLE? CHECK OUT THESE SOLUTIONS

Depending on a number of issues—the complexity of an image, its original file format, and how the image is constructed—you may see that the advertisement doesn't copy and paste or cut and paste as you'd like. You can try one of these tips:

- Check the program preferences. Choose Edit > Preferences > General or Acrobat > Preferences > General (Mac) and select the "Make Select tool select images before text" option. When you paste the image back, the image contents may be stacked differently and the contents visible.

- Select the contents on the page and drag them to the desired position.

# Resizing a Document Page

One page of the document is a converted image where the page's size matches the image's size. To easily check the size of a page, move the pointer to the lower left of the Document pane to show the dimensions in a tooltip (**Figure 2.29**).

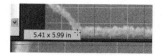

**Figure 2.29** You can check the page size at any time on the Document pane.

Jim and Joe adjust the page's size in the Crop Pages dialog by following these steps:

1. Select page 3, the customer testimonial page in the Pages panel to activate it.

2. Double-click the page with the Crop tool to open the Crop Pages dialog.

3. Select the Fixed Sizes option in the Change Page Size section of the dialog.

4. Click the Page Sizes down arrow and choose Letter (**Figure 2.30**). Click OK to close the dialog and resize the page. The image on the page is automatically centered.

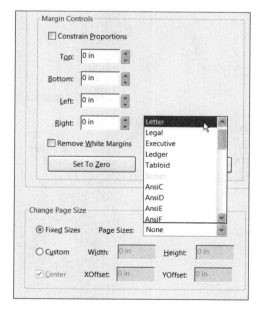

**Figure 2.30** You can choose from numerous preconfigured page sizes.

Most of the pages are now tweaked and resized. The last task to finish the pages layout is to swap the spreadsheet page with another page containing a snapshot of a portion of the spreadsheet.

# Creating a Page from a Snapshot

One page of the presentation document is an Excel spreadsheet that shows the business's sales figures for the first quarter of 2006. Jim and Joe realize it doesn't make good business sense to show their profit for the quarter, although it is shown on the spreadsheet.

They decide to use Acrobat's Snapshot tool to capture the part of the spreadsheet they would like to include in the finished presentation, create a separate PDF document from the snapshot, and then incorporate that into the combo04.pdf document.

## Capturing Content from a Page

Acrobat offers the Snapshot tool, which is a handy way to capture some of the content from a page and use it to create a separate PDF document.

The Snapshot tool is a part of the Select & Zoom toolbar, although it isn't shown on the toolbar by default. To show the tool, right-click/Control-click the toolbar well and choose More Tools from the shortcut menu to open the More Tools dialog. Scroll down the list to the Select & Zoom tools and select the Snapshot tool (**Figure 2.31**). Click OK to close the dialog and add the tool to the toolbar.

To capture a portion of the spreadsheet, follow these steps in Acrobat:

1.  The Select & Zoom toolbar is one of Acrobat's default toolbars, but choose View > Toolbars > Zoom if it isn't displayed in the program. Set the view to 100% on the Zoom toolbar (**Figure 2.32**). You can either click the (+) or (–) button until the view reads 100% or click the value down arrow and choose 100% from the list.

    Whatever size is shown in the Document pane when you capture the snapshot is used in the subsequent PDF document. If you convert at 100%, there is little or no distortion of the snapshot's appearance.

2.  Click the Snapshot tool 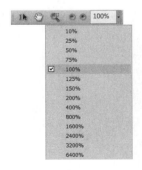 on the toolbar.

3.  Drag a marquee on the page around the content you want to capture (**Figure 2.33**). Release the mouse, and you see the color of the area within the marquee is inverted, that is, dark and light color is swapped, as the snapshot is taken.

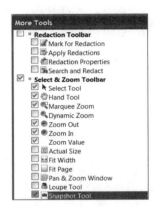

**Figure 2.31** Add the Snapshot tool to its toolbar from the More Tools dialog.

**Figure 2.32** Specify the zoom factor of the page before selecting the content for copying.

| Month | City | 4oz | 8oz | Total Sales | Cost 4oz |
|---|---|---|---|---|---|
| Jan | Laguna Beach | 722 | 1500 | 21,531.78 | 880.84 |
| Jan | Long Beach | 450 | 1452 | 19,102.98 | 549.00 |
| Jan | San Diego | 1200 | 1600 | 25,972.00 | 1,464.00 |
| Jan | San Francisco | 1400 | 1845 | 30,062.55 | 1,708.00 |
| Jan | Portland | 889 | 992 | 17,116.19 | 1,084.58 |
| Jan | Seattle | 1020 | 1550 | 24,164.30 | 1,244.40 |
| Feb | Philadelphia | 677 | 599 | 11,315.24 | 825.94 |
| Feb | Pittsburgh | 458 | 748 | 11,421.94 | 558.76 |
| Feb | Allentown | 799 | 1024 | 16,838.77 | 974.78 |
| Feb | Boston | 1025 | 1555 | 24,254.20 | 1,250.50 |
| Feb | Portland | 644 | 1600 | 22,085.56 | 785.68 |
| Mar | Grand Forks | 555 | 1420 | 19,485.25 | 677.10 |
| Mar | Pierre | 622 | 1852 | 24,701.26 | 758.84 |
| Mar | Des Moines | 499 | 1225 | 16,950.76 | 608.78 |
| Mar | Wichita | 844 | 1020 | 17,109.36 | 1,029.68 |
| Mar | Oklahoma City | 1200 | 752 | 16,652.48 | 1,464.00 |
| Mar | Albequerque | 944 | 887 | 16,346.69 | 1,151.68 |
| Mar | Amarillo | 863 | 655 | 13,230.82 | 1,052.86 |

*Doggone It! Sales 2006*

**Figure 2.33** Drag a marquee with the Snapshot tool around the content on the page.

4. Acrobat tells you the content has been copied to the clipboard; click OK to close the message dialog.

Next, create a PDF document from the content on the clipboard.

## Using Clipboard Content

Acrobat stores content captured with the Snapshot tool on the system clipboard.

 **DOWNLOAD clip.pdf** if you prefer to work with the PDF file created from the snapshot of the spreadsheet as described in the previous section.

Follow these steps to create a separate PDF document from the captured content:

1. Click the Create PDF task button and choose From Clipboard Image.

   The option is now active on the toolbar. Earlier in the project, when you built the combined document, this option was disabled because there was no content on the clipboard.

2. Acrobat automatically converts the clipboard image to a new PDF document.

   Depending on how your Acrobat program is configured and whether you have closed the dialogs previously, you'll see information dialogs explaining that the image PDF needs its content captured and the reading order specified. Click Cancel to close the dialogs.

3. Select the Crop tool on the Advanced Editing toolbar to select it and then double-click the page to open the Crop Pages dialog.

4. Select the Fixed Sizes option in the Change Page Size section of the dialog.

5. Click the Page Sizes down arrow and choose Letter.

6. Click OK to close the dialog and resize the page. The image on the page is automatically centered.

7. Choose File > Save to save the document (the project's file is named clip.pdf).

The final stage of the process is to replace the existing spreadsheet page in the document with the newly created spreadsheet segment.

## Replacing the Document Page

You should now have two documents open in Acrobat—combo04.pdf and the new clip.pdf document. There are numerous ways to swap the pages: You can replace the page or delete the existing one and insert the new one. You can also make revisions by using program commands or visually, as you'll see in this section.

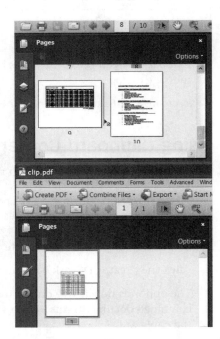

 **DOWNLOAD** You can download the modified document named **combo05.pdf** to see how the extracted portion of the spreadsheet is integrated into the complete document.

Follow these steps in Acrobat to replace the page in the merged document with the new file:

1. From either the combo04.pdf or clip.pdf file, choose Window > Tile > Horizontally to display both documents.

2. For both files, click the Pages icon at the left of each program window to display the Pages panels.

3. Drag the page thumbnail from the Pages panel in the clip.pdf file to the combo04.pdf file, placing it either before or after the existing spreadsheet page (**Figure 2.34**).

**Figure 2.34** Drag the page thumbnail from the Pages panel of the replacement file to the original combination file.

4. Select the original page showing the full spreadsheet and click Delete; a confirmation dialog opens asking if you are sure you want to delete the page. Click Yes; the dialog closes and the page is replaced

   **TIP** You can also select the command from the shortcut menu or by choosing Document > Replace Pages. Because you are already working in the Pages panel, it's simpler to select the command from the panel's Options menu.

5. Save the document with the new content. The sample project is saved as combo05. pdf to differentiate the versions of the document.

The content has been tweaked in many ways, and the document is looking good. As a finishing touch, the Percys decide to add footers to tie the entire document together.

# Adding Unifying Content

One highly useful feature in Acrobat is the ability to add unifying elements to the pages to enhance the integrated appearance of the overall file. In this final construction task of the project, Jim and Joe add a consistent footer throughout the document.

 **DOWNLOAD** Continue working with your own file, or start from the **combo05.pdf** file from the book's Web site.

## Defining the Footer Appearance

Choose options for the footers' contents and placement following these steps:

1. Choose Document > Header & Footer > Add to open the Add Header and Footer dialog (**Figure 2.35**).

2. Define the characteristics of the font to use for the header or footer by clicking the Name down arrow and choosing an alternate font. Specify the size, color, and whether to use an underline.

3. Adjust the page margins as necessary. The defaults provide .5 inches at the top and bottom, and 1 inch left and right on the page.

4. Click the Left Footer Text field to activate it. Click Insert Date to add an automatic field. The default is shown as <<m/d>>, which displays the month and day numerically in the footer.

5. Click the Right Footer Text field to activate it. Click Insert Page Number to add the default number field shown as <<1>>.

6.  Click the Center Footer Text field to activate it. Type `Product Expansion Proposal` and press Enter/Return to break the line. Type `Doggone It!` on the second line.

7.  Click the arrows to scroll through the page previews, which display at the bottom of the dialog.

Choose font characteristics.        Check the pages in the preview area.        Adjust the margins.

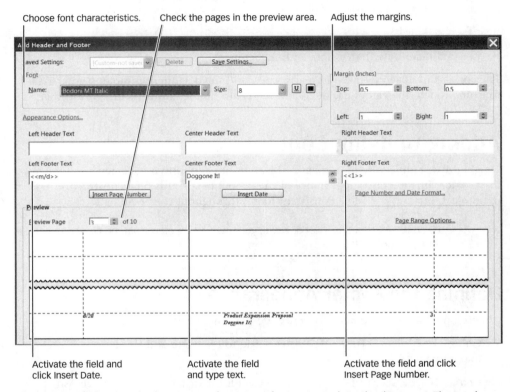

Activate the field and          Activate the field          Activate the field and click
click Insert Date.              and type text.               Insert Page Number.

**Figure 2.35** Configure and select content for custom footers to apply to the document. The numbers on the figure correspond with the steps taken to configure the footer.

The basic footer contents are OK, but Jim and Joe decide to add some customization.

# Customizing the Footers

Choose custom appearances for the date and page number rather than using the defaults by following these steps:

1. In the Add Header and Footer dialog, click Page Number and Date Format to open the dialog (**Figure 2.36**).

2. Click the Date Format down arrow and choose mm/dd/yy from the list.

3. Click the Page Number Format down arrow and choose Page 1 of n from the list.

4. Click the Start Page Number field and type 2. You'll change the page range shortly.

5. Click OK to close the dialog.

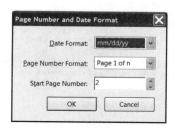

**Figure 2.36** Customize the appearance of the footer's automatic fields.

6. Check the footer text. Earlier you applied the date or page number using the default settings. Now that the settings are customized, you have to click the appropriate buttons to insert the date or page number in the custom formats.

Next up, change the document's pagination.

# Specifying Page Ranges

The first page of the document is a cover page, and doesn't require a footer. Follow these steps to customize the page range for applying the footer content:

1. In the Add Header and Footer dialog, click Page Range Options to open the dialog (**Figure 2.37**).

2. Click the Pages from radio button and type 2 in the first field; 10 is entered in the second field by default since that is the total number of pages in the file.

3. Choose All pages in range from the Subset pull-down menu.

4. Click OK to close the dialog and apply the changes to the preview.

5. Scroll through the preview and check how the footers look on the pages.

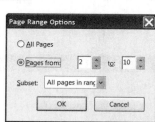

**Figure 2.37** Specify which pages in the document display the footer.

The twins are pleased with the appearance except for the footer on page 4, the converted homepage from their Web site (**Figure 2.38**).

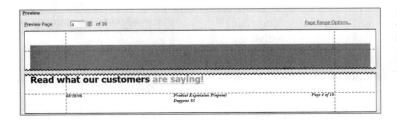

**Figure 2.38** Most of the pages look good, but the text on this page is too close to the footer.

**TIP** If you look through the document and find a typo or want to change the font size, choose Document > Header & Footer > Update to reopen the dialog. Adjust the header or footer as necessary and click OK to close the dialog. The update is applied to the last header or footer applied.

## Automatically Changing Page Content

The last line of the Web page is within the bottom margin of the page and looks crowded. Acrobat 8 Professional includes a spiffy new feature that automatically shrinks the content on a page to fit within the defined margins.

Follow these steps to repair the page layouts:

**1.** In the Add Header and Footer dialog, click Appearance Options to open the dialog (**Figure 2.39**).

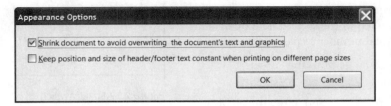

**Figure 2.39** Automatically shrink the pages' content or specify an absolute position for the header/footer in documents having multiple page sizes.

**2.** Select "Shrink document to avoid overwriting the document's text and graphics."

**3.** Click OK to close the dialog. In the preview area, the last line of text that had shown on the page 4 preview is now gone.

**4.** Click OK to close the Add Header and Footer dialog and return to the document.

Looking mighty fine!

There are several ways you can specify how a document displays when it opens. By default, only the first page of the document is displayed in the Document pane and none of the Navigation panels are open. You can choose to display the Bookmarks, Pages, Attachments, or Layers panels. As a finishing touch, Jim and Joe decide to specify the opening view.

### REUSING HEADER AND FOOTER CONTENT

Headers and footers can be applied either to the entire document or to selected pages and can include automatic content, such as the date, or custom content, such as the author's name.

If you find you are re-creating the same headers and footers repeatedly, save their definitions and apply them with a single command by following these steps:

1. Choose Document > Header & Footer > Add to open the dialog.

2. Configure the appearance and content for the header or footer.

3. Click Save Settings to open a dialog and type the name for the header and footer settings.

4. Click OK to close the dialog and save the settings in the dialog.

5. Then click OK again to close the Add Headings & Footers dialog and apply the header and footer to the PDF.

When it's time to reuse the settings, open the dialog, click the Apply Settings down arrow, and choose the custom settings from the list. The headers and footers are added instantly. Click OK to close the Headers & Footers dialog. Nice and quick!

## Setting the View

Using an appropriate view option shows your readers the important navigation content in your file immediately on opening it. They won't have to open any panels, and they'll quickly recognize that you have gone to the trouble of adding a navigation system.

Follow these steps to set the view:

**1.** Set the width of the Bookmarks panel and the Document pane as desired.

2. Choose File > Properties to open the dialog. Click the Initial View tab (**Figure 2.40**).

3. Click the Show down arrow and choose Bookmarks Panel and Page.

4. Click OK to close the dialog.

5. Save the document, and then close and reopen it. You see the Bookmarks panel displayed, and the full width of the page is shown in the Document pane (**Figure 2.41**).

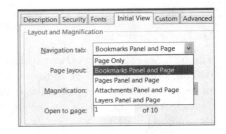

**Figure 2.40** Choose an option to display when the document opens.

**Figure 2.41** The document opens with both the first page and Bookmarks panel displayed.

Bright and early the next morning, Joe and Jim make their pitch over breakfast, and Jan Walford is blown away by their business acumen and quality of their presentation. Of course.

# What Else Can They Do?

Jim and Joe could use some additional features to add to their presentation document if they had more than a few hours to prepare for their meeting. They could customize the bookmarks' text using color or bold/italic text.

They might like to add text labels to some of the pages using separate headers applied to the pages in the same way as the footers were applied in the project.

The brothers might like to configure the document as a presentation. In fact, you can see how they would go about it—if they had the time—in the bonus material for Chapter 2 available from the book's Web site.

All in all, in the short amount of time available, they prepared a valuable and usable document.

# Communicating with Comments

# 3

One of the biggest challenges businesses, both large and small, have to face is managing information. Whether you are in the entertainment business or work for a software company, you use documents as your standard means of conveying information. Managing and controlling what goes into your documents can be a daunting task, especially when many people are involved in communicating and tracking the information. Fortunately, one of the strongest features in Acrobat 8 is its built-in process for managing document reviews.

A *review* is a system in which one member of a team controls and manages the distribution of a document using Acrobat 8 Professional. Reviewers are invited to participate and are given copies of the document. They are also granted rights to use a set of tools to add various types of comments to the document, including graphics and text. The automated reviewing process then returns the comment data from the document to the originator of the review cycle.

Once the review is complete, you can use the comment data in a number of ways for revising the original content. You could use Acrobat's TouchUp tools, for example, to make small changes to text or add additional lines of text, and so on.

Prior to Acrobat 7, only people working with the full version of Acrobat could participate in reviews. In Acrobat 7 Professional, and now in Acrobat 8 Professional, the review originator can enable PDF documents for commenting by anyone working with the free Adobe Reader 7 or 8, expanding the ability to work with comments to millions of additional users.

You can use either Windows or Mac versions of Acrobat 8 for starting, conducting, and analyzing results of the review.

# Follow My Lead

Chris Stevens is an information developer for Lemming Systems, a software company that produces custom database solutions for businesses. As a member of the marketing and communications team, it is his responsibility to circulate draft client documents for review by key employees prior to their publication.

A huge problem has been the decentralized nature of the company, where some people work in the office, others work from home part of the time, and still others work remotely on a full-time basis.

Chris is hopeful that using Acrobat to manage document reviews will alleviate some of the delays, lost copies, late couriers, and other frustrations involved in circulating paper documents.

# Steps Involved in This Project

Chris will use the Comment & Markup tools and workflow Acrobat 8 Professional offers to handle the review digitally (**Figure 3.1**).

He and his assistant plan to prepare the file for distribution, and then initiate the comment and review cycle using an e-mail review, which is managed in the Review Tracker in Acrobat 8 Professional. The review participants use a variety of commenting tools and return the comments by e-mail for integration into the master copy of the review document.

After the comments are e-mailed back, they'll be incorporated into the master PDF document for examination, correction, and reporting.

This is what he needs to do:

- Convert his source Word document to PDF.

- Initiate the review, specifying control and management details, including enabling the document for reviewing by participants using Adobe Reader.

- Invite participants to the review.

- Receive the responses and integrate the comments into the document.

- Examine and sort the comments using the Comments panel.

- Evaluate the comments and decide how to make corrections.

- Integrate the comments into the original Word source document, described in the bonus section on the book's Web site.

- Repeat the process as necessary for further review and, ultimately, approval of the finished piece.

Specify how the document opens to include
important navigation such as bookmarks.

Any PDF file can be used for
commenting and reviewing.

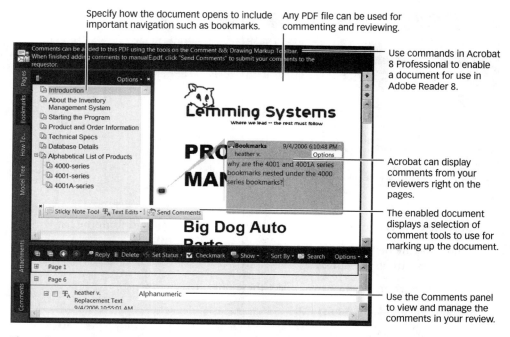

Use commands in Acrobat
8 Professional to enable
a document for use in
Adobe Reader 8.

Acrobat can display
comments from your
reviewers right on the
pages.

The enabled document
displays a selection of
comment tools to use for
marking up the document.

Use the Comments panel
to view and manage the
comments in your review.

**Figure 3.1** Lemming Systems needs a way to manage workgroup input on
business-critical documents.

# Converting the Source Document

Chris constructs most of his manual in Microsoft Word, and the specification sheets are
built as Excel spreadsheets that are then inserted into the Word document. The document also contains database design objects created in Visio. The first step in the process,
once the draft is complete, is to convert it to PDF.

 **DOWNLOAD** If you'd like to convert the source file yourself, download **manual.doc**
from the Web site.

Working in Word, follow these steps to convert the document to PDF:

**1.** Choose Adobe PDF > Change Conversion Settings to open the Acrobat PDFMaker
dialog; the Settings tab is shown by default (**Figure 3.2**).

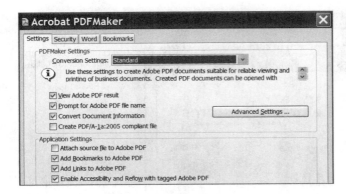

**Figure 3.2** Use the Standard conversion options to produce a basic document for both online and print.

**2.** Click the Conversion Settings down arrow and choose Standard from the list.

Standard is the default setting used in the PDFMaker and will be active unless you've used other settings previously.

**3.** In the Application Settings area, select these options:

- Add Bookmarks to Adobe PDF

- Add Links to Adobe PDF

- Enable Accessibility and Reflow with tagged Adobe PDF

**4.** Select the Bookmarks tab and then click Convert Word Headings to Bookmarks. PDFMaker automatically selects the Heading 1 through Heading 9 options.

The sample project uses modified Word headings, and Chris wants bookmarks for the Heading 1 through Heading 3 headings. Clear those heading levels you don't want to convert to bookmarks (**Figure 3.3**).

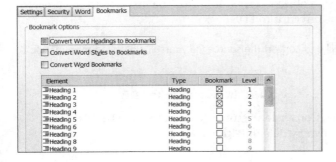

**Figure 3.3** Select Convert Word Headings and the desired heading levels to create PDF bookmarks automatically.

**5.** Click OK to close the Acrobat PDFMaker dialog.

**6.** Click the Convert to Adobe PDF button on the PDFMaker toolbar, or choose Adobe PDF > Convert to Adobe PDF.

The file is processed. As it is converted, several dialogs display showing the print and conversion processes. If the "Prompt for Adobe PDF file name" option is selected on the Settings panel of the Acrobat PDFMaker dialog, a Save As dialog opens for you to specify the file's name and storage location—PDFMaker uses the Word document's name by default. Chris's project is saved as manual.pdf.

## WHY CHRIS CHOOSES THESE SETTINGS

The settings chosen for the PDF document creation are used for specific purposes based on the intended use of the document, its content, or for further manipulation. Chris chose the following settings in the Adobe Acrobat PDFMaker dialog for his project:

- The Standard setting is the PDFMaker default setting. At the end of the commenting-and-markup cycle, Chris will use the High Quality Print option (along with the settings described in the "Converting the Source Document" section) to create the final PDF that he distributes to his client. The High Quality Print setting produces a document at a higher resolution than the Standard conversion option and also uses a higher resolution for color and grayscale images. The Standard setting, however, produces a smaller file size, which is useful for the distributing and commenting phase of the project.

- The Add Bookmarks to Adobe PDF and Convert Word Headings to Bookmarks options are selected to generate the bookmarks for the manual automatically. Chris intends to send his customer a PDF copy of the finished manual as well as a printout.

- Some of the material in the package has links to content on the company's Web site and other external sources. Selecting the Add Links to Adobe PDF option ports the links to the PDF document, which again is useful for the PDF version of the manual.

- The Enabling Accessibility and Reflow with tagged Adobe PDF option is used in this case to make sure the edits can be integrated back into the original Word document correctly, as described in the chapter's bonus material.

## Starting a Review Directly from Word

You can also start a comment-and-markup cycle directly from Word. Instead of choosing the Convert to Adobe PDF setting, click the Convert to Adobe PDF and Send for Review button ⊞ on the PDFMaker toolbar, or choose Adobe PDF > Convert to Adobe PDF and Send for Review. The file is processed, converted to PDF, and opened in Acrobat automatically, displaying the wizard used to set up the review.

Because Chris wants to check through the bookmark structure before starting the review, he chose to convert the file only rather than convert and send for review in one operation.

# Checking the Review Document

After Chris creates the PDF version of the manual, he'll quickly check the bookmarks before starting the review.

Open the document in Acrobat and select the Bookmarks tab to display the Bookmarks panel. The bookmarks are arranged in a hierarchy, nested according to their respective heading designations in Word. That is, a Heading 1 is shown as a first-level bookmark, and Heading 2s are nested within a first-level bookmark as second-level bookmarks (**Figure 3.4**).

It isn't necessary to include bookmarking structures in a document intended for review, but it can be a useful feature. In Chris's project, using bookmarks lets those reviewers in particular subject areas quickly locate the content they want to review. The database manager, for

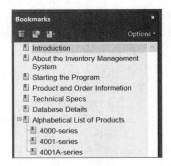

**Figure 3.4** Bookmarks are added to the PDF document and displayed in a hierarchy.

instance, can click the database-related bookmarks to display pertinent content. Also, since Chris intends to start distributing a structured PDF document to his customers, he can show the reviewers how the bookmarks are defined, and they can add comments about the bookmarks as well.

## Specifying the Opening View

Chris wants his reviewers to check the document's bookmark structure along with the content; therefore, he wants to be sure the bookmarks are visible when the document opens. Acrobat allows you to save a setting in the file that defines what the viewer sees when the document opens.

Follow these steps to define the opening view:

1. Choose File > Properties to open the Document Properties dialog, and then click the Initial View tab.

2. Click the Navigation tab arrow, and choose Bookmarks Panel and Page from the list (**Figure 3.5**).

3. Click OK to close the dialog.

4. Save the file to save the specified opening view setting.

5. To test the display, close and then reopen the document. Now Chris can send the document to his reviewers and save a copy of the file for distribution as manual.pdf.

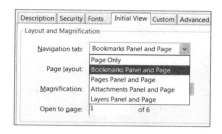

**Figure 3.5** Specify what you want viewers to see when they open the document.

## Initiating a Comment and Review Cycle

Click the Review & Comment icon on the Tasks toolbar, and then click Attach for Email Review (**Figure 3.6**). You can also choose several other options on the menu, including starting a shared review and using the Review Tracker, which is the interface for controlling a review.

> **NOTE** Check out the project in Chapter 4, "Collaborating in a Shared Review" to see how shared reviews work.

The Send by Email for Review dialog opens. This is a three-pane wizard that guides you through the review design and initiation processes, which include:

- Selecting the file.

- Defining recipients and any special instructions.

- Previewing and modifying the e-mail message that is sent to participants.

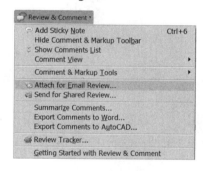

**Figure 3.6** Use the commands on the Review & Comment task button's menu to initiate and manage reviews.

Follow these steps to configure the review settings:

1. Click the down arrow on the Getting Started: Initiating an Email-Based Review pane of the wizard, and choose the file you want to use for the review. If a document is open in Acrobat, its name is shown by default. Chris uses the manual.pdf file.

The first pane of the dialog describes the process. It explains that recipients receive tools and instructions along with the document, and that management of the comments and document can be controlled; it also lists the software required to participate in the review.

2. Click Next to show the second pane of the wizard, Invite Reviewers.

3. Click Address Book to open your e-mail client's address book to select names. Alternatively, type the e-mail addresses in the dialog (**Figure 3.7**).

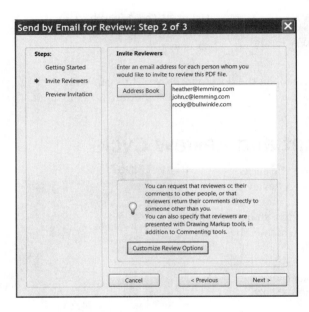

**Figure 3.7** Add the names of the recipients in this pane of the wizard.

4. To modify the review and take advantage of the customization capabilities of Acrobat 8 Professional, click Customize Review Options to open the Review Options dialog (**Figure 3.8**).

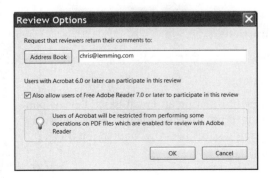

**Figure 3.8** You can customize the way in which e-mails are distributed, including enabling the commenting process for recipients who are using Adobe Reader 7 or 8.

5. Type the e-mail address, or click Address Book to open the Address Book dialog and select the name of the recipient of the review results.

6. Select "Also allow users of Free Adobe Reader 7.0 or later to participate in this review" to enable the document's commenting features in the Adobe Reader. Adobe Acrobat versions 6, 7, and 8 work with the review process.

7. Click OK to close the Review Options dialog and return to the wizard, and then click Next to display the third pane of the wizard.

8. Acrobat 8 includes a default e-mail message for reviewing. It explains the process the user must follow to use the document. Customize the e-mail message as necessary. For example, Chris can add, "Complete the review and return comments by [date]" into the subject line or the body of the e-mail.

9. Click Send Invitation to send the document on its way. The Outgoing Message Notification dialog opens, explaining that the message has been given to your e-mail application.

10. Click OK to close the dialog. Save some time in the future by selecting the "Don't show again" option to hide the dialog permanently.

That's one part of Chris's job done. The e-mail has been sent to his reviewers with the document attached. Let's see how the review works in Adobe Reader 8.

## GRANTING USAGE RIGHTS

Acrobat Professional versions 7 and 8 have the capability to enable documents for Adobe Reader reviewing, and enabled commenting can only be done by e-mail or using a shared folder review. Acrobat also provides methods for browser-based reviews. For users to participate in a browser-based review using Adobe Reader, they must have access to Adobe server products, either Adobe Document Server or Adobe Reader Extensions Server.

Rights are granted on a document-by-document basis. That is, if you are working with Adobe Reader and can comment on one document, that doesn't mean you have the rights to comment on every document you open.

# Participating in the Review

Chris has distributed the document to his reviewers, who receive the manual document as an attachment in their e-mail. The instructions for the review are contained in the body of the e-mail.

When Chris's reviewers open the attachment in Adobe Reader 8, the interface includes several components in addition to the document (**Figure 3.9**):

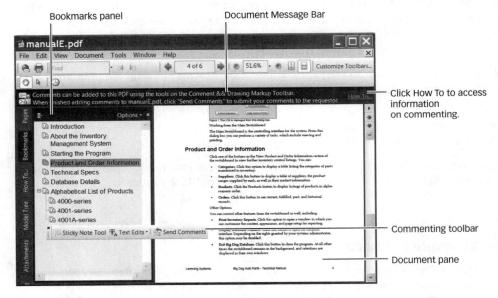

**Figure 3.9** Recipients see the document as well as several other features in Adobe Reader 8.

- The Bookmarks panel and the Document pane are shown as specified by Chris when he saved the document before starting the review.

- The Document Message Bar is shown above the two panes and describes the document's commenting capabilities.

- The Commenting toolbar is open, showing its default tools.

# Using Commenting Tools

When a document opens in Adobe Reader 8, you only see two tools on the Commenting toolbar. In a document with rights enabled, like the one used in the project, the Customize Toolbar option is shown in the toolbar area at the top of the program window (**Figure 3.10**). Let's follow along with the Lemming Systems' staff members as they review the document.

**Figure 3.10** An enabled document shows the Customize Toolbar label in the toolbar area.

Follow these steps to add additional tools to the toolbar:

1. Click the Customize Toolbar button in the Adobe Reader 8 toolbar area to open a dialog listing the tools available for use in an enabled file (**Figure 3.11**).

2. Select tools to add to the toolbar. The choices you make depend on your usual commenting style or the requirements of the review. **Table 3.1** lists the tools on the Commenting toolbar and describes what each tool, or group of tools, is used for.

3. Click OK to close the dialog and add the tools and tool groups to the Commenting toolbar.

Now that the extra tools are added to the toolbar, it's time to see them in action.

**Figure 3.11** Choose from dozens of additional tools to use in the review.

Table **3.1** Breakdown of tools on the Commenting Toolbar

| TOOLBAR ICON | FUNCTION |
| --- | --- |
| | The Sticky Note tool lets you add notes to the document. |
| | Text Edit tools let you indicate text edits in a document. You can select several tools from the subtoolbar for specific types of edits. |
| | The Stamp tools pull-down menu lets you add a variety of stamps to a document, including custom and dynamic options. |
| | The Highlighting tools work like electronic versions of traditional highlighting pens or ink pens that cross out or underline text. |
| | Attach tools let you add either a file or a voice comment. |
| | Show tools let you access the Comments panel, view comment content, and sort comments in a number of ways. |

# Adding a Comment

Comments are very easy to apply in Acrobat. Choose the tool on the Commenting toolbar that you want to use, and then click the document or drag a marquee.

 **DOWNLOAD** The file version used in this part of the project is named **manualE.pdf** because it has been enabled for use in Adobe Reader. You can download it from the book's Web site or continue with an enabled copy of your own file.

Here's a brief summary of the various Commenting tools; Text Edit tools are covered in the next section:

- **Sticky Note tool.** Notes are generally used more than any other type of comment. Clicking the document with the Note tool opens a pop-up window. When you begin typing, text for the note is inserted (**Figure 3.12**). To save space in the document, click the close box in the pop-up window. You then see a small Note icon on the page; click the icon to open the pop-up window again.

**Figure 3.12** Use the Sticky Note tool to add annotations to the document.

- **Stamp tools.** The Stamp tools are updated versions of old-fashioned ink stamps. Click the Stamp tools icon on the Commenting toolbar to open a set of menus and sub-menus (**Figure 3.13**). Some of the stamps are dynamic in that they add your name and the date or time when you add the stamp to the document. You can also create custom stamps. Click the document where you want to apply the stamp. Like other types of stamps, double-click the stamp on the document to open a pop-up window to type text.

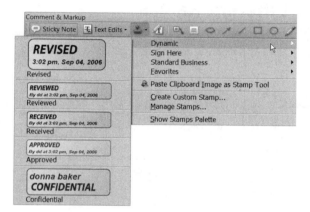

**Figure 3.13** Choose from one of the many available Stamp tools or create your own custom stamps.

- **Highlighting tools.** There are three Highlighting tools in all. Select a tool and then drag it across the text you want to identify. To add text, double-click the highlight to open a pop-up window, and type the text in the window (**Figure 3.14**).

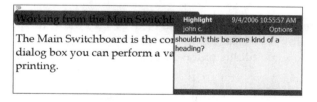

**Figure 3.14** Identify a particular passage on the document using a Highlighting tool.

- **Attach tools.** You can either attach a file or record an audio comment. Select an option from the Attach tools pull-down menu, click the document with the pointer, and then follow the prompts to find the file to attach or record the comment.

  **NOTE** See how to use attachments as part of the document rather than inserted as an attached comment in Chapter 6, "Managing and Organizing E-mail Using Acrobat."

You can modify all comments you add to a document. You can change the appearance or color of icons, add a subject, and reposition comments in the document. To delete a comment, click it in the Comments panel or in the Document pane and then press Delete.

Comments are either collapsed, meaning you don't see any associated text, or open, showing the text in a message box. If the comment is closed, move the pointer over the comment's icon to show the comment's contents in a tooltip.

## The Same Feature, but Different Names

Some of the program features have slightly different names depending on whether you are working in Adobe Reader or Acrobat 8. The features and their names are listed in **Table 3.2**.

**Table 3.2** Comparison of Feature Names

| COMMAND OR FEATURE | NAME IN ACROBAT 8 | NAME IN ADOBE READER 8 |
| --- | --- | --- |
| Toolbar with comment tools | Comment & Markup toolbar | Comment & Drawing Markup toolbar |
| Toolbar command to open tool list | More Tools | Customize Toolbars |
| Dialog name of tool list | More Tools | Customize Toolbars |
| Toolbar containing basic selecting tools | Select & Zoom | Basic |

# Using Text Edit Tools

Chris is particularly interested in his reviewers using the Text Edit tools, because then he can integrate the changes directly into the source Word document. He decides to give each reviewer a list of instructions for working with Text Edit tools.

In a perfect world, all the comments intended for edits would be done with the Text Edit tools, but Chris is quite aware that until his colleagues get the hang of working with commenting tools, he will have to do some editing of the document manually. Oh well, maybe in future reviews!

The Text Edit tools, a subset of the Comment & Drawing Markups toolbar, work in the same way as writing comments on a printed page but are much more efficient.

Here's how Chris explains the workings of the Text Edit tools for his reviewers in an e-mail.

—*Start of Chris's e-mail*—

There are two approaches to adding comments to the document that let me make changes in the original files automatically. Basically, the difference is whether you select the text to change with the specific edit tool or whether you select it with a general tool and then apply the edit type. I'll describe the methods, starting with the Text Edit commenting tools.

# Using the Text Edit Toolbar

You can either use the tools on the Comment & Drawing Markup toolbar or choose Tools > Comment & Drawing Markup > Text Edits and choose the specific tool.

Please follow these steps to use the tools to indicate changes you want made to the content of the document:

1. Click the Text Edits down arrow to display the list of tools, and then click the Indicate Text Edits tool to activate the Text Edits tool [Ir]. The first time you use the tools a dialog displays, showing short descriptions of the tools and how they work. Click OK to close the dialog and get to work.

2. Each text edit displays differently on the page, but all show a highlighted border circling the edit location on the page. Add your edits by doing one of the following:

   - **Insert text.** Click in the text of the document and type to insert text. On the document, you see an insertion caret icon, and the text is placed in a pop-up comment box (**Figure 3.15**).

   - **Delete text.** Select the text to delete using the Text Edits tool, and press Delete or Backspace on the keyboard. You see the text crossed-out in the document (**Figure 3.16**).

   - **Replace text.** Select the text with the Text Edits tool and type new text to replace existing text. The text you type appears in a Replacement Text pop-up comment box, the selected text displays a strikethrough, and an insertion caret is shown at the end of the string of text you selected with the tool. The edit's insertion carat shows a highlighted border. When the pop-up comment box is closed, move the pointer over the highlight to show the replacement text in the tooltip (**Figure 3.17**).

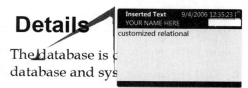

**Figure 3.15** Indicate where you would like new text inserted into the document.

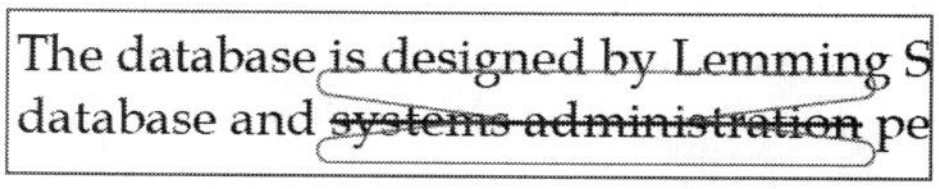

**Figure 3.16** Cross out text that you want deleted from the document.

**Figure 3.17** View replacement text in a tooltip rather than opening the comment.

**3.** Add a comment in the pop-up box that displays when the comment is added if you need to make a clarification or suggestion (**Figure 3.18**).

I know this whole digital editing thing can be confusing, so I'll describe the second method, which might be simpler for some since you start from the document, not in the toolbar.

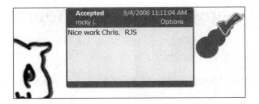

**Figure 3.18** Add additional information about your edits if necessary.

## Starting from the Document Pane

The simplest way to make text edits is to start from the actual page of the document, displayed in the Document pane. You select the content you want to change and then select the tool, which lets you concentrate on the content.

Follow these steps to start editing from the Document pane:

**1.** Click the Select tool ▮ on the Select & Zoom toolbar (Acrobat) or the Basic toolbar (Adobe Reader).

**2.** Drag to select the text on the page (**Figure 3.19**).

**3.** Click the Text Edit down arrow on the Comment & Markup toolbar and choose one of the tools:

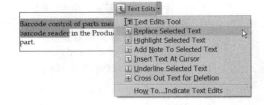

**Figure 3.19** Select the text on the page first, and then apply a text edit comment.

- **Replace Selected Text** replaces the selected text with typed text that is displayed in a pop-up comment box.

- **Highlight Selected Text** highlights the selected text.

- **Add Note To Selected Text** opens a comment box for you to add information about the text that is selected in the document.

- **Insert Text At Cursor** lets you type additional text, which is then placed in a pop-up comment box.

- **Underline Selected Text** places an underscore under the selected text.

- **Cross Out Text for Deletion** adds a strikethrough to the selected text.

There is one more method, and it doesn't require selecting any comment tools.

## Bypassing the Comment & Markup Toolbar

If you select text using the Select tool on the Select & Zoom toolbar, the Select icon displays on the page over the selected text . When you click the icon, the menu displays (**Figure 3.20**). You can choose a number of different comment types from the menu. Note that the menu doesn't contain the entire list of comment types; for some text editing, such as Cross Out for Deletion, you have to use the Text Edit menu option.

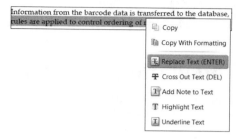

**Figure 3.20** Choose an edit method directly from the Select tool's menu.

## Return to Sender

When you have finished making the edits and adding other comments, send the results back to me. On the Comment & Drawing Markup toolbar, click Send Comments to return the comments to me by e-mail. The comments are attached to an e-mail already addressed to me.

Thank you. I look forward to receiving your feedback.

—*The end of Chris's e-mail*—

When the reviewers are finished with the file, they can send the comments back to Chris directly from the Adobe Reader program. The process is the same from Acrobat 8 aside from the toolbar name differences.

Follow these steps to return the comments from a review in Adobe Reader 8:

1. Click Send Comments on the Comment & Drawing Markup toolbar. The dialog shown in **Figure 3.21** opens.

2. The dialog shows the return e-mail message, which is already addressed using the settings specified by Chris. Modify the text if you want to add your own message.

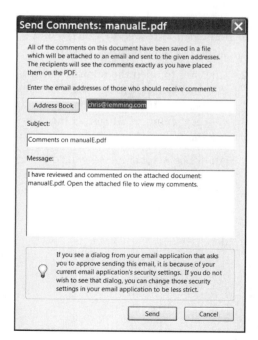

**Figure 3.21** Acrobat uses the subject, message, and e-mail address specified at the start of the review.

3. Click Send to send the comments on their way. The comments are sent as an FDF (File Data Format) file.

Next, Chris integrates the comments into his original PDF file.

# Integrating Comments into the PDF File

Chris works from within Acrobat to import comments into his open PDF file after saving them from the e-mails returned from his reviewers.

 **DOWNLOAD** If you'd like to work with the comment files from Chris's reviewers, download **comments_heather.fdf**, **comments_john.c.fdf**, and **comments_rocky.fdf** from the Web site, and then add them to the PDF file from Acrobat.

Follow these steps to open a PDF file that's part of a review:

1. Open the file originally enabled for the review named manualE.pdf or another copy of the file if you prefer. When the file is opened, Acrobat recognizes it as related to a review and displays a dialog (**Figure 3.22**).

2. Click Yes to open the original tracked document, as in Chris's case. Click No to open the document as a copy or cancel the import altogether by clicking the appropriate buttons.

    An Adobe Acrobat message dialog opens specifying that comments from the copy have been integrated into the original; click OK to close the dialog.

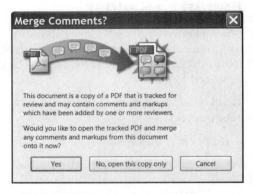

**Figure 3.22** Acrobat recognizes incoming documents as part of a tracked review and offers several options.

3. In the Navigation panels at the left of the program window, the How To panel is active and a description of how to integrate comments from others is displayed (**Figure 3.23**). Read through the information if you are new to the process or need a refresher.

After the file is opened, Chris decides to import the comment files directly from his hard drive where he saved them from the reviewers' e-mail messages.

Follow these steps to locate and add the comment files:

1. Choose Comment > Import Comments to open the Import Comments dialog.

2. Locate and select the file or files you want to import (**Figure 3.24**). Chris selects all three comment files at the same time.

3. If you can't find the file—and are sure you are looking in the right folder—click the Files of type down arrow and choose a different file format from the list.

4. The files are integrated into the document one by one. Depending on the names of the files you use for the review and for adding comments to, you may or may not see a dialog notifying you that the comments come from a different version of the file than the original. Click OK to add them to the document.

5. Save the file after adding the comments.

As Chris receives the replies from his reviewers, he can continue to integrate the comments into his original document while allowing his reviewers to maintain their own copies complete with their comments. Maintaining digital control of the process should help to resolve any issues that can arise when working with paper and trying to reconcile comments from different sources manually—handwritten comments are easier to miss or misinterpret than are those that are typewritten. Also, using the Acrobat review process is extremely time efficient.

**Figure 3.23** Review information about commenting in the How To panel.

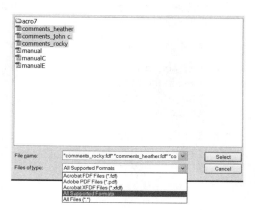

**Figure 3.24** Select the comment file(s) to integrate into the review document.

Once Chris has received the comments and integrated them into his original document, he can save the document using a separate name. Using a distinctive name, such as appending the review date to the end of the original document's name makes it easy to track the progress of a project. He saves the file as manualC.pdf ("C" for comments).

**COMMENT MIGRATION**

You import comments into a PDF document only once. When you are working with multiple versions of a document, it is helpful to save numbered copies. In this way, each time you circulate a document for comments, you have a PDF document that can accept comments. You can also migrate comments, which is a secondary method of adding comments to a document.

Choose Comments > Migrate Comments to open the Migrate Comments dialog and select both the document you are migrating comments from as well as the one you are migrating comments to.

The migration process searches a document and tries to place additional comments in the correct locations based on the document's tags. There may be placement discrepancies based on the differences between the two versions of the document, which you'll have to adjust manually.

Acrobat places migrated comments according to these principles:

- Text comments applied to selected words display within the same words if they exist in the revised document; if the words are mismatched, the comments are placed on the first or last page of the document; if text is deleted, the edit is converted to a note.

- Stamps, notes, and drawing markups are applied according to the original document's structure; if the page is deleted, the comment is placed on the last page of the revised document.

# Managing the Review

In the "old" days, Chris would have to manually flip through the edits he received to see who had finished commenting and whose feedback was still outstanding. He would then have to send out e-mail "reminder" messages. Using Acrobat's Review Tracker and the Comments panel, he can control the information from within Acrobat.

Follow these steps to open the Review Tracker:

1.  Click the down arrow on the Comment & Markup button and choose Review Tracker.

2.  The Review Tracker opens as a separate window (**Figure 3.25**). Choose the review you want to check out from the lists in the left frame of the window.

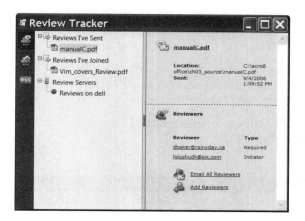

**Figure 3.25** The Review Tracker shows information about reviews.

3.  Click the review's name in the frame on the right to open its information.

    The panel to the right of the window shows the name of the selected review, the storage location of the original review document, and a list of the participants. The participant list is composed of active links. Click a name to open an e-mail dialog addressed to the selected participant.

4.  In the pane on the right in the dialog you can choose:

    ■   **Email All Reviewers** to open an e-mail dialog addressed to those on the review participant list. Add the message and send the e-mail.

    ■   **Add Reviewers** to open the Send by Email for Review dialog to invite additional reviewers. Follow the wizard to add more participants.

It's simple to keep track of a review that has three or four participants; it's much more difficult to control a review with dozens of participants. But the Comments panel makes the task easy by allowing you to sort comments in a number of useful ways.

**NOTE** You can read much more about using the Review Tracker in Chapter 4.

# Using the Comments Panel

Some of the comments in the document are simply text edits intended for reintegrating into the original Word document, whereas others pertain to aspects of the PDF document, specifically the bookmarks, which Chris asked the reviewers to evaluate.

Once comments are integrated into a document, they can be used and examined in a number of ways.

Follow these steps to work with comments in Acrobat:

1. Click the Comments icon ![icon] in the Navigation panel at the left of the program window to display the Comments panel.

   Unlike most of Acrobat's Navigation panels, the Comments panel displays horizontally under the Document pane and any open Navigation panels.

2. Comments imported into the original draft are arranged in the Comments panel according to page by default (**Figure 3.26**).

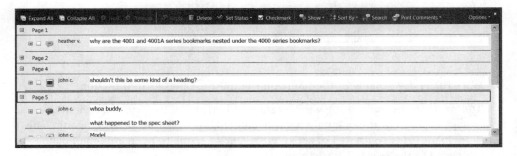

**Figure 3.26** By default, Acrobat arranges comments in a document according to page number.

3. Click the Sort By button's down arrow and choose a sort method (**Figure 3.27**). Chris chooses the Sort By Type option to reorder the list of comments.

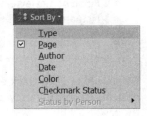

**Figure 3.27** You can choose from among several ways to sort the contents of the Comments panel.

**4.** The sorted list is collapsed. Click the (+) to the left of a name to open the list of comments of a specific type (**Figure 3.28**).

Many of the comments the reviewers added to the document can be transferred to the source Word document, either as edits or comments. To keep track of the edits, Chris will use the Comments panel's Checkmark feature to filter the feedback.

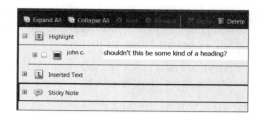

**Figure 3.28** Collapse and expand the headings in the Comments panel to save space.

# Tracking the Comments

Chris intends to export the comments to his source Word document to automatically revise it. He doesn't need all the comments, so he decides to organize the comments he intends to export using the Checkmark feature included in the Comments panel.

Follow these steps to add a checkmark to a comment in the Comments panel:

**1.** Select the comment you want to apply the checkmark to.

**2.** Click the Checkmark icon in the Comments panel.

**3.** The first time you use the feature, an Adobe Acrobat information dialog opens explaining that the checkmarks are internal to your copy of the document only and aren't shared with others in the review. This, of course, is what Chris wants.

**4.** Click OK to close the dialog. A checkmark is shown in the check box to the left of the comment's listing in the Comments panel (**Figure 3.29**).

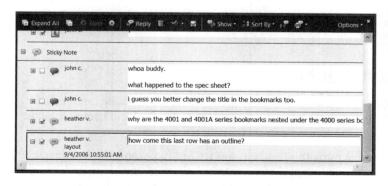

**Figure 3.29** Acrobat offers a checkmark process you can apply according to how you need to identify comments or tasks.

Chris continues through the Comments panel, adding checkmarks for those comments he wants to export to Word to revise the file. The remaining comments are general, and he will note and disregard them.

To check his progress and make sure he hasn't missed any comments, he sorts the comments based on checkmarks by following these steps:

1. Click Sort By on the Comments panel to open the pull-down menu.

2. Choose Checkmark Status. The comments are resorted into two categories—Unmarked and Marked (**Figure 3.30**).

3. Click the Unmarked category to display the list and scan any remaining unmarked check boxes to be sure they are processed.

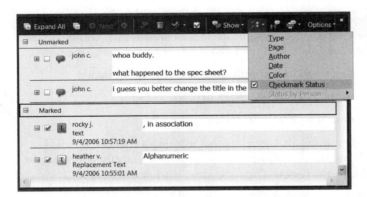

**Figure 3.30** Review the sorted comments to check for outstanding edits.

4. Save the file.

Chris has finished the first round of reviews—without using any paper—and has saved a lot of time in the process.

## Integrating Comments into Word

Chris has a few other options he can choose to continue with his review. He can manually make corrections to the text in the document using the TouchUp Tool and manually adjust the bookmarks according to the comments from his colleagues.

Since the comments are made using the Text Edits tools, Chris can export the comments from Acrobat 8 Professional directly into the source Microsoft Word document (in Windows) to make the corrections automatically and lay out the comments as in the PDF file.

**DOWNLOAD** Read how to export comments into the source Word document and make corrections in the bonus file ch03B1.pdf available from the book's Web site at www.donnabaker.ca/downloads.html. Comment integration is a Windows-only feature.

## What Else Can He Do?

The next phase of Chris's review process is to make the edits in the PDF file, create a new version of the PDF document, and recirculate it to his participant list. When he has approval from all reviewers, his document is ready for printing.

Chris can create a comment summary that can be saved as a PDF document on its own that he can refer to during subsequent review cycles, described in Chapter 12, "Secure Reviewing and Reporting," or he can export the comments to a text or FDF (File Data Format) file in case he wants to send the comments to someone outside the review to integrate into his or her own copy of the review document.

# Collaborating in a Shared Review

Pop quiz: What do town criers, the Pony Express, telephones, teletype, typewritten letters and smudged carbon copies, distributed e-mails, online meetings, and bulletin boards have in common? Answer: All are means of sharing information and collaborating on ideas, devising devious plans, plotting hostile railroad takeover bids, and thwarting invading hordes from the north.

Exchange of information and ideas is an accepted and necessary part of daily life. Looking for a way to efficiently and easily exchange those ideas is also a necessary part of life. Sadly, finding a communication vehicle that is less than efficient or easy to handle is also often a part of life.

One of Acrobat's strongest features is the development of communication methods based on a PDF document and Commenting tools. We've seen an expanding range of functionality, such as enabling a file for use in Adobe Reader and offering tools for measuring objects in a PDF document in Acrobat 7 Professional. That collaborative strength continues in Acrobat 8 Professional with the introduction of a shared review.

Until Acrobat 8, reviews have been of two types, either e-mail reviews (such as the one featured in Chapter 12, "Secure Reviewing and Reporting") or browser-based reviews. A shared review is similar to a browser-based review in that both types let participants view each other's comments as they are added.

A shared review is different from a browser-based review in its simplicity. Anyone having network folder rights can create, distribute, and manage the review, which can easily move shared reviews into the mainstream of many workflows. If you need some quick advice from a few colleagues on a document or design you are working on, drop a copy of the file in your shared folder and invite the gang to weigh in with their comments. In fact, this scenario is featured in the chapter's project.

**NOTE** Acrobat 8 Professional doesn't offer a method to set up a browser-based review, although preexisting browser-based reviews are supported.

# What's Your Preference?

*Vim* magazine is the new kid on the block. In production for less than a year, the fledgling publication is gaining some recognition and, thankfully, increasing sales. *Vim* is a home design magazine catering to the new consumer standard. *Vim* readers are mature in their design esthetic and appreciate a modern design style that focuses on material and workmanship.

Nobody knows the market and their readers better than the cofounders, Lois Lake and Clark Mann. Lois and Clark worked together for many years as architects and designers.

Daisy Trigg is their publishing protégé. Lois and Clark hired Daisy to turn their ideas and knowledge into a publication they can all be proud of. *Vim* offers regular columns and pieces on interiors, exteriors, furnishings, and fixtures. Each issue includes a multipage feature consisting of articles, expert opinions, resources, and advertisers that is not generally seen in magazines catering to their readership. One of the upcoming features revolves around the modern resurgence of art glass.

The interior design of the magazine calls for an opening page for the feature. Rather than gather in a conference room for preliminary discussions, they will offer their opinions in an active review created in Acrobat 8 Professional **(Figure 4.1)**.

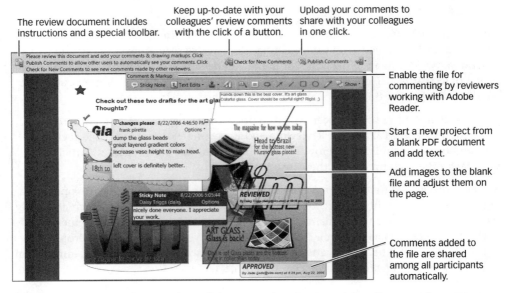

**Figure 4.1** The team at *Vim* magazine collaborate on choosing a special section cover for an upcoming issue using a PDF file assembled in Acrobat 8 Professional.

# Steps Involved in This Project

*Vim* outsources page layout and production, and has a small in-house team. The editorial and art staff collaborates closely. Daisy works her magic by staying organized. She has learned that anything that saves time getting tasks done lets her spend more time focusing on the magazine's content. Daisy thinks she can collect input from her group more quickly and in a more focused manner using an Acrobat shared review, and plans to give it a try today.

To achieve her goal, Daisy has to:

- Produce the PDF file to use for the review.

- Set up the shared review folder.

- Invite participants and specify the deadline.

- Collect and monitor comments as they are produced.

- Collate the comments.

# Preparing the Document

First things first: Daisy has copies of two draft layouts she needs to use for the review. She can assemble the images in Photoshop but decides to use Acrobat 8 Professional exclusively to assemble the review PDF document.

 **DOWNLOAD** If you'd like to create the composite PDF document yourself, download **Vim_coverA.jpg** and **Vim_coverB.jpg** from the book's Web site at www.donnabaker. ca/downloads.html.

# Producing the Review Document

Daisy decides to use the new Acrobat 8 Professional method of using a blank page to start a PDF document. The default new page configuration is a letter-sized page with a Portrait orientation. But using a Landscape orientation is a simpler way for Daisy to present the two images in the review document, so she'll change the program preferences first.

## Specifying blank page appearances

Before Daisy adds images to the document, she changes the program preferences for the new page by following these steps:

**1.** Choose Edit > Preferences (Windows) or Acrobat > Preferences (Mac) to open the Preferences dialog and click New Document in the left column to display the options (**Figure 4.2**).

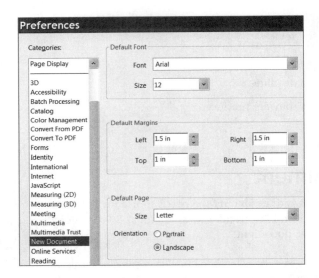

**Figure 4.2** Check the New Document settings before creating the new document.

**2.** Click the Landscape radio button in the Default Page section of the dialog.

**3.** Click OK to close the dialog and set the preference.

Now Daisy is ready to get started.

## Starting a blank file

Daisy will use a blank landscape-oriented PDF file. Follow these steps to create the document for reviewing:

**1.** Choose File > Create PDF > From Blank Page to open a new document. The New Document toolbar opens automatically, and the page shows an active text insertion pointer.

**2.** Type a note at the top of the page. Daisy types Check out these two drafts for the art glass issue's cover. Thoughts?

3. Click and drag to select the text on the page and modify the text appearance if you like (**Figure 4.3**). Daisy clicks the Font down arrow, chooses Arial Rounded MT Bold, and then chooses 18 pt from the Size pull-down menu.

**Figure 4.3** Choose settings in the New Document toolbar to configure text added to a blank page.

4. Choose File > Save to open the Save As dialog. Type a name for the new PDF file and specify its storage location. Click Save to save the file and close the dialog. Daisy names the file covers.pdf.

## Locking the text edits

Converting a file to PDF works differently from creating a new file in Acrobat in that the new document option includes its own toolbar for adding text. However, that text entry functionality has to be locked before you can make other edits or touchups in the file.

Daisy chose the new document route, starting a new blank page and adding configurable text to the page, so she'll follow these steps to finish the document preparation:

1. Prevent the text from being further edited by choosing Document > Prevent Further Editing to open the dialog shown in **Figure 4.4**.

2. Click Prevent Further Editing. The dialog closes, and the Save As dialog opens.

3. Daisy names the document Vim_covers.pdf and saves the file in a shared folder her colleagues can access.

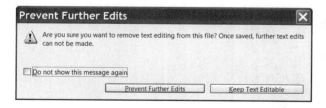

**Figure 4.4** You can prevent or allow editing of text added to a new document.

Once the text entry feature is locked, Daisy can continue with other types of editing. Next she adds the first sample cover image to the blank PDF document.

## Importing the images

Daisy has two alternate draft covers she wants her staff to review. Follow these steps to add the images to the blank PDF page:

1. Right-click/Control-click the toolbar well and choose Advanced Editing to open the toolbar if it isn't displayed in the program.

2. Select the TouchUp Object tool and right-click/ Control-click the page to open the shortcut menu (**Figure 4.5**).

3. Select Place Image to display the Open dialog. Locate and select the first image file, Vim_coverA.jpg, and click Open. The dialog closes and the image is placed at the center of the PDF page within a bounding box.

   In the Open dialog, the Files of type field shows JPEG as the default file format. If you can't find the image in the folder where you thought you stored it, click the down arrow and select a different image format.

4. The pointer changes to crosshairs with arrows. Drag to position the image left of center on the page (**Figure 4.6**).

5. Repeat steps 2 through 4 to place and position the second sample cover image to the right of center (**Figure 4.7**).

**Figure 4.5** Use the TouchUp Object tool to add a new image to a PDF file.

**Figure 4.6** The TouchUp Object tool lets you place a new image in a PDF file. How handy!

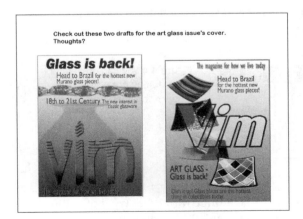

**Figure 4.7** The sample images are added and saved in the new PDF document.

**6.** Save the PDF file again.

Daisy saves the two images with the page. She'll position the images using program tools next.

## Setting and viewing positioning tools

Daisy can eyeball the images' positions on the page but instead decides to check her placement using the guides and grid tools Acrobat provides. She first checks the preferences.

To view and modify grid and guide preferences, follow these steps:

**1.** Choose Edit > Preferences (Windows) or Acrobat > Preferences (Mac) to open the Preferences dialog and choose Units & Guides from the column at the left of the dialog.

**2.** Leave most of the default preferences for the Units and Layout Grid sections as they are except increase the Subdivisions from 3 to 4 per inch by clicking the up arrow to the right of the number field (**Figure 4.8**).

**3.** Click the Guide color swatch to open the small color palette and choose a color that contrasts the page color. The default color for both grids and guides is a medium blue.

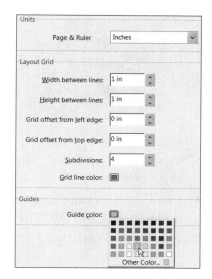

**Figure 4.8** Specify color and spacing preferences that make guides and grids easy to see and use.

**4.** Click OK to close the dialog and save the preferences.

**5.** Display several of the positioning tools located on the View menu by choosing View > Rulers, View > Grid, and View > Guides.

The tools are ready for Daisy to help her position the images just right.

## Tweaking image locations on the page

The two images are on the page but are not evenly placed. Daisy can quickly move them into position by following these steps:

**1.** Click the Hand tool 🖑 on the Select & Zoom toolbar to select it.

**2.** Move the pointer over the upper ruler and then click and drag downward to pull a horizontal guide over the page. Release the mouse when the guide is in the desired position. To adjust the guide's location, move the pointer over the line and click and drag when the pointer changes to a small black arrow (**Figure 4.9**).

**Figure 4.9** Adjust the positions of the images on the page using the positioning reference tools.

3.  Choose View > Toolbars > Advanced Editing to open the toolbar if it isn't displayed in the program. Select the TouchUp Object tool.

4.  One by one, click the images with the TouchUp Object tool to select them, and then drag them into position or nudge them using the keyboard arrow keys.

5.  Choose View > Grid, View > Rulers, and View > Guide to hide the positioning tools again.

    **TIP** You can use any tool to drag a guide from either the horizontal or vertical rulers. However, if you release the guide and click the page by mistake, you activate the tool. It won't cause a big problem and you can undo anything you may do by accident, but I find it just irritating enough to make selecting the Hand tool standard procedure.

### MAIL IT IN

If you need to invite other reviewers who can't use your shared folder because they are outside your local network or away from the office, they can be included as e-mail participants. In that case, Daisy—as the review initiator—sends an invitation for review by e-mail, the recipients add their comments, and the comments are sent back to Daisy. When she opens the comment file, the comments are merged with the review document automatically, using the automated method described in Chapter 3. The comments are merged in her name with the original participant's name in the comment. Slick.

This way, nobody ever has to feel left out of office communications simply because they decide to go on a luxurious cruise vacation for a few days or weeks.

Daisy is ready to set up the review. She's interested to see how it works. To see each reviewer's comments in a shared review, all participants need to have Acrobat 8 (Standard or Professional) or Adobe Reader 8. Anyone with an older program version has to resort to e-mail for commenting.

# Starting the Review

The image PDF file is ready to be loaded into its folder location. A shared review is used only with reviewers who can access the same local shared folder. If a reviewer can't access the file, they can participate only by e-mail.

Daisy follows these steps to get the review underway:

 **DOWNLOAD** Use the file you prepared in the previous section or download the **Vim_covers.pdf** file from the Chapter 4 folder on the book's Web site.

1.  Click the Comment & Review Task button to open its menu and choose Send for Shared Review to open the four-pane Send PDF for Shared Review wizard.

2.  In the first pane, choose a folder location and the PDF file to use for storing the comments. If you have the review file open and active in Acrobat when you start the wizard, the review file's name is listed automatically, like Daisy's choices in **Figure 4.10**. The "Enable Reviewers with Adobe Reader to participate" check box is selected by default. Click Next.

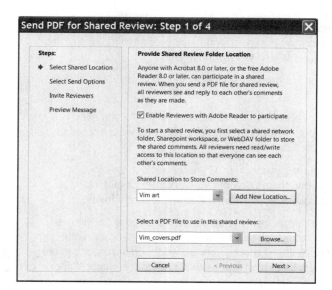

**Figure 4.10** Select the file for sharing and the folder where it is stored.

**3.** Specify how you want the file accessed and distributed. You can send it as an e-mail attachment or as a link to the shared folder. If you like, you can save the file on your computer and e-mail invitations at a later time. Daisy uses the default choice to "Automatically send e-mail invitation to reviewers" and "Attach the PDF file to the message & save a copy locally."

**4.** Click Browse and select a location to save the PDF file copy. Acrobat automatically appends _Review to the end of the file's name. Click Next.

**5.** Specify the reviewers in the third pane of the dialog (**Figure 4.11**). Click Address Book to open your e-mail clients' address list and select the reviewers, or type the names in the Required Reviewers and Optional Reviewers fields. Separate the names with semicolons or line breaks.

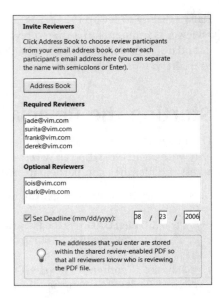

**Figure 4.11** Add reviewers from your e-mail clients' address book or type them manually.

## SHARE AND SHARE ALIKE

The beauty of a shared review is its simplicity. It only takes a few minutes to set up the review. Depending on your work environment, you may never need to consult the IT wizards to set up communications in your workgroup again!

Three types of folders are used for a shared review, depending on how your network is set up. The choices include:

- **Network folder.** The simplest option is to use a network folder. All you need is a shared folder on a local network; reviewers must have read and write access to the shared folder.

- **SharePoint workspace.** If your organization uses SharePoint Services in Windows, place the folder in your shared SharePoint workspace. Again, all reviewers must have read and write access to the document library folder.

- **WebDAV.** If you want reviewers from inside and outside a firewall to participate directly, and your organization uses Web servers supporting the WebDAV (Web Distributed Authoring and Versioning) protocol, your network administrator can set up a shared folder. All reviewers need read and write access to the shared folder.

6. Daisy needs a fast turnaround on the document, so she clicks Set Deadline to activate the date entry fields. She types the date and clicks Next to move to the final pane of the dialog.

7. She then reads the boilerplate subject and content for the e-mail in the dialog. The default text lists the file name as the subject for the e-mail and instructions for participating in the review. You can make changes as necessary, and then click Finish.

8. Depending on your e-mail client's configuration, you may or may not receive a dialog asking for permission to send the e-mail to participants. Send the invitations on their way.

## Sharing Comments

The e-mail invitation explaining how the shared review works is circulated to Daisy's colleagues. Surita is the first to make some time to look at the cover drafts and follows these steps to participate in the review:

1. Open the attachment in either Acrobat 8 Professional or Standard, or Adobe Reader 8. The document displays with a message bar explaining how the process works (**Figure 4.12**).

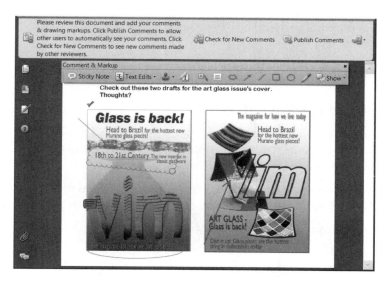

**Figure 4.12**
Instructions are shown when the file is opened for reviewing.

2. Make comments using the Comment & Markup tools, also shown in Figure 4.12. Refer to Chapter 3, "Communicating with Comments" for a full discussion on using and customizing comments.

3. Surita has a clear favorite that she indicates using a checkmark stamp. When she's finished adding her comments, she clicks Publish Comments to attach her comments to the review document in the shared folder.

4. Choose File > Save to save the document locally and close the file.

## Managing Comments

You don't have to worry about forgetting to send comments or not knowing if you have sent them or not. If there are new comments that haven't been stored in the review, Acrobat conveniently keeps track and asks you what to do with the comments (**Figure 4.13**).

You can:

- Click Publish to send comments to other review participants.

- Click Save as Draft to save comments in your document and keep working independently. Publish the comments when you are ready.

- Click Delete to remove comments from the PDF file.

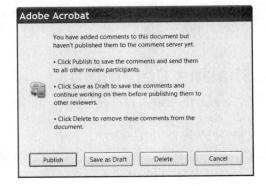

**Figure 4.13** You can't forget to deal with unprocessed comments—Acrobat reminds you.

## Checking the Publishing Status

It doesn't matter whether Surita—or any of the other review participants—is "online" or "offline" when publishing comments. The comments are stored automatically in a queue that is sent the next time the review's shared folder can be accessed.

The document message bar shows an icon describing what sort of connection the file is using. You see one of three different icons:

- A green checkmark on the icon indicates the document is connected to your shared folder

- A yellow caution sign on the icon indicates the document is not currently connected to your shared folder.

- A green rotating disc on the icon means the document is trying to connect to the shared folder.

Once the comments are published to the review document, they are available to Daisy and the other reviewers.

---

**CHECK YOUR PROFILE**

When you first use Acrobat 8 Professional reviews, you see a Review Profile dialog with fields to enter your author name, organization information, and e-mail. Type your details into the fields and then click OK to close the dialog. The information is stored in the program's preferences.

Update your review profile by following these steps:

1. Choose Edit > Preferences (Windows) or Acrobat > Preferences (Mac) to open the Preferences dialog.

2. Choose Commenting from the column at the left and in the Making Comments section of Preferences clear the "Always Use Log-In Name for Author Name" check box if you want to change the author name.

3. Choose Identity in the column at the left of the dialog and edit the name, organization information, and e-mail address as necessary.

4. Click OK to close the Preferences dialog and make the changes.

---

# Following the Comments Online

Acrobat 8 and Adobe Reader 8 offer several ways to follow the course of an active shared review. What you see and in what form depends on what you are doing at the time. For example, if you open the review document in Acrobat, you are notified in a different way than if you are working in another program—where a review notification appears on your desktop's system tray.

## Receiving Notifications

If Daisy or one of the review participants opens the document in Acrobat during the course of the review, a Welcome screen dialog displays (**Figure 4.14**). The dialog provides information on the review since she last opened the document, including a reviewer list and numbers of comments those reviewers have contributed.

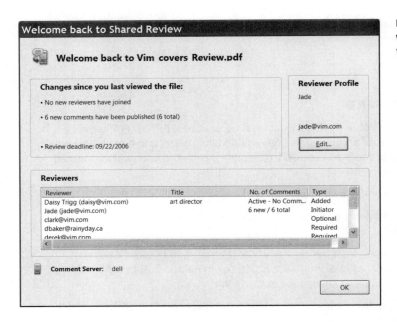

Figure 4.14 Catch up with a review the next time you open the file.

When a participant adds comments to the review, you see a notice in the file identifying the number of comments to be added in a message balloon (**Figure 4.15**).

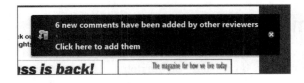

Figure 4.15 New comment activity is shown in a pop-up balloon.

Whether you are working in the file or not, a Review icon is added to the desktop and is located in the system tray. Messages display to notify you of new comments added to the review depending on the notification schedule established.

## Specifying When You Are Notified

Acrobat uses an automatic notification system that checks your system according to a schedule. A program process takes the comments from the storage file and saves a copy locally. You can specify when and where you are notified in the Reviewing preferences. If

Acrobat is open, choose Edit > Preferences (Windows) or Acrobat > Preferences (Mac) and select Reviewing in the left column of the dialog. If Acrobat is not open and you want to save a couple of clicks, right-click/Control-click the Review icon in your system tray to open the shortcut menu (**Figure 4.16**). Choose Reviewing Preferences to open the Preferences dialog with the Reviewing options visible.

**Figure 4.16** Common review tasks are available from the system tray icon's menu.

Set the frequency and location of notifications in a shared review by dragging a slider:

- When the review document is open, drag the slider to specify from 2 minutes to 30 minute intervals between checks for new comments.

- When the document is closed, Acrobat can check for comments in the background; drag the slider to specify a check from once per hour to once per month.

- Specify that the Review Tracker Alerts are shown in the system task bar on an interval ranging from never to 24 hours.

   **NOTE** You don't specify a comments repository or network storage location for a shared review in the program preferences. Network settings are required for browser-based reviews.

In the Preferences dialog you can also establish whether Acrobat notifies you when comments are imported and if the Comment list and Comment & Markup toolbars should be opened automatically. In addition, you can specify the threshold size for sending comments as an FDF (File Data Format) file rather than the entire PDF with comments. Click OK to close the dialog and set the preferences. **Figure 4.17** shows the default program settings for shared reviews.

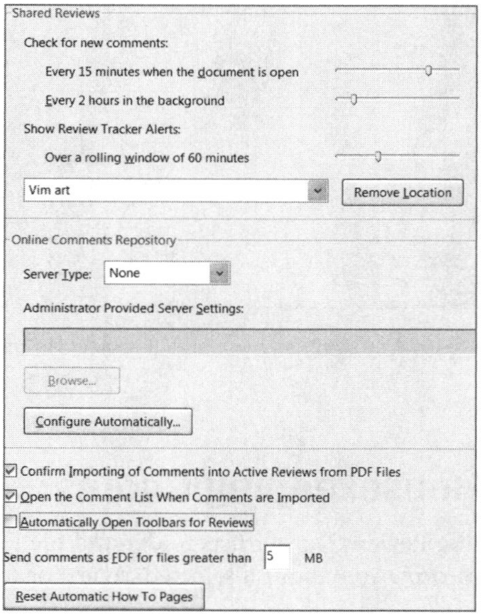

**Figure 4.17** Specify the frequency and location of comment alerts.

# Tracking the Review

To keep an eye on things, Daisy can see details of the review in the Review Tracker. Choose Review Tracker from the Commenting & Review task button's pull-down menu, from the Comments menu, or by double-clicking the Review icon on the system task bar on the desktop.

The Review Tracker opens in a separate window (**Figure 4.18**). Use it to manage reviews and control the reviews you are participating in. If you are working in a number of reviews simultaneously, use the Review Tracker like a switchboard to easily locate and open active review documents.

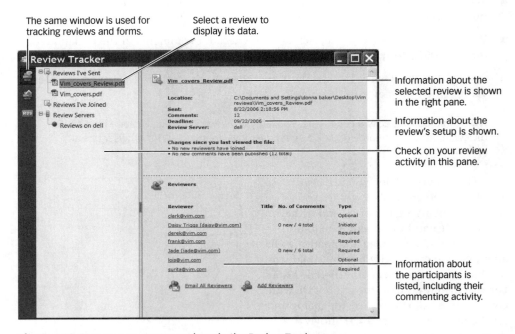

**Figure 4.18** Keep an eye on your reviews in the Review Tracker.

# Housekeeping Chores

The Review Tracker lists folder and file locations in the left pane of the window and information about a selected review or folder in the right pane. If your workflow includes a lot of reviewing, take a few minutes on a regular basis to check out which documents and folders are listed. Although the Review Tracker shown in Figure 4.18 appears roomy, it doesn't take long for dozens of reviews to be listed, both active and finished reviews. Take some time to unclutter your Review Tracker.

Here are a few tasks to keep your files organized:

■ Click one of the headings in the left column of the Review Tracker to expand a collapsed list. For example, in **Figure 4.19** the Reviews I've Sent heading in the left column is selected. In the right column you see two review documents listed. When a review is finished, click the Delete icon 🗑 to remove the review file from the Review Tracker.

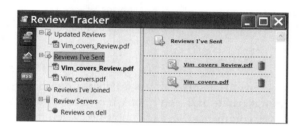

**Figure 4.19** Delete a review's file from the Review Tracker when it is finished.

■ Check out the locations where your review folders are located, and remove any folders that are no longer current. The folder locations for completed work can be removed by clicking the Delete icon to keep the list manageable (**Figure 4.20**).

**Figure 4.20** Remove extra folder locations when they are no longer needed.

■ Right-click/Control-click the review file headings in the left pane to open the shortcut menu. Here you'll find commands for other tasks like reorganizing the location of a file in the folder listings or deleting files and folders.

## Archiving a Copy

One other bit of housekeeping Daisy might want to consider during some of her reviews is to save an archive copy of the review file. She can create the copy from the Review Tracker by following these steps:

1. Double-click the name of the review document in the Review Tracker to open it in Acrobat.

2. Click the Server Status icon at the right on the document status bar to open a small menu and choose Save as Archive Copy (**Figure 4.21**).

**Figure 4.21** Use a command from the document message bar to archive a copy of the review document complete with comments.

3. The Save and Work Offline dialog opens. The File name field displays the review document's name with _Archive appended to it.

4. Click Save to close the dialog.

5. An information dialog opens describing how the archive copy is different from the shared review document in that it is now separate and won't publish or receive comments. It also states the copy contains the comments that were published when it was saved. Click OK to close the dialog and save the archive copy of the review file.

## Information About Information

The information for a selected review is shown in the right pane of the Review Tracker. A shared review shows a great deal of information, or *metadata*, about the review.

Unlike reviews in the past, a shared review can be sent and distributed any way you like. When you set up a shared review in Acrobat 8 Professional, the file is saved with the settings you specify in the wizard—that is, the path to the stored folder, the names and e-mail addresses of the participants, the review initiator, and the deadline date. The neat thing is that it doesn't matter where you work with the file, it is always available. You can open it in a browser window, in Acrobat after saving it to your hard drive, or e-mail it to yourself at home and work on it in your spare time (so much for a quiet weekend away from the office!).

Earlier in the chapter you saw how the storage location, participants, deadlines, and e-mail addresses are included in the file when you start the review. As a result, it doesn't matter where you are located since that data is part of the file. As reviewers publish their comments, they also publish data about their participation. When you next open the file or check it out in the Review Tracker, the current state of the review can be seen.

Daisy decides to call it a day.

# What Else Can Daisy Do?

Daisy is developing more ways to collaborate with her colleagues and is pleased with her first shared review experience. She had two goals for her reviewing experiment, aside from the obvious opinion collection. She wanted to determine how simple or how difficult it would be to set up the document for the review as well as set up the review. She also wanted to see how her staff would respond to writing comments and reading each other's opinions.

There are a number of additional activities she might like to try. For example, if she wants to circulate the review document to more than one set of reviewers, she can use the same source file. Each time she sets up a review cycle the file is given a unique review ID number.

She could also invite others to the review, whether or not they are able to access the shared folder, by inviting others to comment via e-mail. The comments would be sent back to Daisy, and she would merge them with the document in Acrobat. Read about e-mail reviews and merging comments in Chapter 3.

If Daisy needs to produce reports or examine the comments for further tasks, she can work through the Comments list, a Navigation panel that opens across the program window (**Figure 4.22**). Read how to use comments for editing source files in the Chapter 3 bonus.

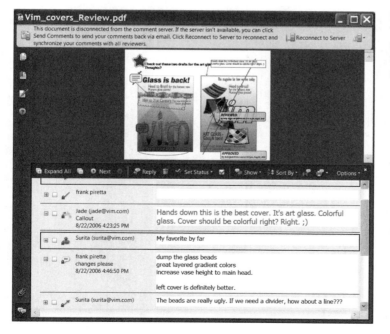

**Figure 4.22**
The Comments List is used to filter, sort, and manage comments collected in a review.

At some point in the future, if *Vim*'s structure grows to encompass telecommuters, Daisy and her staff may find it simpler to collaborate using Adobe Connect, a program that allows online meetings using shared desktops. Participants are invited to attend and may have audio only, voice, or desktop control rights. Read how Acrobat Connect is used in Acrobat's Help files.

# Making Accessible Documents in Acrobat

# 5

Governments all over the world have introduced key legislation, such as Section 508 of the Rehabilitation Act (1998 Amendments to the Americans with Disabilities Act) in the United States, which requires electronic and information technology be accessible to people with disabilities. With such importance now placed on accessibility in technology, it shouldn't come as a surprise that Acrobat 8 Professional contains many options, testing routines, tools, and wizards for making content in your PDF files accessible to people with visual or motor impairments who work with screen readers and other assistive devices. An accessible PDF document can be read in Acrobat 8 or Adobe Reader 8, as well as in earlier versions of the programs.

A whole world lies hidden within a PDF file, and you'll explore that new frontier in this chapter. For example, you'll learn several ways to apply and modify document tags—key elements of accessible PDF files.

Acrobat contains testing features that range from testing high-contrast color schemes, to reading the page aloud, to evaluating the accessibility status of a file. You'll see how to use these features and interpret the results. It's all quite easy to do, and you'll make many people's lives a lot easier if you create files that are truly accessible.

As bonus items on the book's Web site at www.donnabaker.ca/downloads.html, you'll learn how to work with and change the reading order in a file. This is important for those who use screen readers to move through a page. You learn how to define and use articles, which are structures added to a file to control navigation, in the section titled "Controlling a Document with Articles," also in the chapter's bonus file.

# Lend a Helping Hand

Diane Lerner is the executive director of a local community organization called Helping Hands Community Information Services. The organization serves as a clearinghouse of sorts, providing information to the public as well as health and social service professionals. Helping Hands offers brochures, information sheets, and other printed material about the programs, as well as community resources available to those with mental and physical challenges.

In the past couple of years, Helping Hands has launched a Web site that displays information the organization has compiled from its resources in one easy-to-use online resource. The organization has received some very positive feedback from its users.

But many clients have told Diane they find it difficult to make their way through the organization's Web site because they are working with screen readers and other assistive devices, and the Helping Hands Web site hasn't been configured for accessible use. Diane has also learned that many users prefer to download pertinent information that they can access offline.

Diane decides that a useful way to present the information to her clients and enhance the usability of the material is to provide PDF versions of the organization's information and the Web site's content. She also knows that Acrobat can produce accessible documents, so she's willing to invest the time and effort to create material that's useful and accessible for her clients.

# Steps Involved in This Project

Diane plans to test a source document from one of her resources, and she'll convert some of her Web site content to see how easily it can be used in accessible PDF format (**Figure 5.1**). She'd also like to see if a newsletter can be appropriately used by various assistive devices. She hopes to conduct her experiments (in her office, not a dank and gloomy basement laboratory) and present the results at the next meeting of the organization's board of directors.

To complete her project and create content for accessible PDF files, Diane needs to:

■ Test her PDF files for basic accessibility features.

■ Convert a Web page to PDF and append it to an existing file.

■ Check the accessibility status of the documents using Acrobat's accessibility checking features.

■ Make any necessary repairs to her documents in Acrobat according to the files' Accessibility Reports.

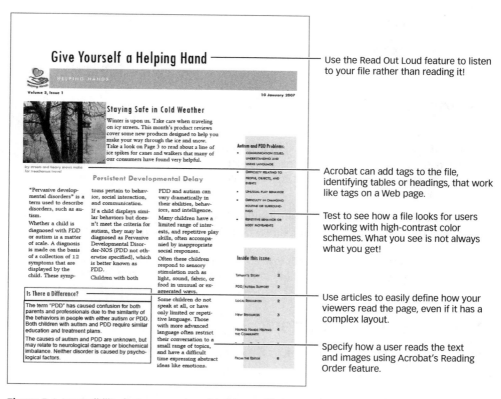

**Figure 5.1** Accessibility features can be added to any file in Acrobat.

- Try the Read Out Loud feature, which simulates a screen reader program.

- Check how the pages look in a high-contrast color scheme.

- Test and configure the file's reading order.

- Add articles—defined paths for readers to follow through a document—to a newsletter to create custom viewing.

- Write a read-me file that users can access to learn how to use Acrobat and Adobe Reader's Accessibility Setup Assistant to configure the programs to work with their assistive devices.

Diane has never experimented with accessible PDF files before. She definitely thinks it is worth the effort, especially considering her users and their needs. The first step in her project is to test the accessibility status of her converted Microsoft Word file, and then add tags to the document.

**DOWNLOAD** The final three topics in Diane's to-do list—configuring reading order, adding articles, and writing a read-me file—are available in a PDF file for Chapter 5 on the book's Web site.

# Testing and Tagging a File

Tags are a primary component of accessible documents. A tagged document contains a collection of tags, similar to those used in a Web page's HTML code, defining relationships among elements in the document, such as tables, lists, images, headings, and text. Like HTML tags in a Web page, you can't see document tags; they are part of the document's information.

Diane's first task is to test the accessibility status and tags of the health_tips.pdf file. She didn't create the PDF file, so she's not sure whether the document is tagged or not.

 **DOWNLOAD**   **health_tips.pdf** to see the original PDF file Diane will work with. You can download the file **health_tips1.pdf** to work with the tagged version of the document.

## Performing a Quick Check

A quick method for checking accessibility is called, simply enough, Quick Check.

Follow these steps to evaluate a file's accessibility status:

**1.** Choose Advanced > Accessibility > Quick Check.

**2.** Acrobat displays the results of the check in a dialog. The Quick Check results indicate that Diane's document isn't structured, meaning it has no tags that define its contents.

**3.** Click OK to close the dialog.

Diane sees that the document isn't tagged, which is fine because she can easily add the tags in Acrobat.

## Adding Tags in Acrobat

Tagging can be done in a source document if you are using a program that has a PDFMaker, or within Acrobat. Acrobat infers the structure of the document from its content and creates a suite of tags.

Follow these steps to add tags:

1. To check for tags, choose View > Navigation Panels > Tags to open the Tags panel. Sure enough, the Tags panel shows the file has "No Tags available" (**Figure 5.2**). Since Diane will be using the Tags panel for a while, she can drag it by its tab and dock it to the left of the program window with the other Navigation panels.

2. Click the Options button on the Tags panel and choose Add Tags to Document. Acrobat processes the file.

3. In the Tags panel, a new label replaces the No Tags available label shown earlier. Now the panel shows a Tags label with a (+) to the left of the label (**Figure 5.3**).

4. Save the document with its set of tags. The project's file is saved as health_tips1.pdf.

After the document is tagged, Diane can check through the list of tags to be sure her document's tags match the content.

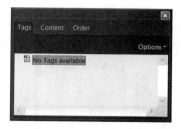

**Figure 5.2** The Tags panel shows that the document isn't tagged.

**Figure 5.3** After adding tags, the label in the Tags panel changes.

## Working with Tags

The list of tags is collapsed within what is known as the *root tag* identified by the Tags label. Click the (+) to the left of the label to expand the hierarchy. The tags in the document are arranged below the root tag. Each tag also has a (+) to the left of its name; click to display the document content that is defined by the tag (**Figure 5.4**).

If you look at the tags in the Tags panel, you'll see various icons to the left of the tags' names. The icons indicate the type of tag, which can range from paragraphs ⊞ to tables ⊞; many tags display the default Tag icon 🏷. Text that is within a container tag, such as a paragraph or heading, shows an icon that looks like a cardboard shoebox 📦—how clever!

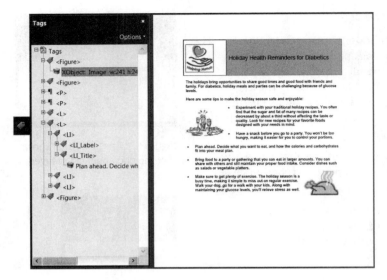

**Figure 5.4** The document's tags are listed in the Tags panel, and each tag shows the content it describes.

When you add tags to a document, Acrobat displays an Add Tags Report in the Recognition Report panel at the left of the Document pane of the program window (**Figure 5.5**). The Add Tags Report for the health_tips.pdf file shows that there are three figures in the document that don't have alternate text, a requirement for an accessible document. You'll learn how to add alternate text later in the chapter in the "Adding Alternate Text" section.

The next step is for Diane to add another page to the existing file. She'll append one of her Web site's pages to test that as well.

> **NOTE** By the way; don't expect the Recognition Report listed in the Navigation panels for every document. The panel option only appears when a document is tagged within Acrobat.

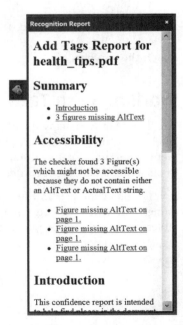

**Figure 5.5** Acrobat shows the results of the tagging process in the Search window area of the program.

# Appending a Web Page to a PDF File

Diane can append a Web page to an existing document using an advanced feature in Acrobat. She'll also review the tags and delete those she doesn't want.

> **NOTE** Chapter 2, "Building a Cohesive Document," discusses converting a Web page to PDF using the Create PDF task button function.

 **DOWNLOAD hh_home.htm** and **helping_hands.jpg** to use for the Web page conversion steps in this section. Either continue with the file hh1.pdf you tagged and saved in the previous section or download hh_tagged.pdf from the book's Web site.

## Adding the Page

Since Diane already has a PDF file open in Acrobat, she'll just convert and add the Web page from Acrobat. Diane can use the From Web Page option (File > Create PDF > From Web Page), but she can also use a command in the Advanced menu that saves her some steps by automatically appending the Web page to her file.

Follow these steps to perform the conversion and add a page in Acrobat:

1. Choose Advanced > Web Capture > Create PDF from/Append Web Page to open the Add to PDF from Web Page dialog.

2. Click Browse to open a dialog. Find and select the file for conversion; in the project, the file is named hh_home.htm. The filename is listed in the URL field in the dialog (**Figure 5.6**).

3. Click Settings to open the Web Page Conversion Settings dialog.

**Figure 5.6** The Web page chosen for conversion is shown in the dialog.

4. Select the Create PDF tags check box (**Figure 5.7**). This way Diane won't have to add the tags again manually, as she did for the first document.

   The other settings are selected by default; these include adding bookmarks, creating headers and footers on each page using information from the Web page, and saving a refresh command.

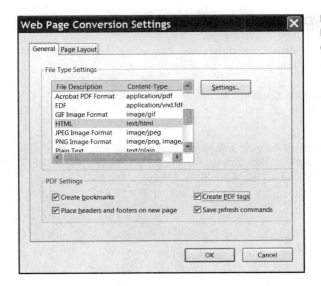

**Figure 5.7** You can specify that tags be added to the Web page when it is converted to PDF.

5. Click OK to close the dialog and return to the Add to PDF from Web Page dialog.

6. Click Create. The dialog closes, and Acrobat processes the Web page.

7. The PDF version of the Web page opens in Acrobat, appended to the hh1.pdf file.

8. Save the file. The project uses the name hh1.pdf for the document composed of both the Web page and the original PDF file.

## Reviewing the New Tags

If Diane checks in the Tags panel again, she'll see additional tags added by Acrobat when the Web page was converted to PDF (**Figure 5.8**).

To find out what a specific tag refers to, follow these steps in the Tags panel:

1. Click the tag you want to identify in the document.

2. Click the Options button in the Tags panel and choose Highlight Content.

3. The tag's content is shown in the document, highlighted by bounding boxes. In Figure 5.8, the <P> tag identifying the first paragraph in the Web page is selected, and in the document you can see the paragraph (below the logo table) framed by a bounding box.

**Figure 5.8** The converted Web page's tags are added to the Tags panel.

## Deleting Extra Tags

Diane notices that at the very end of the converted Web page, there is an extra tag (**Figure 5.9**). The tag was converted from the Web page, which had an extra carriage return at the end of the document. Acrobat recognizes the carriage return as a new paragraph, even though it has no content. Acrobat will attempt to read the paragraph, even though it doesn't contain any content. Talk about a stubborn program!

You can remove unnecessary tags from the document by following these steps:

1.  Click the tag you'd like to delete in the Tags panel.

    If you select the tag, it is deleted; if you select its content, only the content of the tag is removed but the tag remains.

2.  Choose Options > Highlight Content from the Tags panel menu. The content in the document is shown with a bounding box.

    In the project, you see a bounding box on the line following the last table on the converted Web page (shown in Figure 5.9).

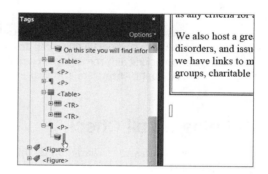

**Figure 5.9** Blank lines in the source document are defined as paragraph tags, even if they have no content.

3.  Press Delete/Backspace on the keyboard, or choose Options > Delete Tag from the Tags panel to remove the tag from the document.

4.  Save the file.

> **NOTE** If you remove a tag and then change your mind, you can't undo the command. Choose File > Revert to return to the previously saved version of the document—a good reason to save your file before starting a new process!

Now that Diane has combined the two files and the tags are adjusted, she'll check the accessibility status of the file.

# Running an Accessibility Status Check

Acrobat offers two ways to test a document's accessibility status. Diane used the Quick Check method when she started with the first document, which checks the document for tags. Now she'll use the Full Check process, which allows her to choose a range of testing options to evaluate the combined file and create a report.

> **DOWNLOAD** If you created and tagged your own files, continue with your document in this section. If you prefer, download **hh1.pdf** to start from this point. The file after checking and correcting is named **hh2.pdf**; the PDF file and its report file, named **hh2AdobePDF.html**, are also available for download.

## Running a Full Check

The Full Check process lets Diane check the status of the document against a number of different collections of Web criteria, as well as Adobe's PDF interpretation of an accessible document. Follow these steps to evaluate the document's accessibility status:

1.  Choose Advanced > Accessibility > Full Check.

    If the document isn't tagged, a message displays telling you to tag the document first and then run the Full Check. Since Diane's document is already tagged, the Accessibility Full Check dialog opens. The options used in the project are shown in **Figure 5.10**.

2.  Select the specific Report and Comment Options needed for your project. By default, the Create Accessibility Report check box is selected; adding hints to the report and identifying the issues with comments are optional.

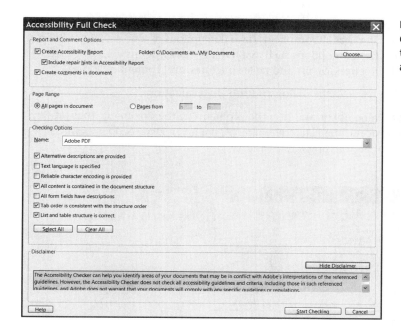

**Figure 5.10** Choose options for evaluating the document's accessibility status.

3.  Click Choose to define a storage location for the report.

    Depending on your workflow, the simplest location to store the report files is with your source documents. If you are doing other activities with the files, such as running batch sequences or working with a large number of files, create a separate folder for the report files.

4.  The "Include repair hints in Accessibility Report" option is selected by default. Unless you are familiar with modifying page structures, leave this option selected to help you make corrections.

5.  To show the results in the actual document as well as the report, select "Create comments in document."

6.  Choose a Page Range. You can select the visible page, a specified range, or the entire document. Diane wants to check all pages.

7.  Select the checking structure to use from the Name pull-down menu in the Checking Options section of the page. Diane uses the default Adobe PDF option.

    **NOTE** Read about other evaluation schemes in the sidebar "Checking Other Standards."

8.  Select checking options and then clear check boxes for those options you don't need to check.

Deselect options depending on the content of your document. For instance, you don't need to include checking that all form fields have descriptions if your document has no form fields. You can check for options such as alternative descriptions, text language, encoding, form field descriptions, list and table structures, and content inclusion.

**9.** Click Start Checking to close the dialog and run the evaluation.

**10.** An Adobe Acrobat dialog opens and lists the problems in the document that prevent it from being a fully accessible PDF document (**Figure 5.11**). Diane's document contains four figures that are missing alternate text.

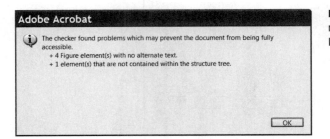

**Figure 5.11** You see the results of the evaluation listed briefly in a dialog.

**11.** Click OK to close the information dialog; the results are shown in the Accessibility Report panel (**Figure 5.12**). You won't find the Accessibility Report panel in the Navigation panels.

Like the Recognition Report described earlier in the chapter, the panel only appears in response to running an Accessibility process in Acrobat.

Diane's document does not contain many errors—just a few related to the images in the file (and one that results from the blank paragraph tag that I added back into the document as an example).

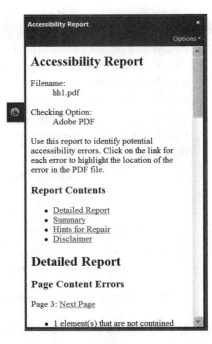

**Figure 5.12** The full report is displayed in the Accessibility Report panel.

### CHECKING OTHER STANDARDS

Rather than testing a page against the PDF standards for an accessible document, Acrobat 8 Professional lets you check a document against national and global standards. In the Accessibility Full Check dialog, choose an option from the Name field of the Check Options. You can choose from:

- Section 508 Web-based intranet and internet information and applications (1194.22)

- W3C Web Content Accessibility Guidelines 1.0

- W3C Web Content Accessibility Guidelines 2.0 (Working Draft 27 April 2006)

In each case, different options are available to choose the accessibility status, such as the options shown in **Figure 5.13** for the Section 508 testing option. You'll also find a link from the dialog to the appropriate Web pages for information on the chosen standard.

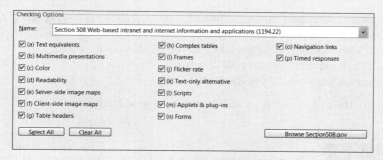

**Figure 5.13** Choose options and check the status of a document against international accessibility standards.

# Interpreting the Results

Acrobat creates an Accessibility Report as an HTML file, which is stored on your computer in the folder you select in the Accessibility Full Check dialog. When you first run the evaluation, the report is shown in Acrobat in the Accessibility Report panel.

If you close the report by closing the panel, you can easily reopen it at any time. Choose Advanced > Accessibility > Open Accessibility Report. Locate and select the file in the dialog that opens. The report again displays in the Accessibility Report panel, or if you prefer, you can open the report in a Web browser.

Since the report is an HTML file, it contains hyperlinks that you can click for more information. The Report Contents section of the file, shown in **Figure 5.14**, has a list of four links you can follow for more information:

- **Detailed Report.** Lists the specific errors.

- **Summary.** Provides a recap of the information that the Accessibility Full Check displays in the Adobe Acrobat dialog prior to displaying the full report (shown in Figure 5.11).

- **Hints for Repair.** Describes the methods you can use to make repairs to the document.

- **Disclaimer.** Explains that the test is done according to the program's capabilities, but the results aren't guaranteed.

To see a specific error to be repaired in the document, click one of the links in the Accessibility Report. The error is highlighted in the document (**Figure 5.15**). In the figure the error is the extra space that was added at the end of the PDF document converted from the Web page.

Speaking of repairs, Diane's next step is to add the alternate text to the file.

**Figure 5.14** Links in the report let you move from section to section.

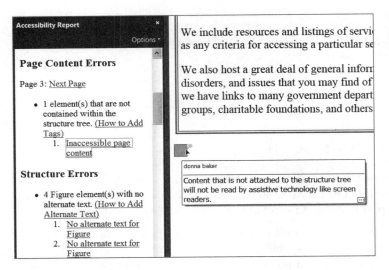

**Figure 5.15** Acrobat highlights a selected error on the page.

# Adding Alternate Text

Viewers using devices such as screen readers have the contents of the document read aloud. If there are nontext elements in the document, such as images, the screen reader can't interpret the objects, and the user misses out on some of your information. One of the most common errors in creating accessible content is omitting a text description of objects such as images. Fortunately, it's also one of the easiest errors to correct. You can attach alternate text to these objects to make them readable. The good thing is that although a picture tells a thousand words, you don't need nearly that many to use as alternate text! Alternate text for Diane's figures should describe the contents of the image, such as "Copy of the Helping Hands logo used next to the page title."

In the settings Diane chose for the Accessibility Full Check, she specified that Acrobat include comments in the document identifying the errors. Move the pointer over the comment icon next to one of the images to display the comment (**Figure 5.16**). The comment's text explains how the alternate text is used by people working with assistive devices.

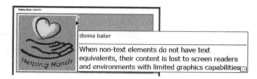

**Figure 5.16** If you choose the option before running the Full Check, the errors are shown in comments on the document page.

> **NOTE** To read more about using comments, see Chapter 3, "Communicating with Comments," Chapter 4, "Collaborating in a Shared Review," and Chapter 12, "Secure Reviewing and Reporting."

# Correcting Document Problems

Acrobat offers several ways to correct alternate text errors. In the Tags panel you can open the tags to find the specific listing for the image, and then choose Properties from the Options menu in the Tags panel. You can also add alternate text through the TouchUp Reading Order dialog, described in the bonus material for this chapter available from the Web site.

Alternatively (and to save a bit of time), rather than scrolling through a long list of tags, use the TouchUp Object tool to select the object instead.

Follow these steps to select and correct an image's content:

**1.** Choose Tools > Advanced Editing > TouchUp Object tool 🖼.

2. Right-click/Control-click the first image in the document with the tool to select the image and open the shortcut menu.

   If you have a lot of repairs to make in a file, instead of scrolling through the document looking for them, select the link in the Accessibility Report to highlight the content in the document. In Diane's document, it's simple to find the error locations.

3. Choose Properties from the shortcut menu to open the TouchUp Properties dialog.

4. Select the Tag tab and type the descriptive text in the Alternate Text field (**Figure 5.17**).

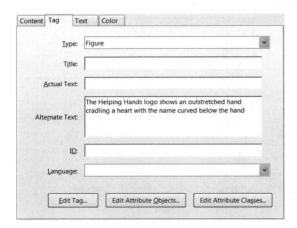

**Figure 5.17** Add the alternate text in this dialog.

5. Click OK to close the dialog.

6. Repeat steps 2 through 5 with the remaining images in the document—there are four images in all.

7. Save the file; the project's file is saved as hh2.pdf.

Diane is pleased with her progress so far. She realizes she can make many of her current files accessible without much difficulty.

## Removing Comments from the File

Before she continues, Diane has to remove the comments from the document because they no longer apply and certainly aren't needed in the finished product.

Follow these steps to remove the comments:

1.  Click the Comments icon in the Navigation panel at the left of the program window to open the Comments panel (**Figure 5.18**).

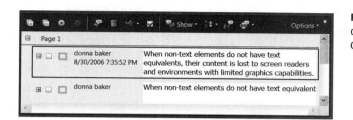

**Figure 5.18** Select the comments for deletion in the Comments panel.

2.  Click the Page 1 listing in the Comments panel.

    Don't click an individual comment because that selects just the single comment; selecting the page lets you delete all the comments from the page with one mouse click.

3.  Click Delete 🗑 on the Comments toolbar to remove all the comments from Page 1.

4.  Click the Page 2 listing in the Comments panel, and click Delete again on the Comments toolbar.

5.  Click the Comments tab again to close the panel.

Diane decides not to include the comments option in the Accessibility Full Check dialog (shown in Figure 9.10) going forward with her project. She finds it simple enough to use the links from the Accessibility Report to highlight content that needs correction, and she'll save time if she doesn't have to remove comments.

> **NOTE** Instead of removing the comments manually, you can remove them through the PDF Optimizer, which you can read about in Chapter 11.

Many users with mobility or vision difficulties rely on screen readers. As an alternative or for testing purposes, Acrobat includes the Read Out Loud feature. Any sort of Reader device depends on proper tagging and reading orders in the document. Now that the file is tagged and accessibility errors are corrected, Diane will check how the document reads as the final step in making sure the file is usable for her clients.

# Read Aloud to Me

Acrobat 8 Professional contains a set of TouchUp tools; Diane uses the TouchUp Reading Order tool to check how the file is read. Acrobat interprets the layout of a page and decides which part of the document is read first, which is read second, and so on.

 **DOWNLOAD** and read the bonus material on the book's Web site, which includes a section named "Evaluating Reading Order" for the skinny on setting, testing, and revising reading order in a document. You'll also learn about artifacts—not the type sought after in the movies, but the type of object that Acrobat can't identify as a specific item such as a graphic or image.

Acrobat's Read Out Loud feature simulates some of the features of a full-blown screen reader program. Diane can test how her file is read right from Acrobat. Before testing the file, however, she'll set some preferences.

 **DOWNLOAD hh2.pdf**, which is the file complete to this point, if you haven't been following along with the project; otherwise, continue with your present file.

## SETTING UP KEYBOARD ACCESS ON A MAC

You can set up full keyboard access on a Mac using system-level preferences. Keyboard access lets Mac users operate screen readers and use a keyboard by following these steps:

1. Choose Apple > System Preferences > Keyboard & Mouse to open the Keyboard & Mouse Preferences dialog.

2. Select the Keyboard Shortcuts tab.

3. Select the Turn On Full Keyboard Access option at the bottom of the dialog.

4. Choose View > Universal Access; select either Enable Access For Assistive Devices to use installed screen reader devices or select Enable Text-To-Speech to use the Mac OS speech technology.

5. Choose System Preferences > Quit System Preferences.

When you open Acrobat in a Web browser, keyboard commands are mapped first to the Web browser. Some keyboard shortcuts may not be available for Acrobat or may not be available until you shift the focus to the PDF document.

# Reading Preferences

Diane needs to change her preferences before testing her file.

Follow these steps to check and change the Reading preferences:

**1.** Choose Edit > Preferences (Acrobat > Preferences on a Mac) to open the Preferences dialog.

**2.** Click the Reading category in the column at the left of the dialog to display the Reading preferences.

**3.** In the Read Out Loud Options section, choose a Volume, Voice, and Pitch (**Figure 5.19**). In Windows, you get what you get—Mac users can choose among numerous voices, including some that aren't even human—just the thing for listening to your favorite alien invasion tale!

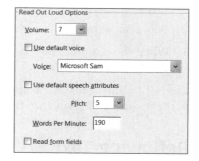

**Figure 5.19** Select characteristics for the Read Out Loud voice.

**4.** Select the Read form fields check box to have text fields, check boxes, and radio buttons in fill-in forms read aloud. Diane has no fields in her documents, so it doesn't matter whether this preference is selected or not.

**5.** Click OK to close the Preferences dialog and apply the settings.

> **NOTE** If you need to make adjustments, you'll have to reopen the Preferences dialog because you can't modify settings in real time as you are listening.

Now that she's chosen a voice and its characteristics, Diane is ready to test the file.

---

**SCREEN READER PREFERENCES**

The Reading preferences include several options for screen readers. You can define whether you want the screen reader to read only the currently visible pages, the entire document, or the currently visible pages in a "large" document from the Page vs. Document pull-down menu. The default size for defining a document as large is 50 pages. Click the field and type a different number to change the definition of a large document.

## Reading the File

Diane has modified and adjusted the tag structure and the reading order in her document. Now she'll test the page.

Start the reading process by following these steps:

1. Choose View > Read Out Loud and select either Read This Page Only or Read To End of Document.

2. The reading starts. The process can be paused and resumed by choosing View > Read Out Loud > Pause / View > Read Out Loud > Resume.

   Diane can also control reading using shortcut keys—Ctrl-Shift-C to pause/resume.

3. When she has read enough, she can choose View > Read Out Loud > Stop or use the Ctrl-Shift-E shortcut keys.

Success! The file reads as she intended, and her clients using screen readers will be able to move through her organization's material without difficulty.

## Reflowing Text

What about people who use magnified screens to view content? Will they be able to see the content clearly and logically (**Figure 5.20**)?

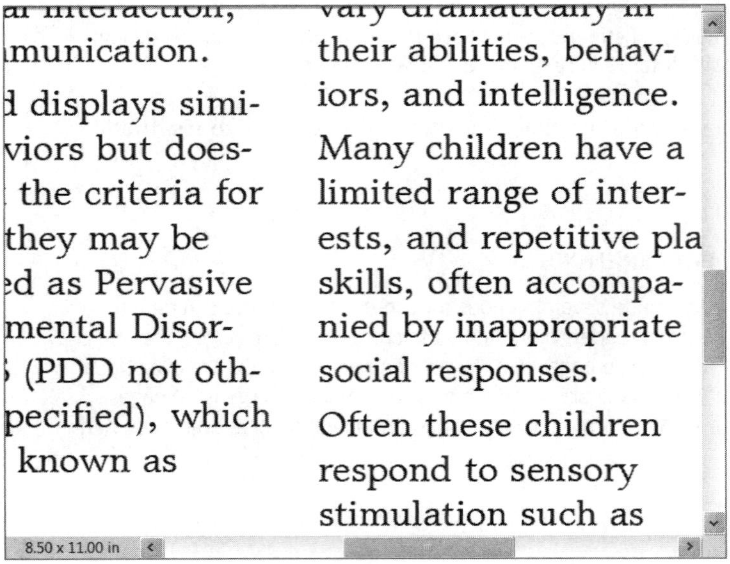

**Figure 5.20** Can you tell your page location when reading at a very high magnification?

The answer depends on the structure of the page. Both Acrobat and Adobe Reader can display content at a high magnification that can still be read clearly using a process called *reflow*, which wraps text to the next line regardless of the page's magnification.

Test reflow by choosing View > Zoom > Reflow. You don't save a reflow view of a document since it is intended only as a method of viewing or testing the document.

Reflow is terrific for basic pages of text because it wraps the text regardless of the layout of the page. It's not so terrific when using a page with a distinct layout, such as columns or pull quotes (**Figure 5.21**). In the newsletter shown in the figure, the date from the upper right of the page appears immediately below the text in one of the columns—there are some reading order issues.

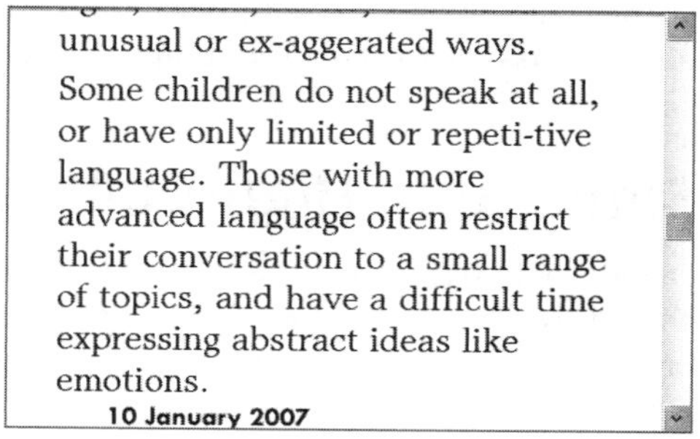

Reflow temporarily places all the text in one column, but not all content is viewable. Text on forms, comments, digital signature fields, and content such as headers and footers aren't reflowed. Vertical text reflows horizontally.

> unusual or ex-aggerated ways.
> Some children do not speak at all, or have only limited or repeti-tive language. Those with more advanced language often restrict their conversation to a small range of topics, and have a difficult time expressing abstract ideas like emotions.
> **10 January 2007**

**Figure 5.21** Quickly check how a document reads by viewing it in a reflow format.

## SCROLLING A DOCUMENT

Another feature Acrobat provides is automatic scrolling through a document, which is useful for viewers who find it physically difficult to use a mouse. Choose View > Automatic Scroll or press Control/Command-Shift-H. The document starts scrolling from the position currently in the Document pane and stops when it reaches the end.

Use the same keyboard shortcut to pause the scroll as well. Or you can click and hold the mouse button—as long as the button is depressed, the page stops. Release the button to restart the scrolling.

Press the Up or Down arrow key to increase or decrease the scroll speed, respectively. On a Mac, the functions are reversed. That is, the Up arrow key decreases the scroll speed; the Down arrow key increases speed. If you reduce the speed to 0, the text will start to scroll in reverse. You can also adjust speed using the number keys—0 is the slowest and 9 is supersonic speed. Reverse the scrolling by pressing the minus key on the keyboard or number pad; press Esc to stop the scrolling.

**DOWNLOAD** and read the bonus information section "Controlling a Document with Articles" from the book's Web site in the Chapter 5 bonus file. Diane wants the newsletters she produces monthly to be accessible to her users, preferably without having to re-create them in a simple unstructured format. She can achieve this goal by using another Acrobat feature, called Articles.

Diane is nearly finished with her project. She wants to check one more simulation—for high-contrast color schemes—that she can set up in Acrobat.

# Simulating High-Contrast Viewers

Diane would like to see how the file will look for users working with modified displays. You always see files in the colors used by a program, those set in your operating system, or custom colors used by the document's author. But some users use modified displays, which they set in either their operating system or particular programs, that allow them to see the content more clearly, often by using high-contrast colors.

Follow these steps to modify Acrobat to use custom colors and text visibility options:

**1.** Choose Edit > Preferences (Acrobat > Preferences on a Mac) and click the Accessibility category in the left column to display the Accessibility preferences.

**2.** In the Document Colors Options section, select the Replace Document Colors check box to activate the options (**Figure 5.22**).

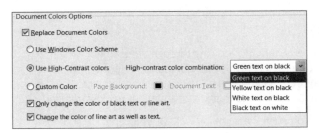

**Figure 5.22** Choose alternate colors for the file display in the Preferences dialog.

**3.** Click the Use High-Contrast colors button, and choose a high-contrast color option from the pull-down menu, such as green or yellow text on black.

**4.** Click OK to close the Preferences dialog.

Diane discovers an interesting problem, one that is commonly seen with high-contrast color schemes. In a section of the newsletter's page (shown in **Figure 5.23**), she sees that the text block at the right side of the figure is difficult to read. In the newsletter file, the text is black on a pale beige background (black on a pale gray background in the book, of course), which looks quite attractive in a regular color scheme. Changing to a high-contrast scheme tells a different story. The light background and the light text used for high-contrast schemes are similar in color, which makes the text hard to read.

**Figure 5.23** Showing the newsletter in a high-contrast color scheme reveals a problem.

If Diane intends to provide accessible content, she'll have to modify the newsletter's layout to prevent the contrast problem by removing the pale beige background from the text blocks. If she wants to make them stand out from the rest of the newsletter's text, she can frame them with a border that won't affect the contrast on the page.

Diane's had much success in her efforts. The last thing she wants to do before finishing the project is to create a read-me file she can distribute to her users to help them work with PDF files more effectively.

## OTHER COLOR OPTIONS

Diane can choose other color options in the Preferences dialog, including Use Windows Color Scheme (in Windows), which uses a custom color scheme the user has set in the operating system. Another option is to use Custom Color. Select the option's check box, and then click the color swatches and choose custom colors. Only custom colors or high-contrast colors can be chosen—selecting one toggles off the other.

She can also select line art and black text changes. If you don't want to change the color of text that is already colored, select "Only change the color of black text or line art"; to change the color of line art, select "Change the color of line art as well as text."

## Read-me, Please

In earlier versions of Acrobat, many of the accessibility settings were available, but they were not easy to find because they were located in a number of different panels in the Preferences dialog. Starting in version 7 and now in version 8 of Acrobat and Adobe Reader, all these settings have come together into one wizard, which is much simpler to use. Please read the "Read-me File" section included as part of the Chapter 5 bonus material available from the book's Web site.

Now that Diane has finished her experiments with accessibility features and processes in Acrobat, she's ready to face the board of directors. They'll be impressed!

## What Else Can She Do?

Diane can set up a real production process for converting her files to accessible PDF documents as soon as she gets the board's go-ahead. Instead of converting each document and testing it, she can instead use a batch sequence and convert a whole folder of files at one time. You can read about batch sequences in Chapter 7, "Assembling a Library."

Another consideration when preparing her files for conversion is for Diane to evaluate the layouts, as she did with the newsletter page, to see if there are any other issues when the files are viewed using high-contrast color schemes.

# Managing and Organizing E-mail Using Acrobat

**6**

One of our most common business tools is e-mail. Organizing and sorting e-mail is often cumbersome. Then there is the question of how to store e-mail: Do you save all the important e-mail messages in folders? What is the best way to organize and manage file attachments? What if you don't necessarily need many of your e-mail files as ongoing working document sources but are required by law or policy to archive them?

If these sound like questions you ask yourself often, this chapter is for you. Acrobat 8 installs a PDFMaker in Microsoft Outlook (Windows) that you can use to automatically convert either a single e-mail, a selection of e-mails, or folders of e-mails into PDF documents. The content of a converted folder is displayed in Acrobat with navigation tools; e-mail attachments can be maintained in their native format.

In Acrobat, you can use the Organizer feature to keep track of your PDF documents. The Organizer lets you sort e-mail and other PDF documents in a number of ways. You can even create virtual folders within the Organizer to use for organizing and managing groups of files in collections.

You can embed attachments in the e-mail and then transport them along with the PDF documents in a secure wrapper—sending the e-mail directly from within Acrobat—as you'll see in this chapter's project. You'll also see how your e-mail's recipients can save attachments from the PDF document, convert them to PDF, or extract them in their native file formats. Very handy features!

Acrobat 8 offers a slick new feature for auto archiving. Rather than manually collecting, organizing, and converting e-mail into PDF, Acrobat can take care of it for you. Specify where the e-mail is located, what you need archived and when, and put that task out of your mind. Now if the program could only walk the dog!

# Sorting the (e)-Mail

This is the story of Angie Johnson, a modern-day businesswoman with a modern-day problem. Angie is a successful distributor for Johnson Outdoors, a garden and landscape contracting firm. Angie is making a name for her company with her use of unusual, new, and environmentally sensitive materials and methods.

Angie prefers to conduct much of her business online via manufacturers' Web site portals and e-mail—clarifying orders, discussing invoices, confirming shipping details, and so on. She often finds it difficult to keep track of the e-mail threads and attachments she includes with her correspondence, and she finds she spends a great deal of time sifting through e-mails for particular information.

Another problem Angie has is maintaining her catalogs of information she sends to customers. Angie maintains up-to-date material and specification sheets for all the products she deals with and makes it a policy to send copies to her customers to help them make decisions on products and materials for their projects.

In addition, she needs to make sure documents are seen by the right people. She sometimes has to send reminder letters and overdue statements, and she worries that someone other than the intended recipients might see the contents.

Angie decides to devise a system that allows her to organize her e-mail content, keep track of her attachments, and send files to her customers that can be secured in a customized Envelope (**Figure 6.1**). And she can do all this using Acrobat 8.

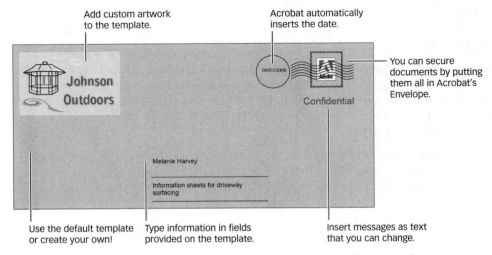

**Figure 6.1** You can create and use a Secured Envelope to securely send your e-mails.

# Steps Involved in This Project

There is no tangible output from this project since it is designed as a demonstration of how you can handle e-mail and attachment control issues using Acrobat 8.

To deal with her e-mails, Angie needs to do the following:

- Evaluate the structure of her e-mail folders. It's simpler to convert entire folders of e-mail files than single files.

- Convert her e-mails to PDF in Outlook. She can convert either one or more selected e-mail files or a folder of e-mails at one time; she can also append new e-mails to an existing PDF document.

- Create collections in Acrobat's Organizer to hold documents for clients and manufacturers.

- Apply a template in Acrobat for a Secure Envelope (a secure wrapper for a document's content).

- Set options in Outlook to automatically archive e-mail on a specified schedule.

Angie decides to start by organizing the folders she has already constructed in her e-mail program, Microsoft Outlook.

Acrobat 8 includes a PDFMaker for Lotus Notes, which is installed as a group of commands on the Actions menu, that provides many of the same features as those used in this project. The one notable exception is that you can't auto-archive messages from Lotus Notes. If you don't use Outlook as your e-mail client, you won't have a PDFMaker to work with to convert files or folders to PDF or append e-mails to existing PDF files. Instead, you can save the e-mails from your program as text files and then convert them to PDF from Acrobat. See the project details in Chapter 2, "Building a Cohesive Document," to learn about creating PDF files in Acrobat.

> **NOTE** The e-mail files used in this project are generic—choose any number of e-mails from your own system and apply the processes described in this project.

# Devising an E-mail Folder System

Angie decides to use the structure she has been working with in Outlook. In **Figure 6.2**, you can see she has a main folder for the client and year named "Harvey 2006," and several folders within the job folder for different aspects of the job.

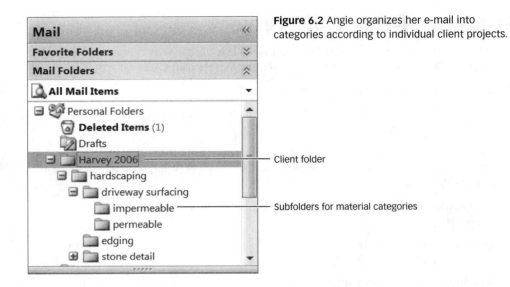

**Figure 6.2** Angie organizes her e-mail into categories according to individual client projects.

She plans to convert the folders of e-mail to PDF files. As you'll see later in the chapter, she doesn't have to worry about attachments to the e-mails—they can be included as part of the PDF files automatically.

# Converting Folders of E-mail to PDF

The simplest way to convert e-mails to PDF in Outlook is to use the Outlook PDFMaker, a menu and toolbar used for converting files to PDF that is installed in Outlook automatically as part of the Acrobat 8 installation process. When you specify conversion settings, the settings are used by default until you change them. For example, if Angie uses the View Adobe PDF Result option, the document opens in Acrobat each time she creates a new PDF file from an e-mail or a folder of e-mails. Before converting files, she takes a minute to check the conversion settings.

> **NOTE** If you are working with a different e-mail program than Outlook or Lotus Notes, convert the files to PDF from Acrobat; you can still use the conversion settings described in this section.

# Adjusting Conversion Settings

Angie takes some time at the outset to build her PDF e-mail system. Before converting any files, she opens and modifies the conversion settings.

Follow these steps to adjust the settings:

**1.** In Outlook, choose Adobe PDF > Change Conversion Settings to open the Acrobat PDFMaker dialog (**Figure 6.3**).

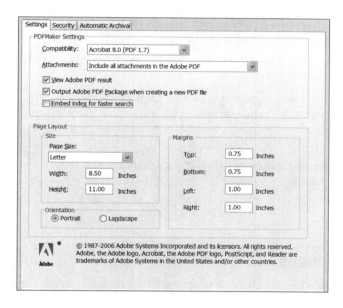

**Figure 6.3** Choose settings for conversion before creating PDF files from e-mails.

**2.** On the Settings tab, choose options for conversion based on how you need to use the e-mails (see the next section for setting these options).

**3.** Select the Security tab and add the desired security settings.

**4.** Define archival methods and frequencies on the Automatic Archival tab (see how Angie sets up an archive in the section "Automating the Archive Process" at the end of this chapter).

**5.** Click OK to close the dialog.

**FILING AND SORTING**

There are as many ways to organize e-mail as there are e-mail users. Unless you are bound by government or business regulations, find the method that works best for your e-mail habits.

Whichever organization scheme you choose, it is important to plan ahead. When you want to convert e-mails and attachments in Outlook to PDF versions, keep these few ideas in mind:

- Organize the e-mails you want to convert into folders. You can choose a folder and convert its entire contents to PDF with one mouse click.

- Name the folders using a meaningful name—when you convert the folder to PDF, the folder name is used as the PDF filename.

- You can create a series of collections in the Organizer that parallels your e-mail folder structure. Using the Organizer means you can access the folders' contents directly from within Acrobat to prepare content for mailing, to do a search for specific terms, and so on.

- If you are working with an e-mail client other than Outlook, create the folders for the collections on your hard drive.

## Choosing conversion options

The default settings for converting e-mail in Outlook's PDFMaker are shown in Figure 6.3. By default, the PDFMaker uses the Acrobat 8 Compatibility option, which allows creation of a PDF Package—a collection of separate PDF files within one named PDF file.

You can choose to include attachments or not using options from the Attachments pull-down menu. Because Angie wants her attachments included in the converted e-mails, she leaves the default option.

The next three check boxes pertain to how and when the converted document is displayed. Since Angie is converting batches of folders, she clears the View Adobe PDF Results option to save time. Otherwise, each time she converts a folder, it will open in Acrobat. She intends to use a navigation structure in Acrobat for working with the e-mail files, so she leaves the "Output Adobe PDF Package when creating a new PDF file" option selected. She clears the "Embed index for faster search" option since she doesn't need the index attached. The index adds to the file size, and since she's not working with many long documents, she can quickly search the e-mails without using indexes.

Angie decides to leave the Page Layout options at their default settings. Using these options, her converted e-mails are shown on letter-sized pages with standard margins and a portrait orientation. With this basic page layout, Angie can easily print PDF versions of the e-mails.

Now it's time to convert the files. Drum roll, please!

## Processing the Files

Converting folders of e-mails in Outlook to PDF is a simple one-click process. Angie has organized her content into folders, and now she decides to convert her client's folder into a packaged PDF document.

Follow these steps to create the PDF:

**1.** Select the folder for conversion in the All Mail Items listing in Outlook (the folders are shown in Figure 6.2).

**2.** On the PDFMaker toolbar, click the Convert Folders ⬚ icon to open the Convert folder(s) to PDF dialog (**Figure 6.4**).

**3.** Click to select the folder or folders for conversion. To save time, Angie selects the "Convert this folder and all sub-folders" check box at the lower left of the dialog. She wants all the client's e-mail converted in one action.

**4.** Click OK to close the dialog and open the Save Adobe PDF File As dialog.

**5.** The name of the selected folder is shown as the PDF filename. Leave the default name or type an alternate name, and then select a folder location. Angie is converting the Harvey 2006 project folder contents, so she'll use the default names throughout.

**6.** Click Save.

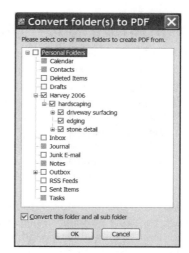

**Figure 6.4** Choose the folder for conversion from the dialog.

**7.** The Creating Adobe PDF dialog opens (**Figure 6.5**). A progress bar shows the files as they are being processed. The dialog includes the name of the mail folder. As each file is processed, the mail subject is shown in the dialog as well. When the PDF document is assembled, the dialog closes automatically.

**8.** Repeat the folder and file selection and conversion process as necessary.

It's simple to add additional content to an existing PDF version of your e-mail files in Outlook using another PDFMaker tool, as Angie discovers next.

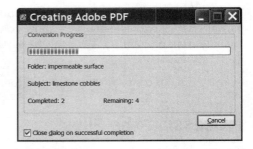

**Figure 6.5** You see information about the conversion progress in this dialog.

# Appending E-mail Documents to PDF Files

Managing a folder of active e-mails on a specific thread or topic is an ongoing process, and the ability to add new content to an e-mail is an important element for successfully managing your e-mails. Rather than manually converting individual e-mails to a new PDF, opening the existing e-mail PDF in Acrobat, and then appending the new e-mail PDF to the file, Angie can use a PDFMaker tool in Outlook to automatically add new content to e-mails.

> **NOTE** If you aren't working with Outlook, you will have to follow the manual conversion method described in the previous section.

Although the following steps describe appending an e-mail to an existing PDF e-mail file, the same principle applies regardless of the content of the PDF you are appending to. That is, instead of appending an e-mail to another PDF e-mail file, Angie can append an e-mail to any PDF file she likes.

Follow these steps to include another e-mail in an existing PDF document:

**1.** Select the e-mail message to be appended to an existing PDF; then Control/Ctrl-click to select multiple messages.

**2.** Choose Adobe PDF > Convert and Append to Existing Adobe PDF > Selected Messages. The Select PDF File to Append dialog opens.

**3.** Select the file to which you want to append the new e-mail (**Figure 6.6**).

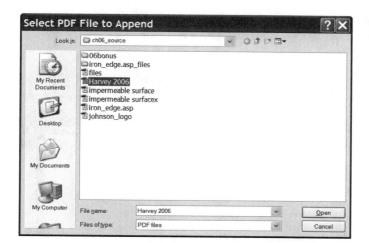

**Figure 6.6** Select the file to append to the new e-mail.

**4.** Click Open to close the dialog and process the document.

It is certainly possible to convert a single e-mail to a PDF document in Outlook as well. Follow these steps to create the PDF:

**1.** Select the e-mail message in your e-mail program's folders.

**2.** Click Convert Messages [icon] on the PDFMaker toolbar.

**3.** In the Select PDF File to Append dialog name the document and select its storage location. Click Save to close the dialog and save the PDF document.

After Angie has processed all her e-mail messages, she can take a look at what she's produced in Acrobat.

# Viewing Converted E-mail Documents

As mentioned earlier, Angie selected her conversion settings and included the default option "Output Adobe PDF Package when creating a new PDF file." In this section, you'll see how Acrobat extracts information from the e-mails, such as the subject or date, to use for the PDF Package interface.

> **NOTE** If you aren't working with Outlook but have combined files into a single PDF file, you'll find a single bookmark in the Bookmarks tab for the file in Acrobat, but you won't have the PDF Package interface described in this section.

Angie opens the converted e-mail file in Acrobat. When the document opens, she sees the first e-mail as well as the PDF Package listings (**Figure 6.7**).

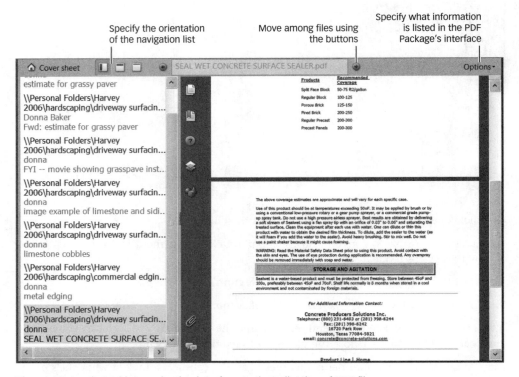

**Figure 6.7** Acrobat adds a navigation interface to the collection of PDF files.

The PDF Package interface shows a list of the e-mail messages and information about the messages, and displays the active message in the document pane of the program window.

> **NOTE** Check out Chapter 9, "Assembling and Preparing Legal Documents" and Chapter 12 "Secure Reviewing and Reporting" for much more on using PDF Packages.

What if you need to look for specific information? Not to worry. You don't have to open all the bookmark categories—just use Acrobat's Search feature.

# Searching E-mail PDFs

It's true that it takes a bit of time to construct a set of PDF documents from your e-mails. If you need to find information in those e-mails, however, you'll be glad you made the effort! Unlike searching e-mails in your e-mail program, which can be frustrating and imprecise, Acrobat's Search feature lets you find precise words or phrases in any number of e-mail PDF documents and files regardless of the method used to create the files.

Because she often refers to information she's shared with customers as well as suppliers, Angie needs to find information in her e-mails on a regular basis. Let's follow through a search example as Angie looks for references to a product in the Harvey 2006 PDF Package.

Follow these steps to search a PDF Package of e-mail files:

**1.** Click the down arrow next to the Find text field [Find] on the File toolbar in Acrobat to open its menu, and choose Open Full Acrobat Search. The File toolbar is one of Acrobat's default toolbars. If the toolbar isn't visible, choose View > Toolbars > File to open it.

**2.** The Search window opens atop the program window and can be moved and resized as desired.

**3.** Type the search term you want to find in the "What word or phrase would you like to search for?" field in the dialog (**Figure 6.8**). Angie types in limestone.

**4.** Click one of the radio buttons, either to search the current PDF document open in Acrobat, in selected PDF files, in the entire PDF Package, or to search a location on your hard drive or server. In Angie's search, she's looking for all references to a particular building material in her converted e-mail files, so she chooses the entire PDF Package.

**5.** Choose other criteria for searching if you wish, such as searching for whole words, using case-sensitive options, or searching bookmarks and comments.

**6.** Click Search in the Search window.

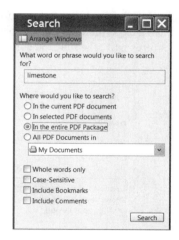

**Figure 6.8** Type the word or phrase you want to find in the dialog and specify the search location.

**7.** The search is performed and the results displayed in the Search window (**Figure 6.9**). You see the search term(s) listed as well as a summary of the results. The search result is highlighted and shown in context, making it easy to find the proper document.

**8.** In the Results area, click the (+) to the left of a document name to open its list of matches. If you move your pointer over a listing, you see the page number in a tooltip.

**9.** Click a results listing to display the document in Acrobat. The search result is highlighted in the document (**Figure 6.10**).

**10.** Click Hide to close the Search window.

> **NOTE** You can also perform advanced searches to specify other criteria for searching. Advanced searches are described in Chapter 7, "Assembling a Library."

Angie is pleased with her progress so far. Next she'd like to experiment with Acrobat's Organizer to see if its features will take her one step closer to e-mail nirvana.

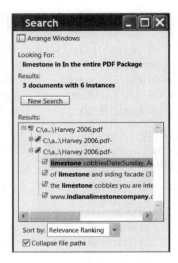

**Figure 6.9** Results from a search are listed in the window by document name and page number.

**Figure 6.10** Acrobat highlights the search results in the document.

# Organizing Files in Acrobat

Angie plans to build a folder structure in the Organizer called *collections*, which are virtual folders that are used within the program only; they have no impact on your system's file folders. You can add new collections, or add and remove files from those collections, without affecting your system folders in any way.

Follow these steps to name a collection and add new files in the Organizer:

1. Click the Organizer icon 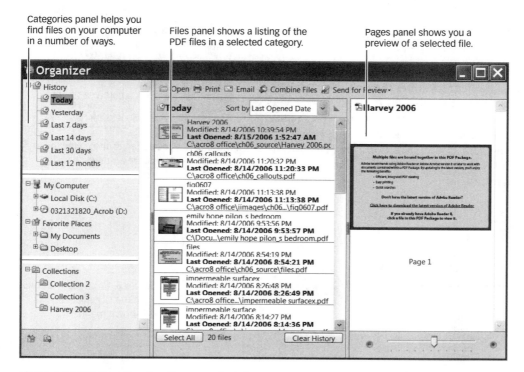 on the File toolbar or choose File > Organizer > Open Organizer. The Organizer opens in a separate window.

2. Acrobat includes three collections named collection 1, collection 2, and collection 3 by default; the collection list is part of the Files panel at the left of the Organizer window (**Figure 6.11**). You can drag the splitter bars between the frames to resize each frame as you are working.

Categories panel helps you find files on your computer in a number of ways.

Files panel shows a listing of the PDF files in a selected category.

Pages panel shows you a preview of a selected file.

**Figure 6.11** The Organizer is a three-panel window you can use to manage PDF documents.

3. Right-click/Control-click a collection name to show its shortcut menu (**Figure 6.12**). Click Rename Collection to activate the default name's text.

4. Type a name for the collection. In Angie's case, she names the first collection "Harvey 2006."

5. Right-click/Control-click the collection's name again, and choose Add Files from the shortcut menu to open the "Select files to add to your collection" dialog.

6. Locate and select the files you want to add to the collection, and then click Add to close the dialog; the files are added to the collection (**Figure 6.13**).

7. Close the Organizer when you have finished adding files.

Once Angie has her collection built, she can access her files either through the Organizer or through Acrobat. In Acrobat, she can click the down arrow to the right of the Organizer button on the File menu to open a menu. Then she clicks Collections, the name of the collection, and the file she wants to view (**Figure 6.14**).

**Figure 6.12** Choose a command for working with collections from the shortcut menu.

**Figure 6.13** Files added to the collection are listed on the Organizer window.

**Figure 6.14** Choose options from the Organizer's pull-down menu.

# Managing Collections

Once you have named your collections and added files to them, you can add more content or delete existing files as necessary. When you click a collection's name in the Categories panel, you have the following options:

- **To remove a collection:** Choose Delete Collection from the shortcut menu. A confirmation dialog opens telling you that removing the collection will have no effect on the actual files on your computer.

- **To add more files to a collection:** Choose Add Files from the shortcut menu and select the new files in the "Select files to add to your collection" dialog.

- **To rename the collection:** Choose Rename Collection from the shortcut menu to activate the text and type the new name.

You certainly aren't limited to three collections. You can add as many collections as you need for your particular project. Either choose Create a new Collection from the shortcut menu or click the Create a new Collection button at the lower left of the Organizer window.

In addition to working with collections, Angie can also access her files in other ways in the Organizer.

# Other Organizer Options

The Categories panel of the Organizer allows Angie to find files in a number of ways. The more she works with the Organizer, the more familiar she becomes with its uses and how to integrate its options into her workflow.

In addition to the Collections category, described in the previous section, the Organizer includes the History and Favorite Places categories, and My Computer, which displays the computer's folder structure.

## Using History files

Acrobat's Organizer includes a History category, which stores information about all the files you have opened during a specific time frame regardless of where they are stored on your computer. This can be handy if you recall you worked with a particular file last Tuesday but can't remember its exact name. Any file you open in Acrobat, whether selected using the File > Open command, from a collection in the Organizer, or from your system's folders, is added to the History.

To work with the History, located in the Organizer's Categories panel, click a time frame from the History listing. A list of the PDF files you have opened during that period is displayed in the Files panel. To clear the listing for any point in time, click the option in the History listing—such as Yesterday—to display the content in the Files panel, and then click the Clear History button at the bottom of the Files panel.

> **NOTE** Use caution when clearing the History. Clearing a History setting such as Last Week also clears all History listings of shorter duration, such as Today or Yesterday.

The History contents are also available in the File menu. Choose File > History and one of the date options (**Figure 6.15**). The History command is conveniently listed above the last documents opened in the File menu.

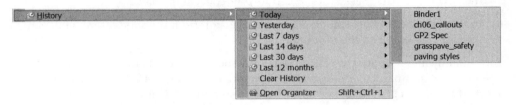

**Figure 6.15** Acrobat arranges the documents you have opened in the History listings.

## Defining Favorites

In the Organizer, right-click/Control-click the Favorite Places listing and click Add a Favorite Place or click the Add a Favorite Place button 🏠 at the lower left of the Organizer window. A Browse for Folder dialog opens. Locate the folder you want to add and click OK. The selected folder is added to the list (**Figure 6.16**).

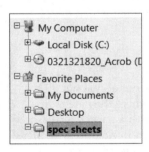

**Figure 6.16**
You can add folders to your Favorite Places for quick access in the Organizer window.

# Working with Organizer Content

Angie can work with her files in other ways in the Organizer as well. She can find, sort, and preview files in the Organizer window. She can also perform some actions on the files right from the Organizer.

## Viewing and Sorting Documents

In the Files panel, Angie can view the content of a selected folder or collection. The files are listed in the Files panel in alphabetical order. You can sort the documents using many different methods. Click the Sort by down arrow and choose an option from the list (**Figure 6.17**).

When you select a file, it appears in the Pages panel (**Figure 6.18**). You can zoom in or out of the document using the (+) and (–) buttons at the bottom of the panel, or drag the slider to show the file's contents. You'll see scrollbars when the view is magnified, when you select more than one document in the Files panel, or when there are multiple pages in the document.

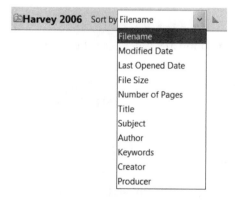

**Figure 6.17** You can sort documents in the Organizer in a number of different ways.

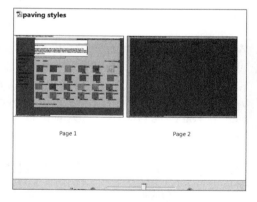

**Figure 6.18** Preview pages before opening PDF files in the Organizer.

## Working with Files in the Organizer

The Organizer also contains a set of tools that Angie can use to work with PDF documents in Acrobat, as shown in **Figure 6.19**:

- Click Open to open selected file(s) in Acrobat.

- Click Print to print selected file(s).

- Click Email to open an e-mail window with the selected file(s) attached.

- Click Combine Files to open Acrobat's Combine multiple files into one PDF file dialog (described in several chapters in the book, such as Chapter 2).

- Click Send for Review to initiate an e-mail review right from the Organizer window. You can read more about working with review cycles in Chapter 3, "Communicating with Comments," Chapter 4, "Collaborating in a Shared Review," and Chapter 12, "Secure Reviewing and Reporting."

**Figure 6.19** Perform a number of common document functions right from the Organizer window.

Whether Angie is working in Acrobat or organizing and managing files in the Organizer, she is sure to save time in her work.

When she created the original PDF documents from e-mail folder contents, Angie chose to attach the source files to the PDF documents in the PDFMaker's settings. In the next section, you'll see how she works with attachments in Acrobat.

# Using PDF File Attachments

In Acrobat 8, Angie can attach files of any type to a PDF document so that the attachments are included with the PDF for storage or for e-mailing. The recipient can open the PDF file, and the attachments are included right along with the document—a simple fact that fills Angie with delight.

In her business, much of the exchange of information with both clients and suppliers is conducted by e-mail. But attaching files to e-mails can be tricky business. Attachments are difficult to manage, and it's easy to forget to include an attachment when sending an e-mail. In addition, attachments simply get "lost" on others' computers. By including the attachments with a PDF, there's no loss of information anywhere, and the recipient can always access the content directly from the PDF. If you move the PDF file on your hard drive, the attached files or pages automatically move with it, saving time in organizing and maintaining your files.

# Displaying Attachments

Angie converted e-mails to a PDF Package and included the attachments. So, she can view the list of attachments by clicking the Attachments icon 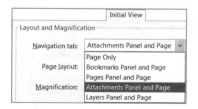 in the Navigation panel at the lower left of the Acrobat program window. Angie has a Web page and text file attached to one of the e-mail PDF files, shown in the Attachments panel in **Figure 6.20**. When she e-mails a file to her clients, they'll see the attachment listed in the document, provided she specifies that the document shows the attachment when it opens.

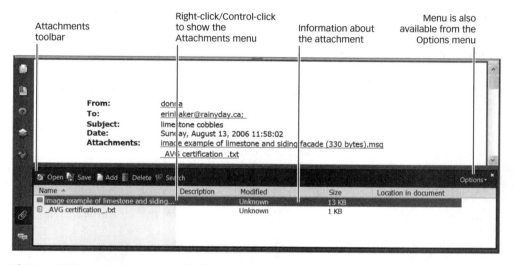

**Figure 6.20** Read about and work with file attachments in the Attachments panel.

You can specify that attachments be seen when the PDF is opened in Acrobat by doing one of the following:

- Click Options in the Attachments panel and choose "Show attachments by default."

- Choose File > Document Properties > Initial View. On the Initial View tab, choose Attachments Panel and Page from the Navigation tab pull-down menu, shown in **Figure 6.21**.

**Figure 6.21** You can specify that a document shows the Attachments panel automatically when it opens.

Angie can also add more information to an existing PDF in the form of attachments. Let's say she's having a problem with one of her suppliers' products. She can attach the e-mails outlining the problem to the e-mails she sends to the supplier. If she wants to extract just the pertinent information from an e-mail PDF, she can select the content, copy it to the system clipboard, and create a new PDF document from it to attach to her e-mail (see how to work with clipboard content in Chapter 2).

## Adding More Attachments

Attachments can be added in two ways—either as attachments to the actual document or as comments attached to a particular location. Angie decides to try both methods.

To attach another document to the active PDF file from the Attachments panel, follow these steps:

**1.** Click the Attachments icon to display the Attachments panel across the bottom of the program window.

**2.** Click Add ![icon] on the Attachments panel toolbar to open the Add Attachment dialog.

**3.** Locate and select the file to be attached to the document.

**4.** Click Open to close the dialog and add the attachment to the document's Attachments panel.

**5.** In the Attachments panel, the new attachment is listed on the Attachments tab (**Figure 6.22**).

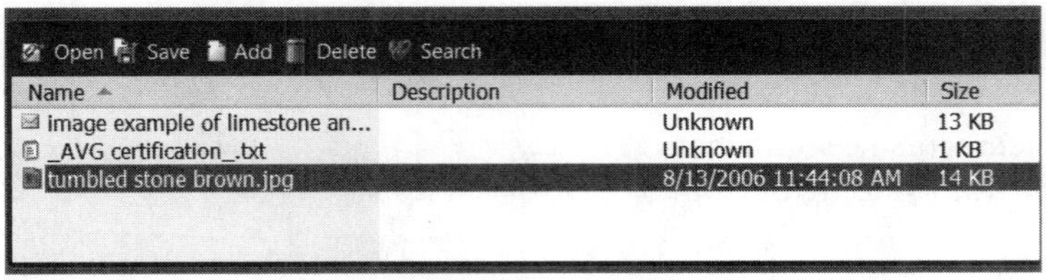

| Name ▲ | Description | Modified | Size |
|---|---|---|---|
| image example of limestone an... | | Unknown | 13 KB |
| _AVG certification_.txt | | Unknown | 1 KB |
| tumbled stone brown.jpg | | 8/13/2006 11:44:08 AM | 14 KB |

**Figure 6.22** You can attach a file to the active document.

**NOTE** If the Attachments panel isn't open, you can click the Attach a File tool on the File toolbar.

Instead of attaching a file to the document at large, Angie can attach it to a specific location. This is referred to as attaching a file as a comment. As her viewers read the document, they see an icon indicating that there is a file attached. A document added in this way is a good method of notifying the users that there is additional information as they are reading.

To attach a file to a document in Acrobat as a comment, follow these steps:

1. Click the Attach a File as a Comment tool on the Comment & Markup toolbar.

2. Move the pointer, which looks like a push-pin, over the document to where you want to display the icon indicating an attachment is embedded.

3. Click the document; the Add Attachment dialog opens.

4. Locate and select the file you want to attach. Click Select to close the dialog.

5. The File Attachment Properties dialog opens. If you like, you can choose an alternate icon or change the color or opacity of the attached file's icon on the Appearance tab of the dialog (**Figure 6.23**).

6. Select the General tab to display fields where you can modify the attachment's name, your name, and a description of the attachment. Angie's selections are shown in **Figure 6.24**.

7. Click Close.

8. The Attachment icon is shown where you clicked on the page and included in the list in the Attachments panel (**Figure 6.25**). In the Attachments panel, the Location in document column shows the number of the page where you attached the file as a comment. Information added in the File Attachment Properties description is shown in the Description column of the Attachments panel.

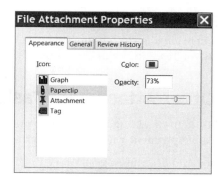

**Figure 6.23** You can customize the appearance of the attached file's icon.

**Figure 6.24** Add text describing the content of an attachment in this dialog.

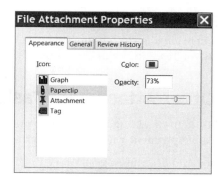

| Name | Description | Modified | Size |
|---|---|---|---|
| _AVG certification_.txt | | Unknown | 1 KB |
| image example of limestone an... | | Unknown | 13 KB |
| paving styles.pdf | suggested stone layouts | 8/14/2006 10:28:10 PM | 162 KB |
| tumbled stone brown.jpg | | 8/13/2006 11:44:08 AM | 14 KB |

**Figure 6.25** Descriptions added in the File Attachment Properties dialog are shown in the Attachments panel.

**9.** Save the document.

There are a few other functions or tasks you can do with a PDF file's attachments as well, as you'll see in the next section.

# Other Attachment Tasks

Aside from adding more attachments in Acrobat, there are several other activities Angie can experiment with. She can do the following:

- Add descriptions.

- Open the attachments or convert the attachments.

- Export the attachment from Acrobat.

- Save or delete attachments.

- Search PDF attachments.

If you add an attachment as a comment and enter text in the File Attachment Properties dialog, that text is seen as a description in the Attachments panel (as shown in Figure 6.25).

Add a description to any attachment in a document by following these steps:

**1.** Select the attachment in the Attachments panel.

**2.** Choose Edit Description from the panel's Options menu.

**3.** In the Edit Attachment Description dialog, type the text you want to use for the description (**Figure 6.26**).

**4.** Click OK to close the dialog and add the description to the file's listing.

**Figure 6.26** Add a description to any attachment that is included in the Attachment's panel's listing.

## Opening attachments

To open an attachment, double-click a listing in the Attachments panel, click Open on the Attachments toolbar, or choose the command from the Options menu. A PDF file opens automatically. If the attachment is another file format, you see a warning dialog that describes the hazards of opening documents that might contain macros, viruses, or other possible problem makers. Click Open to open the document, or click Do Not Open to stop the process and close the dialog.

## Saving the attachments

Click Save ▥ on the Attachments toolbar or from the Options menu to save the attachment as a separate file. In the Save Attachment dialog, choose the storage location for the file. The file uses the name shown in the Attachments panel (which you can change). Click Save to close the dialog and save the file.

## Deleting the attachments

Click Delete to delete an attachment ▥ . Be careful when deleting attachments! If you delete an attachment, it's not in your system's Recycling Bin in case you need to restore it—it's removed completely from the document. If you delete an attachment and change your mind, choose Edit > Undo to restore the attachment to the file.

## Searching the attachments

You can also click Search ▥ to open the Search window and search the contents of the attached files. The Search window provides you with a Search Attachments button automatically. Type the word or phrase you want to find in the attachments, and then click Search Attachments. The results are listed for both the PDF document you are working with and its [PDF] attachments.

Angie is quite pleased with the extra functionality she has discovered in Acrobat 8. She is sure it is going to make document management a lot simpler for her, her customers, and her suppliers. She has one worry, though, and that is about the documents' security. If she could just find a way to ensure the information attached to an e-mail will be seen by only the right people... (cue the dream sequence music).

---

### USING ATTACHMENTS IN OLDER VERSIONS OF ACROBAT

Opening PDF files with attachments in Acrobat 7 is the same as in Acrobat 8. The attachments to Angie's PDF files can also be accessed by those working with Acrobat 5 and Acrobat 6, as long as she has specified that attachments be seen when the PDF is opened, using one of the two methods described earlier in this section.

When you open the document using Acrobat 5 or 6, an information dialog appears and explains that the file contains attachments you can view in the program. Click OK to close the dialog, and then choose Document > File Attachments to open the File Attachments dialog, which lists the attachments according to their locations. Document file attachments are listed first, followed by those attached using the Attach a File as a Comment tool.

# Securing File Attachments

Needless to say, Acrobat has the answer to Angie's concerns, and she's not dreaming! Acrobat 8 Professional contains a feature called a Secure Envelope, which is used as a secure wrapper for a document and its attachments. A Secure Envelope is the digital equivalent of a courier-delivered package—the courier cycles into your office, waits for a signature, and then hands over the package. Acrobat can do much the same thing, without leaving any tire treads in your lobby. Envelopes even look like envelopes!

Encryption using a Secure Envelope doesn't modify the file attachments in any way. Just like a courier package, once you "break" the seal on the document—that is, once your recipient extracts the file attachments and saves them—the files are no longer protected.

Angie can send an e-mail to her customer, attach an invoice, embed the attachment in a Secure Envelope, encrypt the Secure Envelope using a password or certificate security method, and then e-mail it. Only the person with rights to open the Secure Envelope can see the content. Angie has to inform her e-mail recipient of the password needed to open the attached files, which she does by telephone. She decides that the passwords for files are the clients' last names, which makes it easy for both her and her clients to remember.

> **NOTE** You can read more about encryption in Chapter 12.

Acrobat 8 Professional includes a set of three default Envelope templates, which are simply PDF files with an image and a few form fields, as you'll see in the next section. Instead of using one of the defaults, Angie could also create her own custom template. Read how to create and use a custom template in this chapter's bonus material on the book's Web site at www.donnabaker.ca/downloads.html.

# Using a Secure Envelope in Acrobat

The default templates for Secure Envelopes are familiar and serve a useful purpose (**Figure 6.27**). There's no doubt in recipients' minds what the file is when they open it and see the envelope.

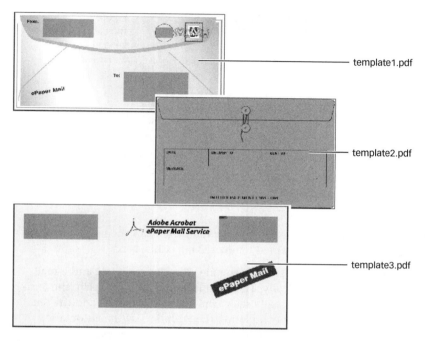

Figure 6.27 You can choose from three default templates for the Envelope.

 **DOWNLOAD johnson_logo.jpg** if you'd like to try creating your own template using the information in the bonus material for this chapter on the book's Web site. You can also download **johnson_outdoors.pdf**, which is the finished custom template. The original template file used in the project is the **template2.pdf** file, located on your hard drive.

Angie will use the wizard to create a Secure Envelope with one of the default templates.

## Using the Wizard

Apply a Secure Envelope using a wizard in Acrobat by following these steps:

**1.** Choose Advanced > Security > Create Security Envelope, or click the Secure task button and choose Create Security Envelope. The five-step Creating Secure Envelope wizard opens.

**2.** In the first panel of the wizard, select the documents to attach to the PDF (**Figure 6.28**). Click "Add file to send" to locate and select additional files, and then click Next. If you add a file by mistake, you can click "Remove selected file(s)" to delete it from the list.

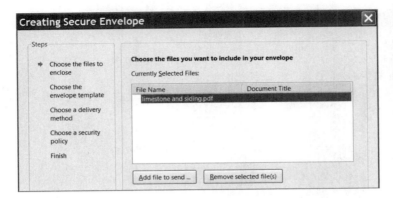

**Figure 6.28** Specify the files you want to send in the Creating Secure Envelope dialog.

3. The second step of the wizard displays. Choose a template from the list (**Figure 6.29**). Angie selects the default template named template2.pdf. Click Next.

4. Select a delivery method option for sending the file. You can complete and e-mail the envelope manually or automatically. The default option is to complete the template automatically, although you usually select the manual option to add the text in the fields (which Angie does after completing the wizard). Use the automatic method if you have built a custom template that doesn't need any customization added. Click Next.

5. In the next panel of the wizard, which is used to specify a security policy, click Show All Policies to display the list of policies (**Figure 6.30**).

6. Select a policy to use for the Envelope. Angie decides to use the default password policy named Password Encryption. Click Next.

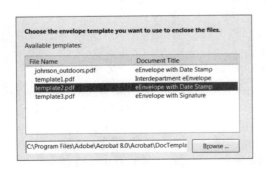

**Figure 6.29** Select a template to use for the Envelope's appearance.

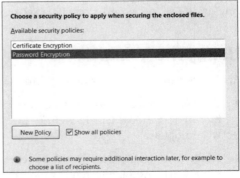

**Figure 6.30** Select a security policy to use for the Envelope.

**NOTE** If you have not previously set up your identity for Acrobat 8, a dialog opens for you to enter identity information. Fill in the required fields and click OK to close the dialog and return to the wizard.

**7.** The final panel of the dialog shows a list of the options you have selected in the other panels. Click Finished to close the dialog.

**8.** Because Angie chose to use a password to protect the document, the Envelope's wizard is replaced by the Password Security - Settings dialog (**Figure 6.31**).

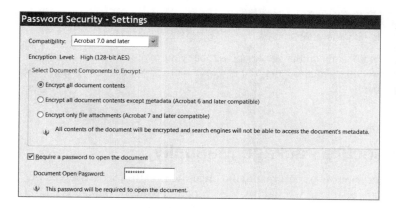

**Figure 6.31** The options available depend on the version of Acrobat you choose in the Compatibility setting.

**9.** Choose an option from the Compatibility pull-down menu (see the sidebar "Encryption Options" for more information). Angie chooses an Acrobat 7-compatibility option.

**10.** Select the document components you'd like to protect. Angie uses the "Encrypt all document contents" option.

**11.** Type a password in the Document Open Password field.

**12.** Click OK to close the dialog and display a confirmation dialog. Retype the password and click OK to finish the wizard.

If you chose to send the Envelope automatically, one of the delivery options available in the wizard and described in Step 4, enter your recipient's e-mail address in the e-mail dialog that opens, and click Send to send it on its way.

Angie chose a manual delivery method in the wizard. Her template requires her to enter her recipient's name in the field, so she'll do that next.

**ENCRYPTION OPTIONS**

In the Password Security - Settings dialog, Angie has three choices based on the version of Acrobat she wants the file to be compatible with. Acrobat 5, 6, and 7 have different encryption capabilities:

- Acrobat 5 encrypts the entire document and its attachments.

- Acrobat 6 encrypts all content except for metadata, which is advanced information about the document's content. (You can read about metadata in Chapters 4, 9, and 10 and in Acrobat's Help files.)

- Acrobat 7 encrypts only the attachments.

The option you choose depends on the version of Acrobat your recipients are working with, as well as your security requirements. You can read more about encryption and security policies in Chapter 12.

## Finishing the Secure Package Manually

Since Angie chose to complete the wizard manually, once the Creating Secure Envelope wizard closes, the template opens in Acrobat in a new program window named Creating Secure Envelope (SECURED). The files she's attached are listed in the envelope's Attachments panel (**Figure 6.32**).

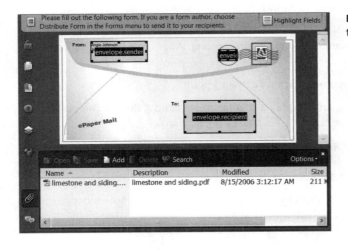

**Figure 6.32** Add information in the fields on the envelope.

To finish the Envelope and send it, follow these steps:

1. Click the envelope.sender field on the template and type the sender's name or e-mail address. Angie types `Angie Johnson, Johnson Outdoors`.

2. Click the envelope.recipient field on the template and type the recipient's name.

3. Choose File > Save to save the file and apply the security settings.

   You don't have to add the date in the envelope.date field manually. When you use a template that has a date field, the date is inserted in the field automatically as soon as you save the file.

4. Open your e-mail program, attach the PDF file to a new message addressed to your recipient, and then send the e-mail.

When the recipients click to open the attachment, they can open the Envelope only if they type the correct password in the Password dialog that displays.

Angie's managed to tame her unruly e-mails and likes the convenience of finding her files and correspondence quickly. But there is one more feature she decides to look into: Rather than adding additional e-mail messages to her e-mail archive, she wants to have Acrobat do it automatically.

# Automating the Archive Process

Being organized is a wonderful thing. Having a program automatically organize and perform ongoing, boring, and time-consuming tasks is even more wonderful. The Outlook PDFMaker in Windows includes an automatic archival feature.

1. Choose Adobe PDF > Setup Automatic Archival to open the Acrobat PDFMaker, which displays the Automatic Archival tab (**Figure 6.33**).

2. Click Enable Automatic Archival to activate the options on the tab.

3. Specify when you'd like the files to be processed. You can include a log file and embed an index if you like.

4. Click Add in the Choose Folders for Automatic Archival section to open the Convert Folder(s) to PDF dialog, shown in Figure 6.4 at the beginning of the chapter.

5. Select the folder to use for storing the archive file and click OK. The Save PDF Archive File as dialog opens.

6. Select an existing PDF document from the dialog, or type a new name in the File name field. Click Open. The selected or newly created file is listed in the PDFMaker dialog.

7. Add other folders and files for archiving as needed. You can add, remove, or change files and folders using the corresponding buttons at the lower part of the dialog.

8. Click OK to set the archiving process in motion. The files will be archived and added to the specified files according to your chosen schedule. Or, if you want to archive the files immediately, you can click Run Archival Now and then click OK.

**Figure 6.33** Specify settings for automatic archiving of your e-mail files as PDF documents.

Angie is pleased with her organization efforts. There are other feats of Acrobat wizardry Angie might want to look at in the future.

# What Else Can She Do?

Angie can further develop her e-mail management system in the future if she likes. Rather than combining files into a PDF package, she could combine selected messages into a single PDF file for compact storage. Learn how to create a single PDF file from multiple files in Chapter 2.

To bring all her files up to date, she can use a feature in Outlook or Lotus Notes that converts older types of archive files to Acrobat 8 PDF Packages. Choose Adobe PDF > Migrate Old PDF Archives to PDF Packages. Select the older file, and Acrobat will update the files to the newer format.

She can convert or attach other business documents to e-mail threads for further reference or include other files in a number of additional folders. That way, the content is readily accessible through Acrobat, and she can search through attachments as well as PDF files to locate content easily.

Angie can create and use a custom template for the Envelope (**Figure 6.34**). Instead of using one of the preconfigured templates, she can save time filling in fields as well as give her work a more custom look by building her own template. You can learn how Angie builds a custom template in the bonus material for this chapter available on the book's Web site.

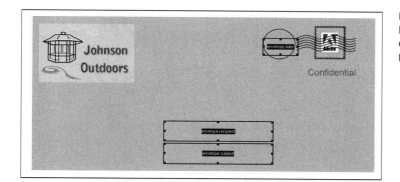

**Figure 6.34** Angie can build and save her own custom Secure Envelope template.

If you are working with an e-mail program other than Outlook or Lotus Notes, consider using the batch sequence process described in Chapter 7 to save yourself time when converting large numbers of files.

# Assembling a Library

# 7

In the old days, governments, organizations, and businesses maintained typing pools and stored paper records in centralized file storage areas. As computers became the norm for most of the workforce by the 1990s, workers assumed responsibility for creating and maintaining their own documents, making the file room redundant and decentralizing control over records.

While U.S. federal law requires all government agencies to archive documents that will be of historical significance, many organizations and private companies voluntarily archive documents for legal and historical purposes.

Suppose you have hundreds of records and historical documents in various formats—paper, digital source files, and PDF pages—that need to be stored for safekeeping, and also suppose that you need to regularly search for specific information in those files. Finally, suppose that in addition to you and your colleagues, a sizable number of people who will also be searching those files have little or no understanding of what they are looking for or how to find it!

Collecting and converting all those documents is a monumental task. However, standardizing the storage of files in PDF format and ensuring the files adhere to an international standard designed for long-term archival storage of documents will help ensure that the exercise will not have to be repeated.

One way of managing documents using Acrobat 8 Professional is through its Catalog feature. *Cataloging* is the process of assembling a collection of documents and indexing it to create a formal catalog. Using PDF documents as the basis for maintaining and storing collections of business-critical and historical documents allows you to do full-text searches of content using the two search functions that are part of the Acrobat program and Adobe Reader.

# Of Course, You Can Drink the Water

Henry Dickens is a progressive kind of guy. He has worked in different capacities as a marine biologist for a number of years before recently taking over as manager of the Midlakes Regional Water Conservancy (MRWC). The MRWC—known simply as the Conservancy—serves as an information repository and clearinghouse for government agencies and departments, local and municipal authorities, and residential and commercial builders.

Accessing the right information can be a difficult task: The Conservancy has stacks of binders stored in a government building that have been accumulating for years, and a surprising amount of information has gone missing or been misplaced. Even when the information is available, the process of sorting through the binders is labor-intensive and a bit haphazard. Visiting researchers may or may not become aware of all the pertinent documents, and if they do, they may not be able to find them.

It's important that the Conservancy's government, industrial, and private customers be able to access the information they need when they need it, whether from past research or other government and environmental sources.

Henry recognizes that there is a significant problem for the Conservancy's users, and he has been encouraged by the Board to explore solutions to the problem. He believes users' problems would be solved if the organization found a way to do the following:

■ Effectively archive and store the organization's information to preserve the content.

■ Manage the information in a way that allows staff and visitors to easily access it without wasting time searching for missing documents.

■ Maintain the collection to prevent lost or missing documents.

# Steps Involved in This Project

After considering and dismissing a number of options as too costly—for example, having the organization's documents captured by a database developer—or too inefficient and time-consuming—having copies made of all documents and bound for sale—Henry decides the simplest and most effective way to handle the situation is to use PDF documents (**Figure 7.1**).

Henry plans to build a PDF catalog that contains documents converted from newer source files and documents scanned from historical records.

This is what he needs to do to complete his document collecting and cataloging project:

■ Collect the source documents in Microsoft Word and convert them to PDF from the desktop.

■ Create a watermark that he can add to all files.

- Design a batch process to automatically add a watermark to all files, identifying them as part of the collection.

- Scan a representative historical document and convert it to a searchable PDF format in Acrobat that complies with the PDF/A standard (see sidebar on next page).

- Apply the watermark to the file using the batch process.

- Create a searchable index.

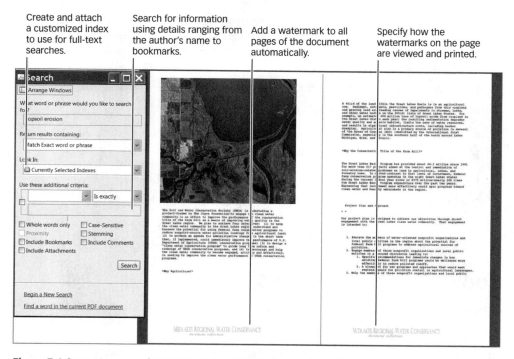

**Figure 7.1** Convert or scan documents from different sources to PDF files.

The first step in the process is to convert the Word documents stored on hard drives all over the office to PDF. Or is it the first step? Henry will check the settings and test a conversion, but he won't actually convert the files. Instead, he'll let some advanced Acrobat program features handle the job for him.

**PDF/A STANDARD**

PDF/A is an international standard for archiving documents using PDF. It is designed to preserve documents for long-term storage and maintain their usability without depending on external technologies, code, or other factors. For example, Acrobat 8 allows you to embed Flash movies in a PDF document. According to the standard, because a Flash movie depends on an external technology (a Flash player), the document isn't considered compliant with the standard.

The PDF/A standard can use one of two color systems: RGB (Red/Green/Blue) color, designed for onscreen reading and basic printing, or CMYK (Cyan/Magenta/Yellow/Black) color, designed for color separations for commercial printing. The Conservancy document collection uses RGB color.

To comply with the PDF/A standard, a document must meet the following criteria:

- It can include only text, raster images, and vector objects.
- It can't include scripts.
- It must have all fonts embedded.
- It can't contain security options such as passwords or other types of encryption.

The Conservancy document collection is designed to comply with the standard.

# Converting Source Files

A major part of Henry's task is to convert all the available text documents that the Conservancy has been storing both digitally and on paper. With the help of two summer interns, the many files the Conservancy has produced over the years are assembled in one folder location. Henry can save a lot of time working from the desktop after checking settings in Word. All he needs to do is locate and select the files from the desktop instead of opening each one in Word and selecting the Acrobat PDFMaker commands.

## Modifying PDFMaker Settings

Using Word's PDFMaker, Henry can add features like links, bookmarks, and tags to the documents. The only requirements for this project are that the files comply with the PDF/A archival standard. Henry realizes that these files are often larger than the Word files instead of smaller, which usually happens when converting to PDF. The assurance of usability 50 years from now makes the file size increase unimportant.

To modify Word's PDFMaker settings from within the Word program, follow these steps:

1. Choose Adobe PDF > Change Conversion Settings to open the Acrobat PDFMaker dialog (**Figure 7.2**).

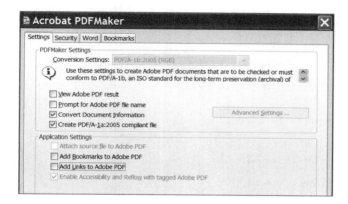

**Figure 7.2** Check the PDFMaker settings before converting Word documents.

2. On the Settings tab, shown by default when the dialog opens, click the Conversion Settings down arrow and choose PDF/A-1b:2005 (RGB). Some of the settings on the dialog are automatically adjusted and disabled.

   Henry's organization has decided to apply the international PDF archival standard to its files, although not mandated by law. In the future, the standards may become mandated, so the organization doesn't want to have to reassemble the collection.

3. Deselect "View Adobe PDF result" and "Prompt for Adobe PDF file name." Because Henry intends to convert a large number of files simultaneously and use the documents' existing names for their PDF filenames as well, deselecting these options saves a lot of time.

4. In the Application Settings area in the dialog, deselect the remaining active options for bookmarks and links.

   The documents were created by different people using a number of templates, and Henry doesn't need bookmarks for any individual file's contents, nor does he need links. The PDF/A conversion option automatically selects the tags setting and disables the option to attach the source files.

   **NOTE** Tags describe the content of the document. For example, an image tag is used to describe the actual image included in a document; a paragraph tag describes the actual content of a paragraph of text; and so on. You can read more about tags in Chapter 5, "Making Accessible Documents in Acrobat."

**5.** Click OK to close the Acrobat PDFMaker dialog.

Now Henry is ready to do the conversions and will work strictly from the desktop. To be more precise, he'll hand off the task to his interns, and they'll work from the desktop.

## Converting Files from the Desktop

Henry's interns get to work, following these steps to convert a batch of documents:

**1.** Open the Windows Explorer window and create a new folder.

**2.** Drag the source Word documents to the folder.

**3.** Select all the files. Then right-click/Control-click and choose Convert to Adobe PDF (**Figure 7.3**).

The Save Adobe PDF File As dialog opens and shows the documents' names by default. Since you have a new folder for the set of files you are converting, you don't need to select a folder location for each file.

**4.** Click Save to close the dialog. The Converting to Adobe PDF dialog opens, listing the number of files processed as well as those pending (**Figure 7.4**).

The progress of each file's conversion, as well as that of the entire batch, is shown in the progress bar. As each file is processed, you see a progress bar that stays open until the entire batch of files is converted.

**5.** As each file is converted, the Save Adobe PDF File As dialog opens. Click Save each time to close the dialog and save the file. After the files are processed, the Adobe PDF Status dialog closes automatically.

That was a quick task! Henry decides to separate the files by type, leaving just the PDF versions of the files in the original folder and moving the Word files to another location on his hard drive.

Next, Henry wants to design a watermark to apply to the files as part of the collection. He'll develop the watermark as part of a batch sequence.

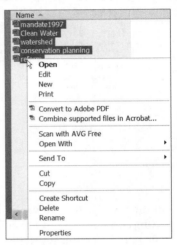

**Figure 7.3** Use the shortcut menu to convert a batch of documents quickly.

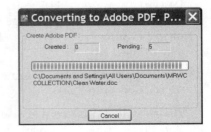

**Figure 7.4** You can track the progress of the file conversion process in this dialog.

# Constructing a Batch Sequence

Converting the source Word files to PDF from the desktop is quick, but there's more to be done. Henry wants the documents identified as part of the collection so he'll add a watermark to the files' pages. But his collection consists of thousands of pages and hundreds of documents. Do he and his interns have to open each document manually, and then add the watermark to each document? Not on your life! Those tasks alone could add days to the project.

## Designing the Batch Process

Thanks to Acrobat 8 Professional, Henry can create and apply a batch sequence to all the files that will automatically make the changes to the documents with a couple of mouse clicks. All he has to do is make four decisions before building a batch sequence. He needs to decide:

- Which commands he needs to run and their details.

- Which files to use.

- Where to store his finished files.

- What format to use for the finished files.

   **NOTE** Acrobat includes eight default batch processes, including some for common tasks such as removing attachments, opening a number of files, or printing chosen files, and you can easily write your own custom sequence. You don't need to have documents open in Acrobat to apply a batch sequence to them.

## Selecting Batch Commands

When you create a batch sequence, many of the commands you choose must be configured, as you'll see in Henry's example. Before the batch sequence's configuration is complete, he has to choose settings in the respective dialogs for Acrobat to apply when the batch sequence is run. For example, Acrobat can't read his mind and choose settings for the watermark; he has to specify the details in the Add Watermark dialog.

Follow these steps to configure a batch sequence:

**1.** Choose Advanced > Document Processing > Batch Processing to open the Batch Sequences dialog.

**2.** Click the New Sequence icon. A small dialog opens to name the sequence. Type the name of the sequence and click OK. Use a meaningful name for the sequence: Henry names his batch sequence Conservancy_pdf. The Edit Batch Sequence-Conservancy_pdf dialog opens.

**3.** Click the Select Commands button to open the Edit Sequence dialog (**Figure 7.5**).

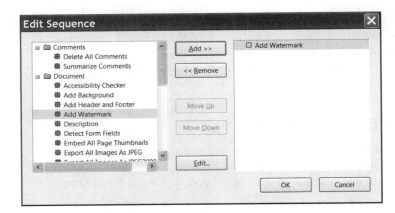

**Figure 7.5** Add and configure commands for the batch sequence.

**4.** To open a category of action, such as Document, in the left column, click the (-) to the left of the folder icon.

**5.** Select a command, and then click Add to move the command to the list on the right. In the sample project, the Add Watermark command is selected in the left column and added to the list on the right.

**6.** Select other commands from other categories as necessary. If you add multiple commands, you can reorder them by clicking the Move Up and Move Down buttons, or delete an action by clicking Remove.

Now that Henry has chosen the command he wants to use in the batch sequence, he has to specify the settings Acrobat will apply when the batch sequence runs. He first tackles the watermark setting.

## Configuring the Watermark

Henry wants to automatically apply a watermark to each page. He wants the watermark to be visible on the page, wants it to print, and wants it to resize itself according to the printed pages' sizes.

 **DOWNLOAD** If you would like to follow along with Henry's design process, you can download the file **MRWC_logo.pdf** used in the project from the book's Web site at www.donnabaker.ca/downloads.html.

Follow these steps to configure the watermark:

1. From the Edit Sequence dialog, double-click the Add Watermark command in the right column of the dialog, (or click the Add Watermark command and then click Edit) to open the Add Watermark dialog (**Figure 7.6**).

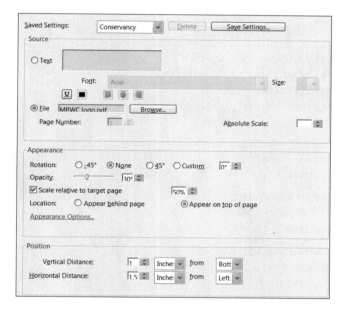

**Figure 7.6** You can add a watermark to each page of a document using a batch sequence.

2. Click File in the Source area of the dialog. Click Browse to display the Open dialog and locate the file to use for the watermark. Henry chooses the MRWC_logo.pdf file and clicks Open to close the dialog and list the file as the source image on the Add Watermark dialog.

3. In the Appearance area of the dialog, specify your preferences for the Rotation, Opacity, and Scale options. In Henry's project, Opacity is set to 30%, and the scale is left at its default, which is "Scale relative to target page."

4. Define the Location for the watermark. Henry chooses Appear on top of page.

5. Click Appearance Options to open another dialog (**Figure 7.7**). Choose the options for when you want the watermark to appear: Henry uses the two default options to Show when printing and Show when displaying on screen. Click OK to close the dialog.

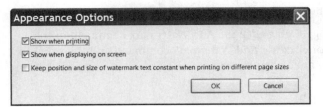

**Figure 7.7** Decide on the appearance of the watermark in relation to print, onscreen view, and on different sized pages.

6. Position the watermark vertically and horizontally. Henry's watermark is placed 1 inch from the bottom vertically, and 1.4 inches from the left horizontally. Drag the sliders or click the arrows to set the values.

7. View the page preview in the dialog (**Figure 7.8**). As you make changes to the watermark, they are shown in the preview area.

   If there are open documents when you create a batch sequence, you see the first page of the active document in the preview area.

8. Click Save Settings at the top left of the Add Watermark dialog to open a field to type a name. Henry types Conservancy and clicks OK. The settings chosen are now available for use in the future, and he will use them again when working with scanned files.

9. Click OK to close the dialog and return to the Edit Sequence dialog.

**Figure 7.8** View the changes you make as you make them in the preview area.

When the batch sequence runs, the watermark is applied to each document automatically. Henry can use the batch sequence for any types of files he uses, and he plans to use it first for the PDF files he created and later for the PDF files he creates from scanned documents.

> **TIP** Henry doesn't have to change all the files to PDF first. He can apply the batch sequence against any files that can be converted to PDF on his system, such as an Excel spreadsheet, PowerPoint presentations, and so on.

Now Henry has to make some final decisions on how to use the batch sequence.

# Finishing the Batch Sequence

The command Henry specified for the file conversion is listed in the Edit Batch Sequence Conservancy_pdf dialog (**Figure 7.9**). All he has left to do is specify how the batch sequence is run, and then give it a try.

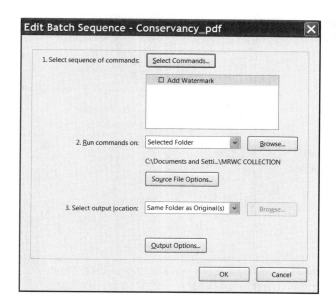

**Figure 7.9** The commands for the batch sequence are listed in the dialog.

# Specifying How the Sequence Runs

To specify features for running the batch sequence, follow these steps:

**1.** Click the "Run commands on" down arrow and choose an option from the list for running the command based on the project's requirements. In this case, Henry chooses the Selected Folder option and then clicks Browse to select the MRWC COLLECTION folder. The name of the folder is displayed in the dialog.

If Henry wants to apply the batch sequence to files of other types stored in the folder, he can specify file formats by clicking the Source File Options and choosing from the list displayed.

**2.** Click the Select output location down arrow and choose an option for storing the processed files. In this case, since the files will be stored in the same folder, Henry leaves the default as is.

Henry can also select a number of features for the files that are processed by clicking the Output Options button to open a dialog containing choices to add prefixes and suffixes, and save files in a range of output formats.

**3.** Click OK to close the Edit Batch Sequence – Conservancy_pdf dialog and return to the original Batch Sequences dialog. The new sequence is added to the list (**Figure 7.10**).

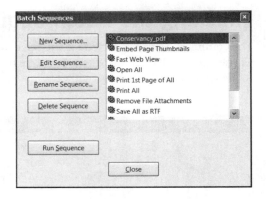

**Figure 7.10** The original batch sequence is added to the list and available for future use.

---

**OPTIMIZING FILES**

You also have the option to run the PDF Optimizer, a process that checks for different elements in a document—ranging from the presence of annotations to the resolution of images—that can be modified as part of the sequence. In Chapter 9, "Packaging and Preparing Legal Documents," read about using the Examine PDF process, which is essentially a subset of the full PDF Optimizer; read about the PDF Optimizer in Chapter 11, "Building a Powerful Interactive Document."

---

## Processing the Files

Henry is ready to give his programming a try. The Batch Sequence dialog shown in Figure 7.10 includes options to edit, rename, remove, or as Henry has done, create new sequences.

After tapping an impressive drum roll on the edge of his desk, Henry clicks Run Sequence. A dialog opens listing information to confirm the sequence's particulars, including the folder of files and location, the chosen and configured command, and the output location. He clicks OK to close the confirmation dialog and start the process.

A small progress window displays as the documents are processed and tested. When the files have finished processing, Henry clicks Close to close the Batch Sequences dialog, and then opens one of the processed files (**Figure 7.11**). The watermarks look great!

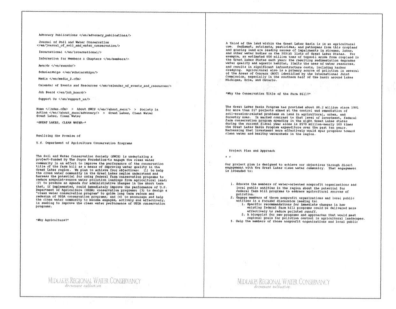

**Figure 7.11**
The finished files now include the watermarks applied by the batch sequence.

At a later time, when he has another batch of files to process, Henry can reopen the Batch Sequence dialog, select the new sequence, and then click Run Sequence. After applying the batch sequence to the files, Henry may want to revise the folder location if he uses a storage folder to hold new material on an interim basis before adding it to the collection.

The other files Henry has to deal with are PDF files generated from documents scanned into Acrobat 8 Professional.

# Scanning in Acrobat

One part of the collection Henry is compiling is made up of historical documents that are available only as printed pages. Instead of rekeying the documents, he can scan them into Acrobat. Acrobat works with your scanner software directly and opens the scanner's dialog within the Acrobat program window. Any scanner that is properly configured for your computer can be used with Acrobat.

**NOTE** In this section, you learn how to work with single documents. For a large project, you might want to investigate working with dedicated scanning software or automatic scanning using high-speed scanners.

Follow these steps to scan a document into Acrobat:

1. Choose Document > Scan to PDF or click the Create PDF button and choose From Scanner to open the Acrobat Scan dialog (**Figure 7.12**).

Figure 7.12 Choose settings before scanning a document into Acrobat.

2. Select your scanner from the Scanner pull-down menu—any scanners you have configured for your system are shown on the list.

3. Choose Front Sides or Both Sides from the Sides pull-down menu. If you have two-sided documents and you have a duplex scanner—that is, one that can scan both sides of a document—choose the Both Sides option; otherwise, leave the default Front Sides option selected.

4. Select a Color Mode from among Color, Grayscale, and Black and White options. The default for scanning is black and white—the optimal choice for capturing text.

5. Choose the resolution for the scanned PDF. Henry leaves the default 300 dpi setting, because that is sufficiently high resolution for capturing the text but not too high as to add unnecessarily to the file's size.

6. Specify a destination for the scanned page (**Figure 7.13**). If you have open documents, Acrobat offers a choice between a new document and appending the scan to the active open document. In Henry's case, the documents are scanned as separate files.

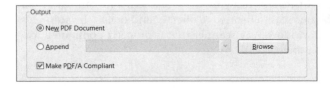

Figure 7.13 Scanned documents can be saved as separate files or appended to an open document.

**7.** Select the Make PDF/A Compliant check box. Henry intends to have his collection move toward compliance with the standard, even though he isn't presently mandated to comply.

**8.** In the Document section of the dialog, Henry drags the slider to decrease the file size versus increasing the quality of the scan (**Figure 7.14**).

The goal is to produce a file that is as small as possible without compromising the quality of the captured text. Click Options to open the Optimization dialog and choose precise settings. Read how to optimize settings for scanned files and converted images in the Chapter 2 bonus section on the book's Web site.

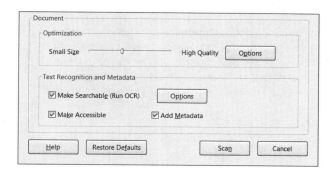

**Figure 7.14** Define how the file should be converted and if the text should be recognized as text.

**9.** In the Text Recognition and Metadata area, select Make Searchable (Run OCR), Make Accessible, and Add Metadata. The default option is to use the OCR (Optical Character Recognition) process to create a searchable document, meaning the content of the document is converted to words and images that you can then use with Search and Find features.

**10.** Click Scan; a Save Scanned File as dialog opens. Name the file and specify its location. Click Save to close the dialog and start the scan.

**11.** The page is scanned, and the Acrobat Scan dialog opens. Click either Scan more pages to continue scanning or Scanning complete, and then click OK.

Additional dialogs may open depending on the options selected, such as making the file accessible (described in Chapter 5) or PDF/A compliant. Respond to the dialog(s) as indicated.

# Working with a Scanned Document

PDF files created by scanning documents using older versions of Acrobat or from programs such as Photoshop create image PDF files, which means you can read and print the document, but the text on the page isn't interpreted and converted to letters; therefore, you cannot search the document for specific words or phrases. Instead, the document contains information about the shapes that make up the letters. Therefore, you should take advantage of Acrobat's OCR (optical character recognition) feature.

## IS IT AN IMAGE, OR IS IT TEXT?

If you open a document and aren't sure if it contains images and text or an image of the page, click the page with the Select tool on the Basic toolbar. Select the TouchUp Object tool ![icon] on the Advanced Editing toolbar and click the text on the page (**Figure 7.15**). If you click a text area in the document and the entire block of text or page is selected, you have an image of the text. If you see the content of each word selected, the page contains searchable text.

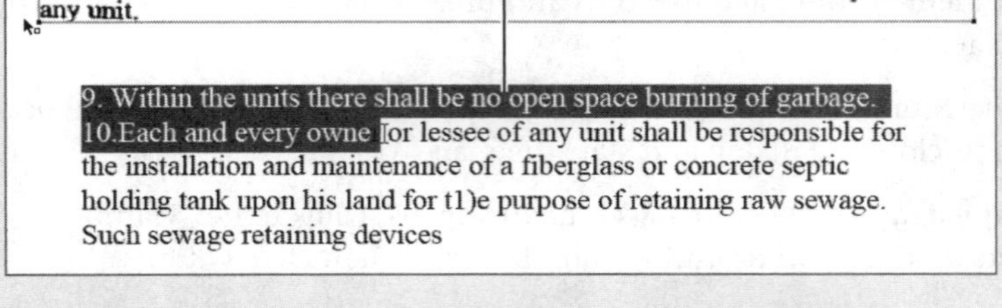

This is an image of text; the entire image is selected.

This is captured text and can be selected.

7. No building waste or other materials of any kind shall be dumped or stored on the unit except for clean earth for the purpose of leveling in connection with the erection of the dwelling house or the immediate improvement of the grounds.
8. No animals other than household pets normally permitted in private homes in urban residential areas shall be kept within the units. No dog or cat that is deemed by the Corporation (on reasonable grounds) to be a nuisance shall be kept within any unit.

9. Within the units there shall be no open space burning of garbage.
10.Each and every owner or lessee of any unit shall be responsible for the installation and maintenance of a fiberglass or concrete septic holding tank upon his land for the purpose of retaining raw sewage. Such sewage retaining devices

**Figure 7.15** You can tell if text is an image or captured text using the TouchUp Object tool.

# Capturing File Content

To capture the content of a scanned or image PDF, follow these steps:

1. Choose Document > OCR Text Recognition > Recognize Text Using OCR to open the Recognize Text dialog. The page information from the file is shown in the Pages area of the dialog. Henry leaves the default page settings as is (**Figure 7.16**).

2. Read the active options in the Settings area of the dialog. To make changes click Edit to open the Recognize Text – Settings dialog. Then make your choices for language, output style, and resolution, and click OK.

   Read about the different types of OCR output in the sidebar "Specifying an Output Style."

**Figure 7.16** Specify the pages for conversion, as well as the characteristics used for the conversion.

3. Click OK to close the Recognize Text dialog and start the capture process.

4. You see several progress bars as the file is processed. The progress bars will close when your file is finished.

When converting a big project like Henry's, try to use the Searchable Image conversion option to make the final PDF cleaner and easier to read. The Formatted Text and Graphics option is rarely used for an archival collection, as described in the sidebar "Specifying an Output Style."

# Finishing the Collection Assembly

Henry has a couple of tasks to finish. Well, perhaps it's more correct to say his interns have a couple of tasks to finish.

To complete the document assembly, Henry and his team have to:

- Scan the rest of the project files and capture the text in the same way as his test file.

- Create a storage file to include copies of all the files they'll use for the indexed collection (that's coming up next).

- Run the Conservancy_pdf batch script to add a watermark to the scanned and captured documents. Read how the files are processed in the section "Finishing the Batch Sequence."

The final stage of Henry's project is to create an index using Acrobat's Catalog feature. Aw c'mon now, this is the fun part!

## SPECIFYING AN OUTPUT STYLE

The setup options for OCR offers three ways to present the captured text. Click the PDF Output Style pull-down menu and choose from the three options:

- **Searchable Image** keeps the foreground of the page intact and places the searchable text behind the image. You'll find this option produces output closest to the original because Acrobat doesn't change the appearance of the document's letters.

- **Searchable Image Exact** keeps the foreground of the page intact and again the searchable text is behind the image. The output visually looks the same as the original, and the converted content is examined more precisely than the generic Searchable Image format.

- **Formatted Text & Graphics** rebuilds the entire page, converting the content into text, fonts, and graphics. This option can often result in substituted fonts and characters that are different in appearance from the original text of the document.

If you choose the Searchable Image option, results can vary depending on the quality of the source document. Scan black-and-white images at 200–600 dpi; grayscale images (made up of shades of gray only) or color images at 200–400 dpi.

Not all fonts and colors scan well. It's best to capture text in black and white, and a font of about 12 points is the optimal size. If your document contains text with smaller point sizes, you can successfully scan it at a higher resolution, such as 600 dpi. Scanning with a higher resolution produces a larger file, but you won't have to rekey the document before converting it. Colored or decorative fonts are difficult for the program to recognize and can lead to search and indexing errors.

However, if you use the Formatted Text & Graphics option, Acrobat actually replaces the text in the document with letters and numbers, and also captures the images. In some cases, the content of the page appears different because Acrobat has assigned different fonts to the document (**Figure 7.17**). Some content may be unrecognizable; characters the program is unable to decipher are called *suspects*. Acrobat contains a method for evaluating a converted bitmap on a suspect-by-suspect basis; the clearer the original document, the less work needed to correct its content.

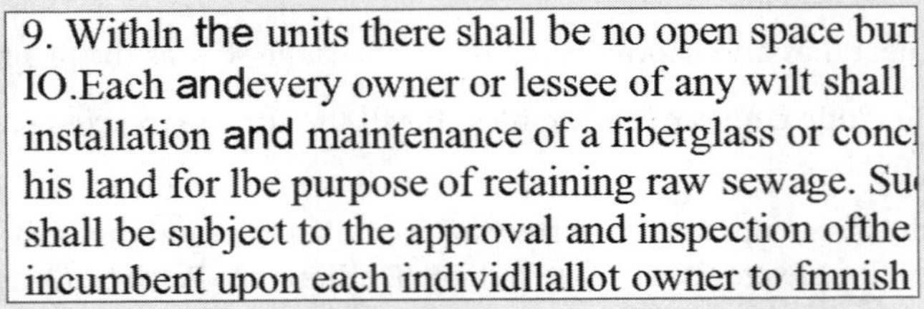

9. Withln the units there shall be no open space bur
IO.Each andevery owner or lessee of any wilt shall
installation and maintenance of a fiberglass or conc
his land for lbe purpose of retaining raw sewage. Su
shall be subject to the approval and inspection ofthe
incumbent upon each individllallot owner to fmnish

**Figure 7.17** The text in a converted document may display several different fonts or misspelled words.

# Designing an Index

The benefit of using an index rather than Acrobat's Search feature is speed. When you are working with hundreds of documents, building an index and including it with the documents it indexes will make searching much quicker.

Henry plans to create a read-me file so users can work with the index more effectively. A read-me file is a set of instructions that accompanies many products, such as software, databases, programs, and other computer content. Using a read-me file is a conventional way of providing additional information to users; the very name of the file says it all.

 **DOWNLOAD** The read-me file Henry created to assist users in working with the collection's index is available from the book's Web site. The file is named **ch07_bonus.pdf**.

## OFFERING USERS MORE OPTIONS

You can also use custom terms to describe a document, including subjects and keywords. These words can then be used as search terms when searching the document collection. Subjects and keywords can be interchangeable, although a document has only one subject. Confused yet? Here's an example: Suppose you are assembling a collection of documents about dogs. The title of one document might be "Bowser's Big Day." That is fine as a title, but almost useless when searching for the document in a collection—unless you are looking for Bowser! If you included a subject, or classification, such as "veterinarian visit," your users would find the document by using "veterinarian" as a subject search term.

Using the same example, you could assemble a number of keywords, such as "doctor," "animal hospital," "checkup," and "vaccinations." If users then search for one of these keywords using the Keywords option in the Search PDF window, they again would see the document in the search results.

Be sure to differentiate the type of words you are using and explain them to your index users. Define a word as a subject or a keyword—not both—for best results. If you search using a keyword term and have used the same term as a subject in some documents, your search results will be inaccurate. For example, if you define "floral arrangement" as keywords in some documents and as a subject in others, searching for the term using keywords returns only those documents having the term as keywords; searching for the term as a subject returns only those documents having the term as a subject.

# Building and Applying an Index

Now that Henry has assembled his documents in the shared folder he's using to store the collection and index, he's ready to build his index.

Follow these steps to configure the index:

**1.** Choose Advanced > Document Processing > Full Text Index with Catalog to open the Catalog dialog.

**2.** Click New Index. The New Index Definition dialog opens. Add information to the dialog to name and describe the index, and select the folders you want to include, as well as any you want to exclude (**Figure 7.18**).

**3.** Click Options to customize the index by adding or removing content from the index (**Figure 7.19**). Read about the options in the sidebar "Customizing Your Index Options."

**4.** Click OK to close the Options dialog and return to the New Index Definition dialog.

**5.** Click Build to open the Save Index File dialog. Name the index file and save it with the document collection.

**6.** Click Save to close both the Save dialog and the New Index Definition dialog. The index is created and the results appear in the Build dialog.

**7.** Click Close to close the Build dialog.

The index creates its own subfolder and files, including the index.pdx file (the index's database file) and a log file. Don't delete or move any of the indexing folders or files, or you will corrupt the index.

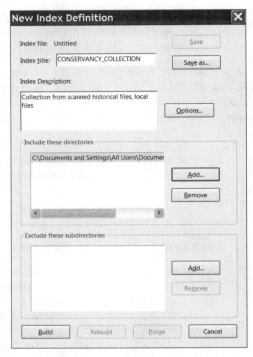

**Figure 7.18** Select the files and write descriptions for your index.

**Figure 7.19** Customize the index using specific features in this dialog.

## CUSTOMIZING YOUR INDEX OPTIONS

You can customize your index in a number of ways using the Options dialog shown in Figure 7.19:

- Select the "Do not include numbers" check box if you want to omit numbers from the index. Use this option if your indexed documents contain a lot of numerical information that isn't likely to be searched, because including the numbers adds to the search time.

- Select the "Add IDs to Adobe PDF v1.0 files" check box if you are working with very old PDF files; unless you have files created with Acrobat versions 1 or 2, you don't need to select this option.

- Select the "Do not warn for changed documents when searching" check box to prevent viewing a warning dialog.

- Click the Custom Properties button to open a dialog that lets you specify custom document properties to include in an index. The custom properties are then included as a search option in the Search PDF window. Custom properties, such as those used in Microsoft Office files, can be included in an index.

- Click the XMP Fields button to open a dialog that lets you select custom XMP (Extensible Metadata Platform) fields, which are indexed and included as a search option in the Search PDF window. XMP fields are imported XML content that can be included with a document's contents.

- Click the Stop Words button to open a dialog in which you can specify words to exclude from the index—words such as "the," "an," and "and." Be sure to tell your index users though. If they search for an exact phrase, such as "The Five and Dime," they won't have a return on the search.

- Click the Structure Tags button to open a dialog to choose tags that can be used in searching. For example, you might want to use <image> to search for images in a document collection.

# Testing the Index

Once the index is created, it's time to test it using Acrobat's Search function. You can perform simple searches in a single document using the Find toolbar (**Figure 7.20**). Choose View > Toolbars > Find, or right-click/Control-click the toolbar well and click Find. Type a search term in the field, and click Previous or Next to move within the document to the next occurrence of the word, which is highlighted on the page. Click the Find down arrow to open a list of additional search criteria.

**Figure 7.20** You can set preferences that apply options to new indexes automatically.

# Setting Preferences

For Henry, building an index is a one-shot deal. His normal workday won't include creating and manipulating indexes on a regular basis. On the other hand, his interns, who will maintain the index, may want to set preferences in Acrobat that are applied automatically to any new index that is built.

To do so, choose Edit > Preferences (or Acrobat > Preferences on a Mac) and click Catalog in the Categories panel at the left of the dialog to show the Catalog preferences. The Catalog preferences include the same options as those used to customize the index shown in Figure 7.19, as well as several other options, such as creating a log file or forcing an ISO standard (**Figure 7.21**).

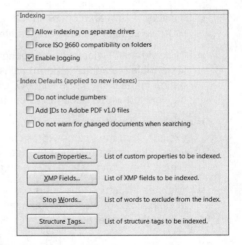

**Figure 7.21** Use the Find toolbar to locate content in a single document

If you intend for an index to be cross-platform, you might want to choose "Force ISO 9660 compatibility on folders." This option applies the ISO standard document-naming process automatically to filenames to comply with MS-DOS filenames, which are names of less than eight digits with no spaces. This preference renames the files, but you'll have to rename folders manually to comply with the standard.

Most of these preferences are self-explanatory and include items like choosing drive locations for storing the index files and excluding numbers from new indexes.

# Maintaining the Index

The Catalog feature has to be rerun whenever changes are made to the contents of the documents in the index. This includes adding new documents, making changes to existing documents, and moving or renaming documents. If documents in your collection are changed in any of these ways, you have to rebuild the index because it no longer points to the content accurately.

In Henry's project, the content of existing documents isn't changed, but new documents are added on a regular basis. Therefore, to maintain an accurate index, his interns needs to rerun the Catalog feature whenever new documents are added.

To maintain the index, follow these steps:

1. Choose Advanced > Document Processing > Full Text Index with Catalog to open the Catalog dialog.

2. Click Open Index and select the index's PDX (Catalog Index File) file from the indexing folder.

3. Click Open to replace the dialog with the New Index Definition dialog (shown in Figure 7.18).

4. The buttons at the bottom of the dialog are active when you open an existing index. Click Rebuild to repair and reconfigure the index; to delete an existing index, click Purge.

# What Else Can He Do?

After working with the index for a while, Henry should get feedback from his users as to how they are using the index and if it is meeting their needs. There are a few things that he may want to change over time. For example, users may find it useful to have keyword searching, which can be added to the documents through the Document Properties dialog.

There are many ways in which Henry could assemble, convert, and process the files for his collection. For example, he chose the files for the initial conversion to PDF from the desktop. Instead, he could build a batch sequence to convert the files. He could use the Combine PDF Files feature and convert and combine the contents to a single megafile, or use the Combine PDF Files feature and build a PDF Package.

For ease of use, Henry could use a PDF home page for the collection and add shortcuts to the home page on the computers accessing the collection. If he attaches the index to the home page, his users can search without having to attach the index. Locating and attaching the index is described in the Chapter 7 bonus material available from the book's Web site.

# Communicating with Technical Drawings

8

Acrobat 8 Professional, as in the previous two versions of the program, offers the ability to work with layered technical drawings that originate in Microsoft Visio or AutoCAD. In addition to using images having multiple layers, you can also manipulate data stored within the PDF version of the drawing. *Metadata* is embedded in the source program in Windows, either in AutoCAD or Microsoft Visio, and can be read in Acrobat or Adobe Reader using the Object Data tool.

In this chapter, you'll see how an interior designer shares a floor plan, which is created in Microsoft Visio, with the client firm's office manager who uses Adobe Reader 8 to read and work with the embedded data in the PDF file.

Acrobat 8 Professional includes several measuring tools that you can use to identify perimeter, distance, and area in a drawing. The scale drawing lets the designer and her clients communicate about details in the drawing using precise measurements.

The first part of this project, converting the Visio drawing to PDF, is exclusive to Windows; however, manipulating the drawing, signing it, and sending it for review can be done in either Windows or Mac OS.

# That's the Plan

Emily Hope is an interior designer specializing in office design and development. She works with numerous local office furnishing and supply companies, and most of her clients are referred by commercial property owners.

Emily is preparing a floor plan for Lemming Systems, a small computer company. The company has rented suites in a commercial building, and she's ready to send the first draft of the plans for the administration suite to the company's office manager, Joyce Delgado. Emily develops the basic floor plans in Visio for discussion with her clients. When the layouts are approved, she sends the drawings to her contractor's draftsperson for conversion to blueprints, which will be used by various subcontractors to complete the work.

She is trying to streamline communication to and from her clients and contractors. The current work process includes distributing multiple e-mails and copies of plans in different file formats to view in different readers, as well as e-mailing lists of specs and requirements.

Emily hopes that for the purposes of discussing requirements and nailing down a contract she can use a single file format, PDF. She wants to embed information about project components right in the PDF, and fortunately she can do that using Acrobat 8 Professional. She has learned she can add measurements of different project elements as comments in the PDF document before sending the file to her client, and her client can add measurements in response.

To simplify communications among everyone involved, Emily can enable PDF versions of the drawings to let her clients examine the drawing's data, which provides details on project materials. Her clients can work with commenting and measuring tools directly in the PDF drawing, in either Acrobat 7 or 8, or Adobe Reader 7 or 8.

Emily is one smart cookie: She wants a drawing that can be easily transmitted and read, can display metadata, and can be measured and commented on. Let's see how she meets these lofty goals using a PDF file (**Figure 8.1**).

> **NOTE** You can't duplicate the appearance of the drawing shown in Figure 8.1. It was developed by a trained professional on a closed course, and attempting this feat yourself may result in injury. I'm kidding about the trained professional bit but not about what you see in the image. The drawing is a composite showing the different features used in this project. While you can view all the elements shown, you can't see them at the same time.

Specify layer behavior like visibility and locks.

Show and hide content in the drawing.

Use a scale embedded in the drawing for measuring in Acrobat and Adobe Reader.

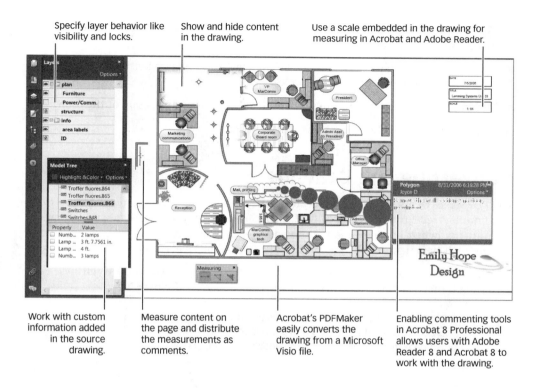

Work with custom information added in the source drawing.

Measure content on the page and distribute the measurements as comments.

Acrobat's PDFMaker easily converts the drawing from a Microsoft Visio file.

Enabling commenting tools in Acrobat 8 Professional allows users with Adobe Reader 8 and Acrobat 8 to work with the drawing.

**Figure 8.1** The floor plan can be enabled and used for multiple purposes.

# Steps Involved in This Project

Emily has a number of steps to complete in this project. You know, of course, that it will all work out in the end! Emily needs to:

- Convert her Visio drawing to PDF and include the embedded data in the drawing for her client to view.

- Add measurements as comments in the PDF drawing for her client to use to examine the contents.

- Protect the document from changes using a password.

- Enable the drawing so Joyce, who is working with Adobe Reader 8, can use it.

- E-mail the file to Joyce.

- Ask Joyce to use the Commenting & Drawing Markup tools in Adobe Reader 8 to work with the drawing.

- Have Joyce add a dynamic stamp to the document that places her name and the date on the file before sending the comments back to Emily.

- Receive the comment data from Joyce and add it to her source copy of the drawing.

First up, Emily converts her Visio drawing.

# Converting the Drawing

The PDFMaker that Acrobat 8 installs automatically in Visio has the capability to convert multilayered Visio drawings to PDF, maintaining the layers as individual PDF layers. In Emily's drawing, however, maintaining all the individual layers isn't important for sharing with her client, so she'll export the PDF with the layers grouped.

The conversion process has two parts: Emily first has to choose conversion settings according to her drawing's use, and then she has to convert the drawing.

 **DOWNLOAD** If you use Microsoft Visio and would like to convert the source file yourself, download **LSOffice.vsd** from the book's Web site at www.donnabaker.ca/downloads.html. Download **LSOffice.pdf** to see the converted file.

## Choosing Conversion Settings

As previously mentioned, Emily doesn't need all the separate layers for her drawings, so she'll flatten the drawing to layer groups.

Follow these steps to choose conversion settings for the drawing:

1. In Visio, choose Adobe PDF > Change Conversion Settings to open the Acrobat PDFMaker dialog (**Figure 8.2**).

2. Click the Conversion Settings down arrow and choose Standard if it isn't shown by default. Emily wants to print the plan as well as view it onscreen, and the Standard setting allows her to do both.

3. In the Application Settings portion of the dialog, leave the default "Include Visio custom properties as object data in the Adobe PDF" option selected, and then deselect "Exclude Visio objects with no custom properties."

   In Emily's project, all of the content on the page is part of the drawing.

4. Click OK to close the dialog.

Once the conversion settings are chosen, Emily can create the PDF version of the drawing.

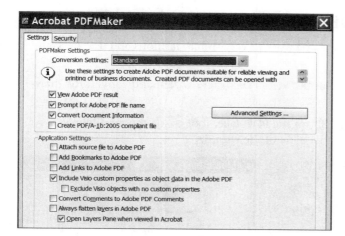

**Figure 8.2** Visio includes a PDFMaker for converting files to PDF with or without layers.

## WHAT YOU SEE; WHAT YOU DON'T SEE

Emily's drawing is constructed in a few layers. She'd like to define the drawing's appearance to show most of the layers as the PDF file's default appearance. She'd also like to lock layers so they are always visible in the PDF drawing. In Visio, choose View > Layer Properties to open the Layer Properties dialog (**Figure 8.3**). Assign Visible, Print, and Lock status to the different layers according to the drawing. The settings are included in the file and define how the layers behave in Acrobat or Adobe Reader.

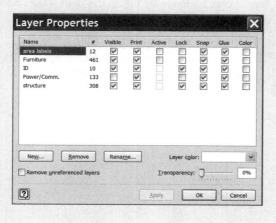

**Figure 8.3** Establish the characteristics for the drawing's layers in Visio before conversion.

# Generating the PDF File

The PDFMakers in Visio and AutoCAD work in very similar fashions and use the same sequence of steps and options.

Follow these steps to work through the Visio PDFMaker's wizard and convert the drawing to PDF:

**1.** Click Convert to Adobe PDF  on the PDFMaker toolbar, or choose Adobe PDF > Convert to PDF to open the first pane of the wizard.

**2.** The conversion settings option to include custom properties (object data) is shown again in the first pane of the wizard. Leave the option selected and click Continue.

**3.** Choose the layering option for the page (**Figure 8.4**). The default is to Flatten all layers. Although Emily is using all layers in the drawing, she wants to organize them into a group, so she selects the "Retain some layers in the selected page" option. This option allows her to arrange groups of layers as well as select specific layers. Click Continue to move to the next pane of the wizard.

**Figure 8.4** Choose one of several methods for converting drawing layers.

**4.** Select the layer or layers in the Layers in Visio Drawing list on the left and click Add Layer(s) to move the layer names to the Layers in Adobe PDF list on the right (**Figure 8.5**).

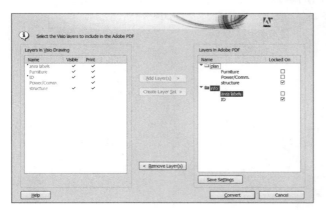

**Figure 8.5** Specify how the layers are organized in the PDF file and whether to group layers in sets.

**5.** With the layers still selected click Create Layer Set. A small text field appears. Emily types plan to name the layer group.

A hierarchy is formed using the group name with the selected fields as nested layers of the named group. When the PDF file is opened in Acrobat, the two layer group labels are listed in the Layers panel as the default display for the file.

**6.** Continue adding other layers and forming layer groups as desired.

**7.** Click Convert to open the Save Adobe PDF File As dialog.

**8.** The Visio document's name and folder location are used by default. If you like, change the name and choose an alternate storage location. Emily uses the default, and her drawing is saved as LSOffice.pdf.

**9.** Click Save to close the dialog and convert the drawing.

Now that Emily's drawing is converted, she can open it in Acrobat and check it out. She first wants to make sure the layers are behaving as necessary before sending the file to her client.

## Checking Out the Layers

The drawing opens in Acrobat, displaying the page as well as the Layers panel. If the panel is closed, open it by choosing View > Navigation Panels > Layers (**Figure 8.6**).

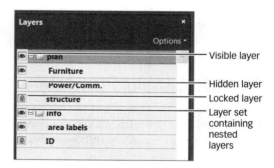

The icons to the left of the labels in the Layers panel correspond with different states for the layers that Emily established in Visio and the PDFMaker. Clicking the (+) to the left of the layer group labels shows the nested layers in the group. As specified in Visio, the layer showing the power and com-

**Figure 8.6** The icons on the Layers panel identify layer characteristics.

munications outlets, named Power/Comm., is hidden. The layers showing the drawing identification (ID) and walls (structure) are locked and visible.

The arrangement works quite well, but Emily wants to make a change or two before e-mailing the file.

## Defining a Reference Layer

Emily is afraid that the Layers panel and its different icons will be confusing to her clients and decides to simplify the Layers panel's contents. She'll convert the two locked layers in the drawing to reference layers.

Layers are classified either as *view* layers, where their visibility can be toggled on or off, or *reference* layers, which keeps the layer visible. The first change Emily makes is to define the two locked layers as reference layers by following these steps:

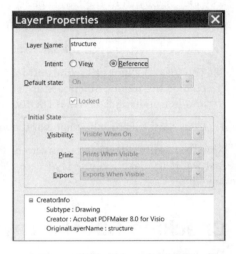

1.  Right-click/Control-click the structure layer's label in the Layers panel and choose Layer Properties to open the dialog.

2.  Click Reference to switch the active intent from View to Reference. Notice that the rest of the dialog is inactive when you make the selection (**Figure 8.7**).

3.  Click OK to close the dialog.

Emily wants to alter another layer's properties next.

**Figure 8.7** Defining a layer as a reference layer deactivates other layer properties.

## Changing Layer Properties

The ID layer is also locked, and Emily intends to convert it to a reference layer after she changes its other properties. It's important that the identifying information for the drawing be visible regardless of how or where the drawing is used.

Follow these steps:

1.  Select the ID layer in the Layers panel and choose Options > Layer Properties from the Layers panel or right-click/Control-click the layer and choose Properties to open the Layer Properties dialog.

2.  In the Initial State section of the dialog, click the down arrow for:

    ■ **Visibility,** and choose Always Visible.

    ■ **Print,** and choose Always Prints.

    ■ **Export,** and choose Always Export.

3.  Click the Reference Intent button at the top of the dialog. When the Reference intent is selected, the other settings are disabled as a result of the new options Emily selected.

4.  Click OK to close the dialog.

    The referenced layers are listed in the Layers panel in italics and have no prefacing icon, making the list of layers simpler to understand (**Figure 8.8**).

5.  Emily saves the file using another name. The project file is named Lemming01.pdf.

Emily's next task is to add some measurements in Acrobat. (By the way, she can also add measurements in the Visio drawing, but that's the subject of a different book!)

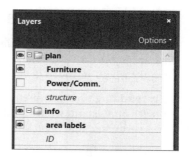

**Figure 8.8** The referenced layers are shown in italics in the Layers panel.

# Measuring Objects

Acrobat 8 Professional includes several tools you can use to measure elements on a page, such as the distance between two columns of text or the space between two objects in a PDF drawing. If you are working with a scaled drawing, as Emily is in her project, you'll even be able to assign a scale. (You can choose from a number of values, such as pixels, inches, or even miles!) If you add annotations to the measurements, the values are converted to comments in the PDF file. For more information on working with comments in general, see Chapter 3, "Communicating with Comments," Chapter 4, "Collaborating in a Shared Review," and Chapter 12, "Secure Reviewing and Reporting."

 **DOWNLOAD** Lemming01.pdf if you'd like to practice adding measurements to the drawing. The drawing, complete with measurements, is available as well: Download **Lemming02.pdf**.

## Adding Visualization Tools

While she's in interface arrangement mode, Emily adds tools to the Select & Zoom toolbar to use for checking out the drawing.

1.  Right-click/Control-click the toolbar well and choose More Tools to open the dialog.

2.  Scroll down to the Select & Zoom toolbar area and choose Marquee Zoom and Dynamic Zoom.

3.  Click OK to close the dialog and add the tools to the toolbar.

## Measuring to Scale

The original drawing uses a scale of 1:64, which is included in the document's metadata. Once in Acrobat 8 Professional, Emily can set the scale to be used automatically for anything measured in the PDF version of the drawing.

Emily is adding one measurement in the drawing to help the Lemming Systems' office manager understand what's in the drawing. The three tools on the toolbar measure distance, perimeter, and area, and Emily uses the area tool in the drawing.

Follow these steps to specify scale and measure an object in the drawing:

1. To open the Measuring toolbar, right-click/Control-click the toolbar well at the top of the program window and choose the Measuring toolbar (**Figure 8.9**).

2. To zoom into the area of the drawing to be measured, select the Marquee Zoom tool, which was added to the Select & Zoom toolbar.

3. Drag a marquee on the drawing to select the area and release the mouse (**Figure 8.10**). The drawing zooms to the largest magnification that fits within the program window.

4. Select the Area tool on the Measuring toolbar. The Area tool dialog opens.

5. Type the scale for the drawing and choose the units of measure in the Units and Markup Settings area at the bottom of the dialog (**Figure 8.11**). Emily types 64 in the field on the right since her drawing uses a ratio of 1:64.

   Once the scale values are entered, they are automatically displayed each time a drawing tool is activated.

**Figure 8.9** Acrobat 8 Professional includes tools for measuring aspects of a document or its contents.

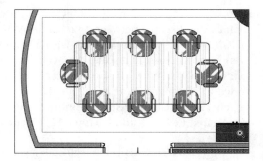

**Figure 8.10** Use specialized Zoom tools to quickly display an area of interest on the page.

**Figure 8.11** Specify the scale for the drawing when you select a Measuring tool.

**6.** Change the name of the measurement if required. Emily types `Conference table area` in the Label field.

**7.** The pointer, now large crosshairs, shows a bounding box when it is over a point on the drawing (**Figure 8.12**).

**8.** Click when the pointer is on the location where you want to start measuring an area.

**9.** Drag to place the second and subsequent points on the drawing.

To limit, or *constrain*, the segments to straight lines as you draw, hold down the Shift key as you drag and click the mouse.

**10.** To close the shape and finish the measurement, click when you see the pointer change to a small circle (**Figure 8.13**).

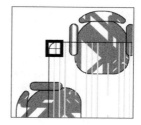

**Figure 8.12** Move the crosshairs on the drawing until they identify a point on the drawing for precise measuring.

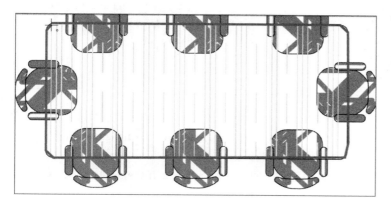

**Figure 8.13** Acrobat tells you when the pointer is over the point of origin of your measurement.

**11.** Select the Hand tool on the Select & Zoom toolbar to disengage the drawing tool. Move the tool over the comment icon at the margin of the area to see the name of the area in a tooltip (**Figure 8.14**).

**12.** Save the file. Emily saves the file as Lemming02.pdf.

Emily has finished adding her measurement to the drawing, which was added to the PDF file as a comment. She'll take a look at the comments listed in the Comments panel next.

**Figure 8.14** The selected area is shown in a tooltip to the specified scale.

# Viewing Annotations

When Emily added the measurements to her drawing, she selected the Measurement Markup check box in the tool's dialog and typed text in the Annotation field. Acrobat converts the text and measurement to a comment. You can view comments by moving the pointer over a measured area and viewing the content in a tooltip, as shown in Figure 8.14 for example. Emily can also work with the comments in the Comments panel, one of Acrobat's Navigation panels.

To view the comments, follow these steps:

1.  Select the Comments icon 🗫 in the Navigation panel at the left of the program window; the Comments panel is displayed across the bottom of the program window (**Figure 8.15**).

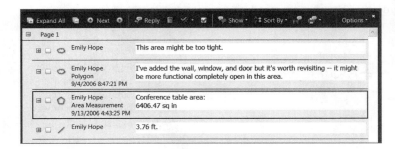

**Figure 8.15**
The measurements are shown as comments in the Comments panel.

2.  Click Expand All 🗔 on the Comments panel's toolbar to open the comments in the page.

    You can also click the (+) to the left of each comment, which toggles to (–), as shown in the figure, indicating the comment is expanded.

3.  Read the comments: The text includes both the annotation typed in the tool's dialog as well as the measurement.

4.  To close the Comments panel, click the Comments icon again.

Save the file. The version of Emily's drawing used to this point in the project is saved as Lemming02.pdf.

The file is complete with Emily's comments. She has a few final items to take care of before sharing the drawing.

# Preparing the Drawing for Distribution

From Emily's perspective, her drawing is ready to go. However, she has to make a few more changes to allow her client, Joyce, to use the file. Emily has to:

- Add a password to protect the contents of the drawing.

- Enable the file so her client can use the commenting tools in Adobe Reader.

- E-mail the file to her client.

 **DOWNLOAD** Continue working with your Lemming02.pdf file in this section. Several versions of the drawing are available from the Web site if you prefer to start from a new file. **Lemming02P.pdf** is the drawing with a password applied; **Lemming02E.pd**f is the password-protected drawing after being enabled for use in Adobe Reader.

## Protecting the Drawing's Contents

Emily needs to protect the contents of her drawing from modifications or changes for legal and professional reasons. She can prevent users without a password from either opening the drawing or making changes to the drawing, and decides to follow the latter route.

### Adding a password

Follow these steps to add password protection to a PDF file:

**1.** Make sure all the changes are finished, and the file is in distribution-ready form.

Once the password is applied, Emily must enter the password each time she wants to save changes to the file—a time-consuming and downright boring task.

**2.** Choose File > Properties to open the Document Properties dialog. Click Security to display the Document Security tab (**Figure 8.16**).

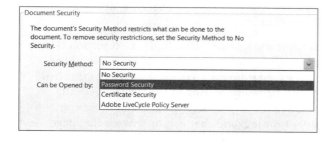

**Figure 8.16** The level of encryption and available options depend on the selected Acrobat version.

3. Click the Security Method down arrow and choose Password Security. The Password Security Settings dialog opens over the Document Properties dialog.

4. Click the Compatibility down arrow and choose Acrobat 5.0 and later from the Compatibility menu if it isn't displayed by default.

   The variety of document components that can be encrypted varies according to the level of encryption applied. Read more about the different encryption options in the sidebar "What's the Password?"

5. In the Permissions section at the bottom of the dialog, select "Restrict editing and printing of the document. A password will be required in order to change these permission settings." Several additional fields are activated in the dialog (**Figure 8.17**).

**Figure 8.17** Specify the changes you want to allow for those using the file.

6. Type a password—Emily types password—in the Change Permissions Password field.

   **NOTE** The password is a very important feature for preserving rights in a document. In a real-life situation, please enter alphanumeric characters that are more unique than those used in this project!

7. Click the Printing Allowed down arrow and choose Low Resolution (150 dpi). Emily wants the recipients to be able to print a copy for quick reference.

8. Click the Changes Allowed down arrow and choose "Commenting, filling in form fields, and signing existing signature fields."

   Emily wants her recipient to add comments, as described in the next section. There aren't any form fields or signature fields to worry about, but they are part of the option. The "Enable text access for screen reader devices for the visually impaired" option is selected by default. It won't have any bearing in this project, so Emily leaves it selected. The option to enable copying of text, images, and other content isn't selected. Emily has allowed for printing, and that is sufficient for this stage of the project.

**9.** Click OK. An information dialog opens explaining that the Permissions Password works throughout all Adobe products but may not work in other products. Click OK. The information dialog closes, and the Confirm Permissions Password dialog opens (**Figure 8.18**).

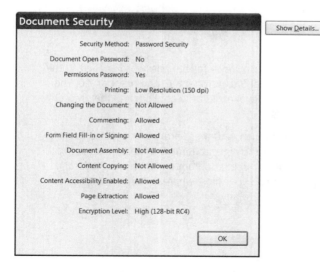

**Figure 8.18** A password must be confirmed before it can be applied to the document.

**10.** Type the password again in the Permissions Password field. Emily types password again, and clicks OK again, which closes the dialog and opens another information dialog stating the security feature isn't stored in the file until it is saved.

**11.** Click OK to close the information dialog; the Password-Security Settings dialog closes automatically, returning Emily to the Security tab in the Document Properties dialog.

**12.** The security settings aren't saved until the next time Emily saves the file. To check the settings before saving, click Show Details to open the Document Security dialog (**Figure 8.19**).

**Document Security**

| | |
|---|---|
| Security Method: | Password Security |
| Document Open Password: | No |
| Permissions Password: | Yes |
| Printing: | Low Resolution (150 dpi) |
| Changing the Document: | Not Allowed |
| Commenting: | Allowed |
| Form Field Fill-in or Signing: | Allowed |
| Document Assembly: | Not Allowed |
| Content Copying: | Not Allowed |
| Content Accessibility Enabled: | Allowed |
| Page Extraction: | Allowed |
| Encryption Level: | High (128-bit RC4) |

OK

Show Details...

**Figure 8.19** Check the password's details before saving the document.

**13.** Once she's checked through the settings, Emily clicks OK to close the dialog, and then clicks OK again to close the Document Properties dialog, returning to the program window.

**14.** Save the file to apply the security settings. Emily saves the file as Lemming02P ("P" for "protected").

## Reviewing the security

Once the password is saved in the document, Emily notices some changes on the program window. The file's name has changed. The file she saved as Lemming02P.pdf is shown as Lemming02P.pdf (SECURED).

She also sees a security icon 🔒 at the top left of the Navigation panel area on the program window (**Figure 8.20**). Click the icon to display the Security Settings panel. Basic information about the password security is shown as well as a link to the Document Properties dialog's Security tab.

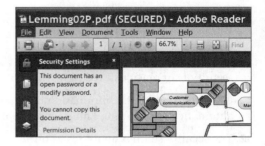

**Figure 8.20** Information about the type of security is shown in the Security Settings panel.

Next, Emily must enable the file to be used by her recipient who uses Adobe Reader, not Acrobat.

**WHAT'S THE PASSWORD?**

Emily uses the default Acrobat 5.0 compatibility level for the password applied to the drawing. She could also choose from Acrobat 3.0, Acrobat 6.0, and Acrobat 7.0. The higher the version number, the greater the level of security applied, and the greater the ability to choose customized settings.

Acrobat 3.0 uses the lowest level of encryption, and there are fewer choices to make. Choosing Acrobat 6.0 or Acrobat 7.0 offers the highest number of variables. Acrobat 6.0 compatibility lets you encrypt all the document content except the metadata, which is important for search engines to find your files; whereas Acrobat 7.0 allows encryption of just file attachments, if there are any.

# Enabling the File for Use in Adobe Reader

Acrobat 8 Professional allows Emily to specify that a user working in Adobe Reader 7 or 8 can access tools for commenting.

Follow these steps to prepare the file:

1. Choose Comments > Enable for Commenting in Adobe Reader

   Emily can also choose Advanced > Enable Usage Rights in Adobe Reader, which provides several types of usage rights including digital signatures, completing forms, and commenting.

2. An information dialog opens, stating that the file has to be saved when enabled, and that certain features such as editing content and changing pages will no longer be available. Click OK to close the dialog and open the Save As dialog.

3. Save the file with an alternate name; the project is saved as Lemming02PE.pdf ("E" for "enabled," get it?).

   Be sure to save an enabled document using a different name. You may have to make changes to the original document in the future and require features that are disallowed in an enabled document.

   It's simpler to edit a document that doesn't have security attached, because you don't have to remove the security and then reapply it. An unsecured PDF file can be changed in Acrobat 8 Professional by anyone using editing and other tools. A document's form fields can be filled in, the file can be signed, and pages can be modified. Once a file is enabled for use in Adobe Reader, some of the editing, signing, and other modifications are restricted.

Emily checks out the security settings for the file after saving the enabled version (**Figure 8.21**). To show the settings, choose File > Properties to open the Document Properties dialog and choose the Security tab or click the Permission Details link in the Security Settings panel. All the options that were selected in the Document Properties dialog are now frozen, indicated by dark gray backgrounds on the fields and disabled buttons.

By first applying a password and then enabling the file, Emily can control user access to features more precisely. For example, she wants to allow Joyce to print a low-resolution copy of the drawing, which she specifies in the Password-Security Settings dialog. If she simply enabled the file, printing would be allowed but not restricted to specific settings.

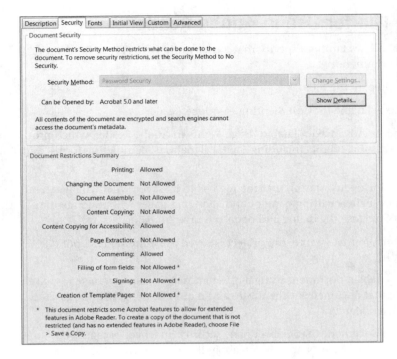

**Figure 8.21** Once a file is enabled for use in Adobe Reader, many of its document properties are frozen.

# E-mailing the Drawing

Finally, Emily sends the file to Joyce.

Follow these steps to e-mail a PDF file from Acrobat:

1.  Open the document you want to send in Acrobat. Emily is sending the Lemming02PE.pdf file.

2.  Choose File > Attach to E-mail or click the e-mail icon 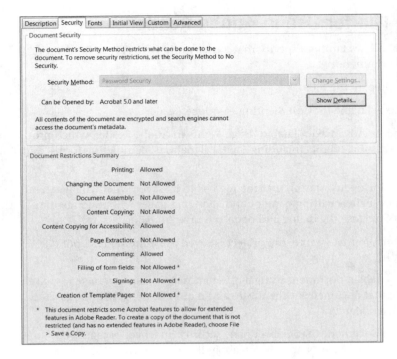 to open an e-mail message window. The e-mail uses the filename as the subject line and includes the open PDF file as an attachment (**Figure 8.22**).

3.  Enter the recipient's e-mail address and send the file.

That's all there is to it! Emily is finished for the day.

Now let's turn to Joyce's tasks. She'll be working with the drawing's embedded data and comments. Since Emily enabled the document's Commenting features, Joyce can work in Adobe Reader 8.

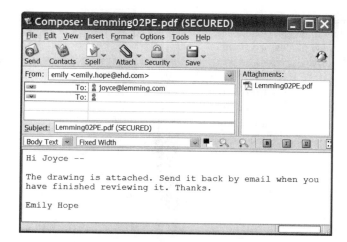

**Figure 8.22** Send a PDF file directly from Acrobat to your e-mail program for mailing.

# Opening the Drawing in Adobe Reader

Joyce saves the e-mailed PDF file and then opens it in Adobe Reader. When the file opens, a few additional features are shown in the program window.

The Navigation panels corresponding to the additional features that Joyce can access are opened. The features include the following:

- **Object Data** ![icon]. Emily created the PDF document in Visio using the embedded information in the Visio file as object data in Acrobat.

- **Layers** ![icon]. The document was created in Visio with a number of layers, which Emily then modified in Acrobat.

- **Security** ![icon]. The document is protected from changes by a password that Emily added and configured prior to e-mailing the drawing to Joyce.

A Document bar displays below the toolbar area explaining that the document contains rights and instructions (**Figure 8.23**). Click Hide to close the Document bar and save screen space.

**Figure 8.23** The rights-enabled PDF document displays information about what Joyce can do with the file.

NOTE If the document had been distributed using Acrobat's Review features, a How To window would also display. Read about using the review process in Chapters 3 and 4.

At the left of the Adobe Reader 8 program window, the Navigation panels are arranged similarly to the layout in Acrobat 8. The How To panel is included and contains links to common tasks that Joyce might be using, such as adding comments (**Figure 8.24**).

Joyce has made her way around the program, checking out the new features. Next she'll examine the drawing's data.

**Figure 8.24** When in doubt, look for help. The How To panel is a quick entry to assistance.

# Viewing Object Data

When Emily created her drawing in Visio, she included custom properties for the objects and groups of objects in the drawing. This information contains details about specific parts of the project, such as types of furniture configurations, light fixtures, and chairs. Recall in the section "Converting the Drawing," Emily included these custom properties and Acrobat obliged by converting them to object data.

## Displaying Object Data

Acrobat 8 Professional and Adobe Reader 8, like their version 7 predecessors, offer the Object Data tool, which you can use to identify and examine data embedded in the PDF file's source file as custom properties. The Object Data tool—the only tool on the Object Data toolbar—is automatically enabled in this project because the file contains the appropriate type of objects.

Follow these steps to examine object data in a project file:

1. Open the Object Data toolbar by choosing Tools > Object Data > Show Object Data Toolbar in Adobe Reader 8.

2. Choose the Object Data tool ![icon] from the toolbar, or select it from the Tools menu.

**3.** When you mouse over an object on a drawing that contains metadata, the pointer changes to crosshairs (**Figure 8.25**).

**4.** Double-click the object to select it: The first click selects all the objects with data on the drawing, and the second click selects just the object below the crosshairs. The Model Tree panel opens once the object selection is complete, and the content of the embedded data is shown in the lower section of the Model Tree panel (**Figure 8.26**).

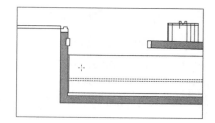

**Figure 8.25** Objects on the page that contain data are identified with a crosshair pointer.

As shown in the figure, the drawing contains a large number of objects that include data. Click through the objects in the drawing to see the data.

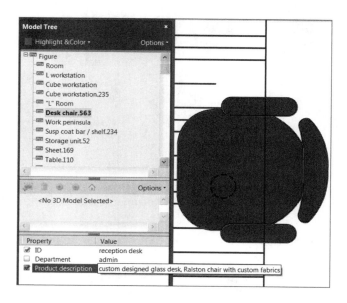

**Figure 8.26** The Model Tree panel shows a selected object's name as well as its properties.

**5.** To work with the drawing's data, click the Options button in the Model Tree panel and select different functions, such as zooming to the selected object, counting similar objects, exporting the data as text or XML, or copying the content to the clipboard.

## Fun with Objects

Here are some experiments you can try with the drawing's object data:

- Click the Highlight Color down arrow in the Model Tree panel to open a color picker, and choose another color to highlight or identify a selected object.

- Choose an object from the list at the top of the Model Tree panel, and then click the Options down arrow and choose Count. An information dialog opens, listing the number of objects that have the same data associations. Some objects are single, whereas others are created in multiples. For example, the object named Sheet.258 is made up of the two chairs and round table that are a part of a parent object named L-shaped workstation. The object, Sheet.258, is one of three objects that has the same object data—there are two additional sets of side chairs and round table in other parts of the drawing (**Figure 8.27**).

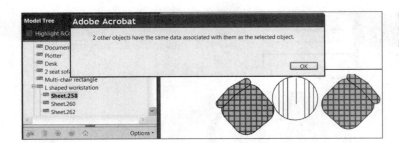

**Figure 8.27** Count the number of times the same object appears in the data.

- Select an object from the Model Tree panel, and then choose Zoom to Selection from the Options menu on the panel. The drawing resets in the Document pane to display the selected object.

- To go back to an object you have previously viewed, choose Previous View from the Options menu in the Model Tree panel.

Enough fooling around—Joyce's got work to do! In the next section, you'll see how she uses a combination of Commenting tools and object data information to add her content to the drawing.

# Adding Comments to the Drawing

Joyce can add comments at will to the document now that the file has been enabled for commenting in Adobe Reader. To learn how to add different types of comments and work in the Comments panel, check out the projects in Chapter 3 and Chapter 4.

There are a few specific types of commenting that Joyce needs to add to the drawing. For example, she has to ask Emily to clarify some details before she can complete her cost estimates. She'll respond to one of Emily's comments first.

 **DOWNLOAD LS_Joyce.pdf** to see Joyce's version of the file complete with her comments, or you can experiment with the version of the file you have opened in Adobe Reader (or Acrobat).

## Responding to Comments

Rather than littering a page with a number of new comments, Joyce can simply reply to an existing comment.

Follow these steps to add a comment response:

1. Select the Comments tab at the left of the program window to display the Comments panel across the program window.

2. Select the comment you'd like to respond to.

3. Click Reply ![reply icon] on the Comments panel toolbar; a Reply row is added to the Comments panel (**Figure 8.28**).

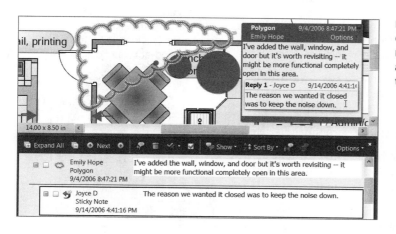

**Figure 8.28** Reply to existing comments rather than adding additional comments to respond.

4. Type the text for your response. Joyce types `The reason we wanted it closed was to keep the noise down.`

When Emily receives the comments back from Joyce, she'll see her response.

Joyce has one more immediate comment to make. Joyce wants to ask Emily a question about one of the plant selections and decides to copy the property and value from the object data into a new comment.

## Using Object Data in a Comment

Select an object either from the drawing or the list in the Model Tree panel using one of the selection options described in the earlier section "Viewing Object Data." Follow these steps to use the object's metadata in a comment:

1. Click the Object Data tool to select it, and then click the object on the drawing to open the Object Data dialog. Joyce wants to inquire about the desk in the reception area, which is called "Work peninsula" in the Object Data dialog (**Figure 8.29**).

2. Click the Options down arrow and choose Copy Data. The information about the desk is stored on the clipboard.

3. Click the Sticky Note tool 📝 on the Commenting and Drawing Markups toolbar.

4. Click the drawing with the Sticky Note tool where you'd like to place the comment. Joyce clicks over the desktop object.

5. A note box opens; choose Edit > Paste or use the shortcut keys Ctrl/Command-V to paste the copied object data into the comment.

6. Type additional text for the comment (**Figure 8.30**).

When Emily reviews the drawing, she'll be able to see immediately what Joyce is referring to without having to use the Object Data tool.

The final phase of this journey is for Joyce to add a custom stamp showing the company logo and her name before she sends it back to Emily.

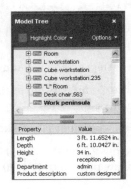

**Figure 8.29** Select the object you want to make inquiries about to take advantage of data copying.

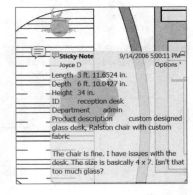

**Figure 8.30** Information copied from an object's data can be used in a comment.

# Stamping the Drawing

One group of Commenting tools is called Stamp tools, and they do indeed work like old-fashioned ink stamps. Of course, since they are digital, the stamps don't need a custom rack or ink-stained drawer for storage. In addition to the dozens of stamps that are included with Acrobat 8 and Adobe Reader 8, you can create an infinite number of custom stamps that are stored with all your other stamps for future use.

 **DOWNLOAD** The source file used to create the custom stamp in this section, named **JDstamp.pdf**, is available from the book's Web site.

## Creating a New Stamp

As a representative of her company, Joyce decides to incorporate the Lemming Systems logo into a custom stamp she can apply to the drawing now that she's finished working with it.

Follow these steps to create a custom stamp:

1. Choose View > Toolbars > Comment & Markup to open the toolbar. The default toolbar shows only the Text Edit and Sticky Note tools.

2. Click Customize Toolbars on the toolbar row to open the Customize Toolbars dialog, which lists the additional tools that can be added to the toolbars (**Figure 8.31**).

3. Select the Stamp tool and click OK to close the dialog. The Stamp tool is added to the Comment & Markup Toolbar.

4. Click the Stamp tool down arrow and choose Create Custom Stamp to open the Select Image for Custom Stamp dialog.

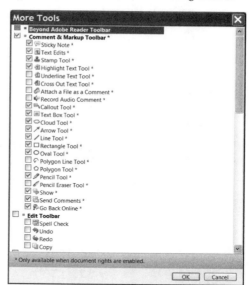

**Figure 8.31** The Comment & Markup Toolbar contains only two tools in its default configuration, but there are plenty more to choose from.

5. Click Browse to show the Open dialog, and then locate the file to use for the custom stamp. Joyce chooses the PDF file named JDstamp.pdf and clicks Select to close the dialog.

6. Check the preview of the stamp in the Select Image for Custom Stamp dialog (**Figure 8.32**). If it is the correct file for the stamp, click OK to close the dialog. The Create Custom Stamp dialog appears.

7. Click the Category down arrow and choose an existing category of stamps, or as Joyce does, type a new category in the field (**Figure 8.33**). Joyce selects Custom.

8. Type a name for the custom stamp in the Name field; Joyce types JD-reviewing.

   The file preview is shown in the dialog. The dialog also offers you an opportunity to pick another file again if you like. No? Let's keep going then.

9. Click OK to close the dialog.

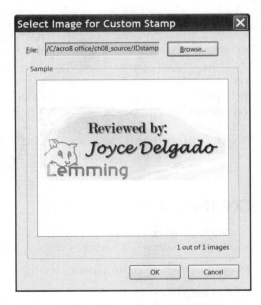

**Figure 8.32** The selected file is shown in the preview; click Browse and select a different file if necessary.

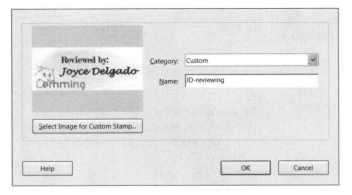

**Figure 8.33** Specify a name and stamp category for the new custom stamp.

## Applying the Stamp Comment

Joyce is now ready to add the stamp to the drawing document.

Follow these steps to select and apply the custom stamp:

1. Click the Stamp tool down arrow and choose Custom > JD-reviewing from the menu. The new category and stamp have been added to the menu (**Figure 8.34**).

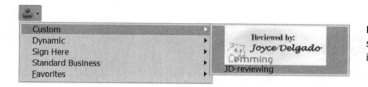

**Figure 8.34** The new stamp and its category are included on the menu.

2. Move the pointer over the drawing to the location where you want to place the stamp and click to apply it to the page.

3. Double-click the stamp to open its message note box and type further information if necessary. Joyce types Let's set up a meeting for Monday.

4. Like other comments, when Joyce moves the pointer over the stamp, the contents of the note are shown in a tooltip (**Figure 8.35**).

5. Save the file. Joyce saves it as LS_Joyce.pdf.

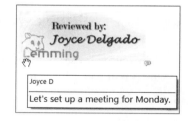

**Figure 8.35** Notes added to stamps display in a tooltip.

Joyce's final task is to send the comments back to Emily. She could use the same method Emily used—that is, e-mail the entire PDF file—or she can send just the comments back, which she decides to try. What could it hurt? She's getting into this digital communication thing.

# Returning the Comments

Joyce could send all the comments back to Emily using the Export Comments command (Document > Comments > Export Comments to Data File), or she can send only her comments back using a method in the Comments panel.

**DOWNLOAD LS_Joyce.fdf** if you'd like to work with Joyce's comments, or try exporting your own.

To send just her comments from the drawing file, Joyce follows these steps in Adobe Reader:

**1.** Click Comments in the Navigation panels to open the Comments panel across the bottom of the program window.

**2.** Click Sort By on the Comments panel's toolbar and choose Author. The comments are sorted under both Emily's and Joyce's names.

**3.** Click Joyce's row in the Comments panel to select it. The row is highlighted with a bounding box (**Figure 8.36**).

**Figure 8.36** A simple sort defines the comments you want Adobe Reader to export.

**4.** Click Options on the Comments panel's toolbar and choose Export Selected Comments.

**5.** Adobe Reader uses the filename and its storage location by default. In this case, the file is named LS_Joyce.fdf.

**6.** Click Save to close the dialog and save the comments file.

**7.** To send the comments file, Joyce opens an e-mail window, addresses it to Emily, and then attaches the LS_Joyce.fdf file.

Shortly thereafter, Emily receives the e-mail from Joyce in her in-box. But suppose Emily doesn't want to work with the file immediately when she receives Joyce's e-mail with the attached FDF file. She can save the e-mail attachment to her hard drive like any other type of e-mail attachment and then later add the comments directly into the open document.

Which option you use is a matter of timing and workflow. If you have the document open, work from the document to import the comments; if not, double-click the attachment in your e-mail program or from its storage location on your hard drive to automatically open Acrobat 8 and the comments' source PDF file. Of course, in the end the results are the same.

# What Else Can Emily or Joyce Do?

In Emily's work, the integrity of the drawing is important, and she can't allow her drawings to be modified. Emily could use digital signatures and certify the drawing, as described in the project in Chapter 12. Or, she could take it a step further and create a custom signature appearance, which is also shown in the project in Chapter 12.

Emily could enclose the drawing in a Secure Envelope for protected transmission to her client, as discussed in Chapter 6, "Managing and Organizing E-mail Using Acrobat." She could create and use a custom Secure Envelope template, which is described in the bonus material for Chapter 6 (on the book's Web site).

Technical drawings, such as the plan used in this chapter's project, can be protected using a security policy instead of password protection to restrict who can view the document and what changes can be made to its contents. Refer to the bonus material for Chapter 12 on the book's Web site to see how to create and use a digital signature. In addition, you'll learn how to exchange digital certificates with others and how to read and extract information from an existing signature file.

Emily might also like to add programmed fields to the drawing that would allow her viewers to click a button and return the comments to her automatically by e-mail. You can read about that process in Chapter 10, "Streamlining Form Development and Data Management."

If Joyce decided to distribute the drawing to staff members to elicit their comments on the design, she could use Acrobat's review process. In that way, she could control the distribution and follow the reviewing and comment-gathering processes through Acrobat's Review Tracker feature. You can read how to set up a review and use the Review Tracker in an e-mail review in Chapter 3, or a shared review in Chapter 4.

# Packaging and Preparing Legal Documents

On a printed page, what you see is what you get since there isn't anything aside from the paper and the ink printed on it. You don't necessarily want everyone to see everything on a written page all the time, and a heavy black marker is all that's needed to mask out sensitive information.

Obscuring confidential information works on a hard copy document. In a digital document what you see isn't all there is. In fact, much of the data that makes up a document is actually hidden below the surface of the words and images—like an iceberg.

*Redaction* is a method used to remove confidential information from a document before final publication. Nowhere is the need for proper redaction, accompanied by appropriate document conversion and storage, more important than in the field of law.

A tremendous amount of paper is generated as part of the daily practice of law, such as complaints, motions, writs, settlement agreements, and evidentiary documents. During the discovery phase of a trial, the use of Bates numbers allows all these documents to be shared by multiple parties with a guarantee that all involved are using the same document.

Adobe Acrobat 8 Professional offers a terrific workflow for managing documents for legal purposes that include converting the files to PDF and storing them in a PDF Package ready for distribution or storage, redacting, removing sensitive information, and numbering the contents.

# Saving Money—and Time

Anthony, Norman & Perkins (AN&P) is a small, three-partner law firm. Over the past year, AN&P has generated enough business to warrant hiring associates. Janet Leigh started her career as a paralegal and hopes she has the opportunity to use and expand upon her experience in her new role as litigation associate.

One area where Janet feels traditional methods have fallen short is in the area of document preparation. She is sure she can convince the partners to realize that their firm can gain a competitive advantage over other firms using electronic discovery. Not only can they increase the speed at which documents are prepared and processed, but they can minimize costs for the firm, and ultimately their clients.

In the past, AN&P experimented with converting files to TIFF for redaction and storage but found the conversions costly and locating specific information very time-consuming.

Always a forward-thinking person, Janet is preparing to pitch the partners on the value of using a PDF-based workflow. She's offering to use her new case, Alfred v. Mother's Motel as an example of how she can save the firm and her client time and money (**Figure 9.1**).

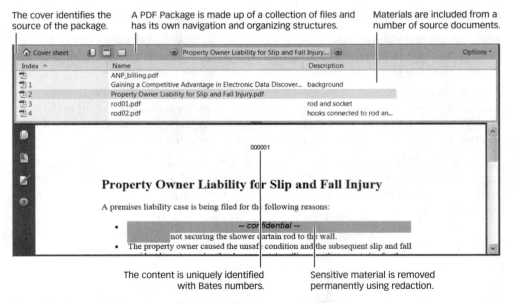

The cover identifies the source of the package.

A PDF Package is made up of a collection of files and has its own navigation and organizing structures.

Materials are included from a number of source documents.

The content is uniquely identified with Bates numbers.

Sensitive material is removed permanently using redaction.

**Figure 9.1** A completed package of legal (or other) documents, including a custom cover.

Janet starts her discussion with some major issues the partners may not be aware of:

- A concern that opening a native file may launch a computer virus

- The need to view files in a common format in a medium that closely resembles paper review

- The need for file formats that are compatible with case management systems

- The value of both TIFF and PDF formats to prevent opposing counsel and other parties from viewing metadata

## Steps Involved in This Project

Janet's plan is to show the partners how she can use PDF files to manage her case materials. She explains that the steps in her demonstration case include:

- Collecting the documents needed for the case and converting them to PDF.

- Creating the PDF Package, complete with a custom page to use as its cover.

- Customizing the appearance and display of the PDF Package.

- Examining the documents for hidden data and other contents.

- Deleting data and other types of information from the documents.

- Applying redaction tools to remove particular content from the pages.

- Searching the pages for additional material to be redacted.

- Using the Bates numbering feature to generate unique numbering for the pages.

Janet's first task is to gather all the documents.

 **DOWNLOAD** The cover page Janet uses for the package is **ANP_cover.pdf** and is available from the book's Web site at www.donnabaker.ca/downloads.html along with the other files demonstrated in the project, including **rod01.pdf**, **rod02.pdf**, **ANP_ billing.pdf** and **injury_note.pdf**. Load some documents from your hard drive to try the project with more source material.

## Producing the Document Package

Some of Janet's materials are on paper and require scanning to incorporate into the package. Other files are documents in Word and WordPerfect, and others are Web pages and PDF files. Although a PDF Package can contain files in different formats, Janet needs to use PDF format for processing. Read more about including documents in various file formats in the sidebar "Adding Other Types of Files."

The PDF Package workflow in Acrobat easily accommodates these various materials.

> **NOTE** The project shows how to combine Word and PDF files into a PDF Package. Chapter 7, "Assembling a Library," describes how to scan documents and capture their contents using OCR (Optical Character Recognition). To learn how to convert and use Web pages as PDF files, see Chapter 2, "Building a Cohesive Document."

Janet follows these steps to construct the PDF Package:

1. Click the Combine Files button on the Tasks toolbar to open the Combine Files dialog.

2. Click Add Files to display the Add Files dialog. Locate and select the files you want to use (**Figure 9.2**).

   If your source files are all in the same folder, choose Add Folder instead, and then locate and select your folder.

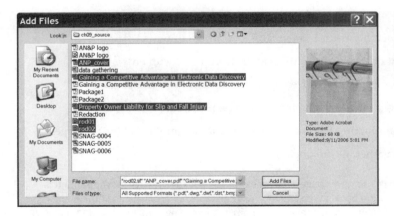

**Figure 9.2** Choose individual files or entire folders to include in the package.

3. Click Add Files to close the dialog and load the selected files in the Combine Files dialog.

4. Adjust the order of the package contents if necessary. The document you will use for the cover sheet should be the first in the list.

   The order can be changed in either this pane of the wizard or the next by selecting a document in the list and clicking Move Up or Move Down to adjust its location.

5. Choose a file size and conversion setting by selecting one of the buttons at the bottom of the dialog. Janet uses the Default File Size, which is appropriate for printing and e-mailing (**Figure 9.3**). Click Next.

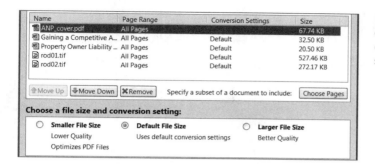

**Figure 9.3** Specify the order of the package contents and conversion settings.

6. Click "Assemble files into a PDF Package." Additional options for the package are added to the dialog (**Figure 9.4**).

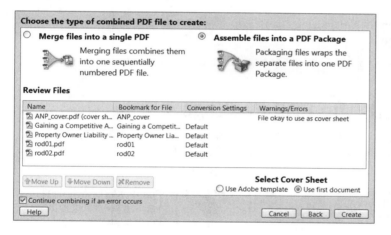

**Figure 9.4** A PDF Package includes a cover sheet that is specified in the dialog.

7. Select "Use first document" in the Select Cover Sheet option at the bottom of the dialog. Acrobat evaluates the file and specifies whether it can be used successfully as a cover sheet.

8. Click Create to show the next pane of the wizard and start the assembly process. Acrobat doesn't use the original files in a PDF Package. Copies of the files are converted to PDF and their status is displayed in the dialog (**Figure 9.5**). Click the arrows to show previews of the documents in the dialog.

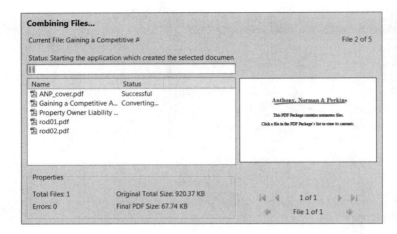

**Figure 9.5** You can watch the assembly of the package as well as the progress of file conversions in the dialog.

9. Click Save to open the Save dialog. Name and save the package. Janet names the package ANP01.pdf.

The PDF Package opens in Acrobat, and Janet takes a look at her new creation next.

# Working with the PDF Package

When the PDF Package opens in Acrobat, it displays a list of the package contents and shows its cover page by default in the Document pane (**Figure 9.6**).

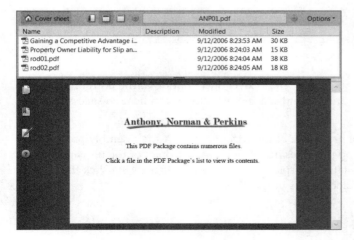

**Figure 9.6** The first thing you see in Acrobat is the cover page.

Janet can make a number of modifications to the PDF Package depending on her needs and how she intends to use the package. For example, she can strip out extra information and leave only the component file's name and creation date, or add a description to make it easier to find a file.

 **DOWNLOAD** The package Janet uses is named **ANP01.pdf**. Either work with your own PDF Package or download a copy from the book's Web site.

## Managing the View

Janet can use some of the existing tools in Acrobat as well as those provided with the PDF Package (**Figure 9.7**). She first checks out how the package contents work in the program window:

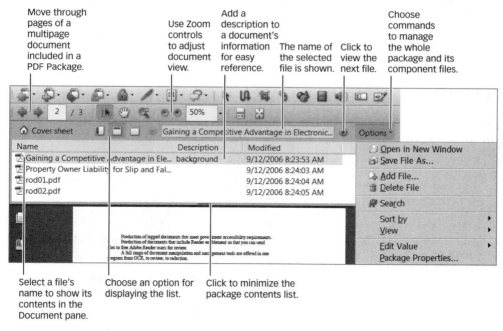

**Figure 9.7** The PDF Package offers many ways to work with contents in multiple files.

- **To move through the package**, Janet clicks each document's name in the list.

- **To move through the package in the same order as that used for listing the files**, Janet can click the View Next button ⊙, or click the View Previous button ⊙ to move backward in the list.

- **To move through a multipage document**, Janet clicks the file's name to show it in the Document pane and then uses the page controls to move through the file's pages. In Figure 9.7, for example, the active document in the PDF Package has three pages with page one displayed in the Document pane.

- **To change the orientation of the PDF Package's list**, Janet can select one of the buttons from the PDF Package toolbar. She can click the View Left button ▣ to move the list to a vertical location at the left of the program window like the Navigation panels. The default view is selected in Janet's project by clicking the View Top button ▣. The size of the document list can be minimized by clicking Minimize View ▢ or dragging the hatched bar on the bottom of the PDF Package's list.

Janet decides that modifying how she views the package contents is terrific, but she then realizes she forgot a file. Fortunately, tools are available to handle modifications to the package contents.

## Adjusting the Components

Janet looks through the PDF Package contents and decides she'd like to add one more file to the package.

To add an additional file to the PDF Package, follow these steps:

1. Click the Options button on the PDF Package toolbar and choose Add File. The Add File Attachment dialog opens.

2. Locate and select the file to add to the package and click Open. The dialog closes, and the selected file is added to the end of the list in the PDF Package contents list (**Figure 9.8**).

3. The new file opens using the view specified in its properties. As you see in Figure 9.8, the document opens showing the form as well as the Document Status Bar that indicates the document contains fields.

4. Save the file to incorporate the new material. Janet names the file ANP02.pdf.

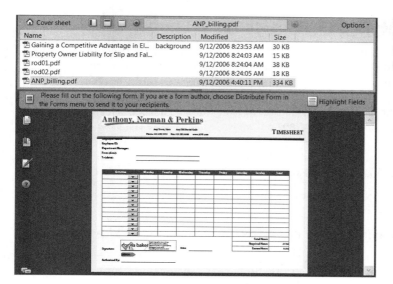

**Figure 9.8** Additional files are added to the end of the list of documents.

## ADDING OTHER TYPES OF FILES

Suppose a document is central to a case and witness testimony depends on how markup appears on a page in a Word document or a comment is modified on an Excel spreadsheet. Not to worry—you don't have to add PDF files to the PDF Package. Instead, choose any sort of file that can be converted to PDF format. When the file is added to the package, you don't see its contents in the Document pane. Instead, all you see is an icon of the file format and choices to Save or Open (**Figure 9.9**). Click Open to convert the file to PDF (at which time the file's content is visible in the Document pane like the other PDF components of the package); click Save to save a copy of the file in its original file format. For the best of both worlds, use a PDF version of the file for searching as part of the PDF Package, and attach the original source file to the PDF, which is stored within the PDF Package. Slick.

**Figure 9.9** Non-PDF files added to the PDF Package show an icon only.

## Modifying the Package Display

Janet thinks she has a winner on her hands! The PDF Package is a terrific tool for organizing the content into a single package. She can easily see how the feature can be used to display information during client meetings or to organize exhibits in court.

 **DOWNLOAD** If you have been following along with the project, continue with your file. If you prefer, download **ANP02.pdf**, which is the package complete to this point.

Janet would like to simplify the display, add short descriptions to some files, and specify a different way for the package to display by default.

She first simplifies how the list of files is displayed and then makes changes by following these steps:

1. Click the Options button on the PDF Package toolbar and choose View to open its menu.

2. Deselect an item to remove it from the display—the menu closes automatically. By default, the Name, Modified, Description, and Size columns are selected.

3. Repeat steps 1 and 2 to remove other items from the display.

4. Adjust the widths of the columns on the PDF Package list by dragging the separators (**Figure 9.10**).

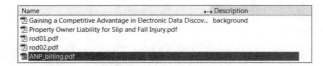

**Figure 9.10** Remove columns you don't need and adjust the remaining columns as necessary.

Next, Janet adds descriptions to two of her component PDF files. To add a description to a PDF file included in a PDF package:

1. Select the file in the PDF Package list.

2. Right-click/Control-click the file's name and choose Edit Value > Description to open a dialog that has an active text field.

3. Type the description for the field. Janet adds descriptions to both PDF files showing images. For rod01.pdf, she types rod and socket; for rod02.pdf, she types hooks connected to rod and fabric and then clicks OK.

4. On the PDF Package's list, move the pointer over a listing to see both the name and description display in a tooltip (**Figure 9.11**).

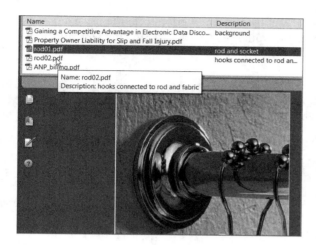

**Figure 9.11** The file's name and description are shown in a tooltip.

Then Janet defines how the PDF Package will open and display. She can define how the list is displayed in relation to the Document pane, what fields are shown on the PDF Package's list, and what pages are displayed.

Janet follows these steps to specify how the PDF Package is shown:

1. Choose Options > Package Properties from the PDF Package's menu to open the Package Properties dialog.

2. Select or clear the check boxes for the titles listed in the Fields column (**Figure 9.12**).

   If you prefer, click the Hide and Show buttons instead of selecting or clearing a column title's check box.

3. Select a field and click one of the command buttons to reorder the fields' columns.

4. Click the Sort by down arrow to choose a sort option. The default set includes Index, Name, Description, Modified, and Size. Janet chooses Index sorting.

5. Click the Sort order down arrow and choose either Ascending or Descending; Janet chooses Ascending.

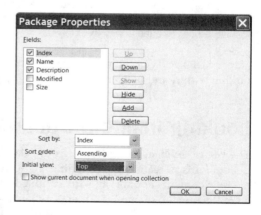

**Figure 9.12** Specify columns of information to include or exclude from the PDF Package's list.

6.  Specify the Initial view for the PDF Package using an option from the list. The choices are the same as those available from the PDF Package's menu: Left, Top, and Minimized. Janet chooses Top.

7.  Click OK to close the dialog.

8.  Save the file to retain the settings. When the file is reopened, the selected options are displayed for the PDF Package (**Figure 9.13**).

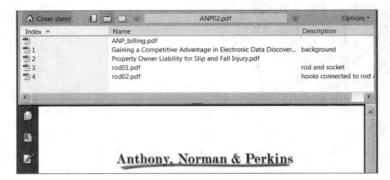

**Figure 9.13**
The configured PDF Package shows the selected columns and layout in the program window.

**NOTE** Janet can quickly reorder or sort the contents of the package at any time by clicking the title at the top of each column. In Figure 9.13, for example, the Index column is actively being sorted, indicated by the small arrow to the right of the title and the highlighted background.

Janet's PDF Package is complete. It's time to check inside the documents to see what's lurking within and beneath the text.

# Looking Inside a Document

The key to understanding how sensitive data and information is embedded in a PDF document is to realize that anything that can be hidden or covered can easily be recovered. Documents contain all sorts of added content and features, some of which are added manually, such as comments, whereas others are included as part of the document structure, such as an embedded search index.

Instead of having to remember where and when to look for information that may be sensitive or extraneous, Acrobat 8 Professional offers the Examine Document process. Janet decides to use the command to check out the files in her PDF Package.

Each document in the PDF Package is examined separately. Follow these steps to examine a document and remove unwanted content:

1.  Select a document from the PDF Package; Janet chooses the case time sheet named ANP_billing.pdf.

2.  Choose Document > Examine Document to open the Examine Document dialog.

    If the file has attachments, an information dialog opens stating that the attachments aren't examined and that you have to open each one and check it. Click OK to close the dialog.

3.  Items that are present in the document are checked in the dialog. Items that aren't present, such as Bookmarks or Hidden layers, are grayed out in the dialog. Clear any check boxes for content that is present but you don't want removed (**Figure 9.14**).

    The range of hidden data and other content that can be found in a document is included in **Table 9.1 (page 225)**.

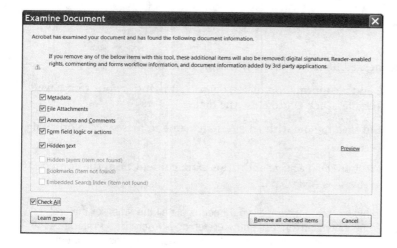

**Figure 9.14** Acrobat examines the document for a range of different objects and content.

4.  Click Preview to display areas of hidden text in the document in the Hidden Text Found in [*name of file*].pdf dialog (**Figure 9.15**). As you can see in Janet's document, checking for hidden text is a good idea! In a multipage document, click the arrows below the preview area to move through the pages; click OK to close the dialog and return to the Examine Document dialog.

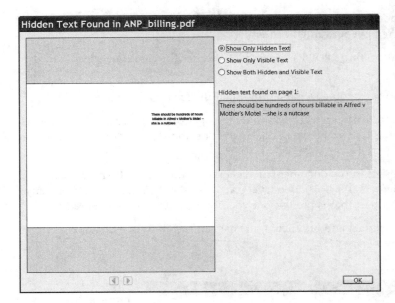

**Figure 9.15** Checking for hidden text can find notes that might be embarrassing if distributed.

5. Click "Remove all checked items" to delete the items from the file.

6. The file is processed, and a confirmation dialog opens listing the actions that have been performed on the file. Click OK to close the dialog.

7. Choose File > Save and save the file with an alternate name to preserve the original PDF document.

Janet checks all the files in her PDF Package and strips extra content from the component files. The package is saved as ANP03.pdf.

> **TIP** If you want to strip hidden content from all your documents all the time, set the preference instead of using the command. Choose Edit > Preferences / Acrobat > Preferences and select Documents from the column at the left. In the Documents options, select either "Examine document when closing document" or "Examine document when sending document by e-mail." Click OK to close the Preferences dialog and make the change.

**Table 9.1** Types of Data and Content

| ITEM | WHAT IS INCLUDED | WHERE TO VIEW THE ITEM | FIND OUT MORE |
|------|------------------|------------------------|---------------|
| Metadata | Metadata contains information about the document that can be used for searching and archiving a file. Metadata can include data about fonts, keywords, camera settings for images, copyrights, and so on. | Choose File > Properties to show the metadata in the Properties dialog. | Chapter 5 and Chapter 5 bonus materials on the Web site |
| File attachments | Files attached to a PDF file either when the original file is converted to PDF or from Acrobat. | Choose View > Navigation Panel > Attachments to see any attached files. | Chapter 6 |
| Annotations and comments | Any comments added in Acrobat using the comment tools or drawing markup tools, or files attached as comments are included. | Choose View > Navigation Panel > Comments to display comments included in a document. | Chapters 3, 4, and 12 |
| Form field logic or actions | Form fields can be input fields, such as those used for typing text, or other form fields such as check boxes, radio buttons, and signature fields. Fields can have associated actions, such as buttons that e-mail a form when clicked, or calculations, such as a field that calculates a total on an order form. Removing form fields flattens the fields, and they are no longer active. | Click Highlight Fields on the Document Status Bar that displays when a document contains form fields. | Chapters 10 and 11 |
| Hidden text | Text in the document that is transparent, the same color as the background, or hidden by other content. | Click the double arrow buttons to navigate pages that contain hidden text, and select options to show hidden text, visible text, or both. | Right here! |
| Hidden layers | Some PDF files contain multiple layers that can contain sensitive information and contribute to the file size unnecessarily; remove the hidden layers to flatten the file to a single layer. | Choose View > Navigation Panel > Layers. | Chapter 8 |

**Table 9.1** *continued*

| ITEM | WHAT IS INCLUDED | WHERE TO VIEW THE ITEM | FIND OUT MORE |
|------|------------------|------------------------|---------------|
| Bookmarks | Bookmarks are text links that open specific pages of a file using a specified magnification; bookmarks may be added intentionally as part of a document's navigation structure or included with default conversion settings. | To view bookmarks, choose View > Navigation Panel > Bookmarks to open the panel and see any existing bookmarks. | Chapter 2 |
| Embedded search index | An index can be embedded into a document to speed up searching. Faster searching requires storing of indexing information within the file, increasing the overall file size. | Choose Advanced > Document Processing > Manage Embedded Index to see if the file contains an embedded index. | Chapter 7 |
| Deleted page and image content | A PDF file that has been modified, such as inserting or removing pages, or changing the size using the Crop tool, contains content that isn't visible. The extra content adds to the file size and may contain sensitive material. | | Chapter 2 |

 **DOWNLOAD** Janet's PDF Package stripped of extra content is available from the book's Web site. Look for the file named **ANP03.pdf**, which is the package complete to this point.

**STOPPING THE DATA AT THE SOURCE**

If you are starting from scratch—creating the source documents, converting them to PDF, and then building a PDF Package—change settings in Word before converting the files to save time.

Before converting your first file, choose Adobe PDF > Change Conversion Settings to open the Acrobat PDFMaker dialog. On the Settings tab in the Acrobat PDFMaker dialog, make these changes from the default settings:

- Clear the check box "Convert Document Information" to prevent converting Microsoft Word metadata to PDF.

- Clear the check box "Attach source file to Adobe PDF," which attaches a copy of the original Word document to the PDF file, basically undoing your metadata seek-and-destroy mission.

# Removing Sensitive Content

On the surface, all versions of Acrobat and Adobe Reader that are capable of applying comments to a page can obscure information on a page by covering it up, which is fine for printing or viewing online. Commenting & Markup tools such as the Rectangle or Highlighting tools can be customized to "black out" or cover up images or text (**Figure 9.16**).

A cover-up is just that: The content still exists in the document and can be revealed as easily as it is hidden (**Figure 9.17**).

**Figure 9.16** Commenting tools can be used to visually black out or obscure content on a page.

**Figure 9.17** A comment is merely an overlay on the page's surface and can be readily moved, revealing the content you are trying to hide.

# Redacting Text and Images

Redaction refers to methods for permanently removing content and replacing it with a space holder of some type, such as a colored box, default text or code, or blank space.

Acrobat 8 Professional includes a set of redaction tools, and Janet plans to show the partners how the tools can save them time, money, and prevent potential litigation issues. She opens a document at random from her hard drive and follows these steps:

1.  Right-click/Control-click the toolbar well and choose Redaction from the shortcut menu to open the toolbar.

2.  Click the Mark for Redaction tool ▨. An information dialog opens explaining that you can use the tool to specify content for removal and then use the Apply Redaction tool to complete the task. Click OK to close the dialog.

    Save a mouse click and a few seconds in the future by selecting "Don't show again" at the lower left of the dialog before clicking OK.

3.  Move the pointer over the page and drag to select content for redaction. You can select single or multiple words, or entire paragraphs. Each item selected displays a bounding box (**Figure 9.18**).

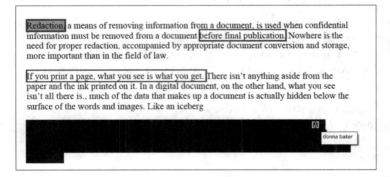

**Figure 9.18** Select words, phrases, or entire paragraphs for redaction.

4.  Move the pointer over a selected object on the page to see how it will look after redaction. In Figure 9.18, the lower paragraph is completely obscured.

5.  When you have finished making the selections, click Apply Redactions ▤. A confirmation dialog opens; click OK to close the dialog and apply the redactions to the file (**Figure 9.19**).

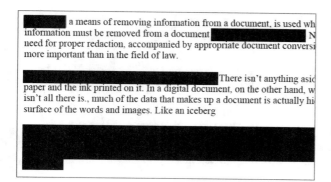

**Figure 9.19** The selected content is removed from the document.

6. A second information dialog opens asking if you would also like to examine the document for other content that can be removed. Click Yes to proceed with the document examination as described in the previous section, "Looking Inside a Document." Since Janet has already cleaned up the files, she clicks No to close the dialog.

7. Choose File > Save and specify a new name for the file to prevent overwriting the original.

In many workflows, it's important to have both redacted and full versions of a document. Once the redacted file is saved, the original content can't be restored. If you apply redaction and change your mind, choose File > Revert to return to the file's status prior to the redaction.

Janet thinks big black blobs on a page bring all sorts of conspiracy theories to mind, and I am sure many would agree with her. Rather than having documents that wouldn't look out of place on an episode of the X-Files, she decides to look into altering the redaction marks' appearance.

## Customizing the Redaction Marks

Acrobat offers several ways to modify the appearance of the redaction marks by using custom colors, text, and specific codes. There aren't any government regulations regarding the color or text used in a redaction mark. The ability to customize how redaction marks appear means you can use an in-house color scheme to represent the types of material redacted, such as instances of different names redacted in different colors.

Before selecting text for redaction, follow these steps to customize the redaction marks:

1. Click Redaction Properties ◢ on the Redaction toolbar to open the Redaction Tool Properties dialog. The default settings specify a solid black fill for the redaction marks.

2. Select Use Overlay Text to activate the rest of the fields in the dialog (**Figure 9.20**).

3. Select options for the text including:

   ■ Selecting a Redacted Area Fill Color if you'd like the areas filled with color other than black

   ■ Choosing Font, Font size or whether to use auto-sizing, and Font color

   ■ Positioning for the text and whether to repeat the text

   ■ Typing custom text in the field that is used on the page

4. Click OK to close the dialog. Continue with the redaction process as described in the previous steps. When the redaction is applied, you see the custom color and text (**Figure 9.21**).

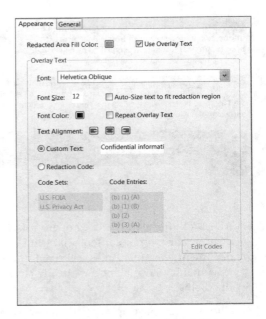

**Figure 9.20** Choose custom colors and text instead of the default black blocks for redacting.

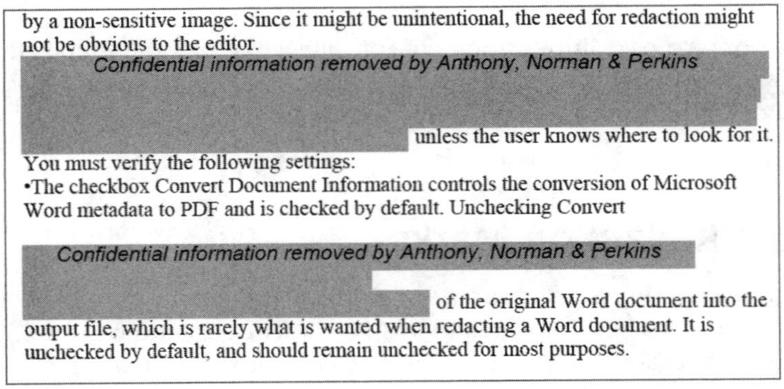

by a non-sensitive image. Since it might be unintentional, the need for redaction might not be obvious to the editor.

*Confidential information removed by Anthony, Norman & Perkins*

unless the user knows where to look for it.

You must verify the following settings:

•The checkbox Convert Document Information controls the conversion of Microsoft Word metadata to PDF and is checked by default. Unchecking Convert

*Confidential information removed by Anthony, Norman & Perkins*

of the original Word document into the output file, which is rarely what is wanted when redacting a Word document. It is unchecked by default, and should remain unchecked for most purposes.

**Figure 9.21** Use a combination of color and text as redaction marks.

Often, Janet finds she has to read through many documents looking for the same content to redact. Acrobat 8 Professional offers an efficient way to handle that task.

**WRITING IN CODE**

If regulations or legislation governing your work requires it, you can specify a code identifying the reason for redaction rather than using text over a solid block of color. In the Redaction Tool Properties dialog, click Redaction Code to activate the code choices. Select a Code Set and a Code Entry.

To edit the codes and add other sets of code, click Edit Codes to open the Redaction Code Editor. Add, modify, export, and import code to meet your requirements. Click OK to close the Redaction Code Editor and return to the Redaction Tool Properties; click OK to close the dialog and return to the document. The next time you use the Apply Redaction tool the custom code is inserted on the page.

# Searching for Content

Janet wants to show the partners how Acrobat 8 Professional can be used to locate and redact certain terms, whether you have one or a thousand documents. The only requirements are:

- The PDF file(s) must contain searchable text, described in the sections on OCR (Optical Character Recognition) and searchable text in Chapter 7. Read some quick solutions to try in this chapter's sidebar "Image or Text?"

- The PDF file(s) must not be encrypted, as described in Chapter 12 "Secure Reviewing and Reporting."

Janet searches a number of documents she's going to add to the case files by following these steps:

1. Right-click/Control-click the toolbar well area at the top of the program window and choose Redaction to open the Redaction toolbar.

2. Click the Search and Redact tool ⊞. An information dialog opens, explaining that the program can only find your terms in searchable text. Click OK to close the dialog and display the Search window.

3. Type the word or phrase to search for in the "What word or phrase would you like to search for?" field (**Figure 9.22**). Janet types `Mother's Motel`.

4. Specify a search location. Janet leaves the default option to search the open PDF file.

    If you have a single PDF file active, the option to search "In the current PDF document" is active; if you have a PDF Package open in Acrobat, the option to search "In the entire PDF Package" is included in the list and active by default. Choose another location or click the down arrow and locate the area to search on your hard drive.

5. Click Search and Redact to conduct the search. The specified files are searched, and the results are displayed in the Search window (**Figure 9.23**).

6. Click the (+) sign next to a document name to open a nested list of occurrences of the word or phrase.

**Figure 9.22** Use Acrobat's powerful Search function to locate terms for redaction.

7. Select the occurrences to mark for redaction. Janet clicks Check All to—you guessed it—select all the occurrences of the term or phrase.

8. Click Mark Checked Results for Redaction to show the terms highlighted on the document page. Close the Search window.

9. To remove the marked items, click Apply Redactions in the Redaction toolbar, and then click OK.

10. Save the document to preserve the changes.

The last item Janet wants to look into is Bates numbering, a method for uniquely referencing document pages. Originally, Bates numbering was done by a time-consuming manual process, either hand stamping or applying labels on every page. Quality control and accuracy are an absolute necessity.

**Figure 9.23** Search results are listed by page number in the Search window.

**IMAGE OR TEXT?**

How do you know if any of your files are composed of images of text rather than captured—and therefore, searchable—text? You don't know for sure. Here are some ways to handle the situation:

- Manually check each file in the package.

- Run a few searches using terms that are common to different documents.

- Create a batch sequence that automatically checks all the documents assembled for a case to find pages that contain images of text, captures the text, and applies OCR (Optical Character Recognition), described in Chapter 7.

- Choose Advanced > Document Processing > Export All Images to extract copies of all the images from the PDF Package, and then check the exported images to see if any are full pages. This method is especially quick when the PDF Package doesn't have any images in it.

**MORE ON REDACTION**

Here are a few sources that you may find helpful:

Microsoft. "How to Minimize Metadata in Office Documents." January 28, 2005. Available from http://support.microsoft.com/default.aspx?scid=kb;EN-US;Q223396.

National Security Agency. "Redacting with Confidence: How to Safely Publish Sanitized Reports Converted from Word to PDF." Available from http://www.fas.org/sgp/othergov/dod/nsa-redact.pdf.

U.S. District Court Web page on Redaction. Available from https://ecf.cand.uscourts.gov/cand/faq/tips/redacting.htm.

# Numbering the PDF Package

Bates numbering is named after the Bates automatic numbering machine where an arbitrary unique numeric or alphanumeric identifier is generated for each page of each document used in a case. The number is unique to the documents disclosed or produced in a case, but there isn't a standardized algorithm for determining the number.

Acrobat 8 Professional offers a Bates numbering feature that is configured through the Add Headers and Footers dialog. You can read more about configuring headers and footers in Chapter 2.

Janet decides to apply the numbers to the files in the PDF Package by following these steps:

**1.** Choose Advanced > Document Processing > Bates Numbering > Add.

An information dialog opens, explaining the selected file is part of a PDF Package and that numbering must be applied to each file separately.

**2.** Click OK to close the information dialog and open the Bates Numbering dialog (**Figure 9.24**).

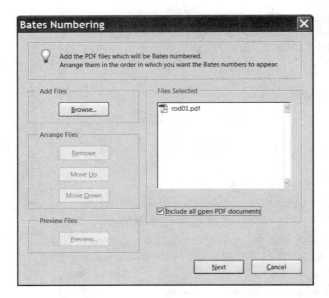

Figure 9.24 Select files to include in the Bates Numbering dialog, including open files.

**3.** Select the "Include all open PDF documents" check box to add the open PDF file to the Files Selected list. Click Next.

**4.** The Bates Numbering dialog closes and is replaced by the Add Header and Footer dialog.

**5.** Click Insert Bates Number to open the Bates Numbering Options dialog (**Figure 9.25**).

Figure 9.25 Choose from a number of options for configuring the page number.

6. Specify the Number of Digits, Start Number, Prefix, and Suffix as required for your naming convention and click OK to close the dialog.

   The minimum number of digits allowed is six. Janet types img into the Prefix field to identify the file as an image. Since two of the files in Janet's project are large images without any text, having a way to identify the file as an image will help her sort her types of PDF content more readily.

7. In the Add Header and Footer dialog, the number is shown in its default position in the upper center of the header (**Figure 9.26**). In the Left Header Text field, the automatic numbering formula is shown and is written as <<Bates Number#6#1#img#>>.

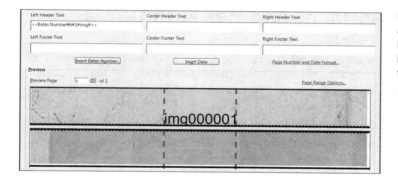

**Figure 9.26** View the automatic number's location on the page in the preview area of the dialog.

8. Click OK to close the dialog; click OK again to close the dialog that states the numbering has been applied successfully. Check out the page and its number in the Document pane (**Figure 9.27**).

**Figure 9.27** You can see how the finished number is placed on the document.

**9.** Save the document.

> **NOTE** Once a file is added to a PDF Package, it becomes a separate file and is not influenced by any changes made to the original; nor does making changes in the PDF Package's document make any changes to the original.

Janet has completed her initial experiment with the PDF Package and the features in Acrobat 8 Professional to assist in her case file preparation. She thinks using her method will improve the firm's ability to prepare cases, minimize administrative costs, and speed up access to information in the case documents.

# What Else Can Janet and Her Firm Do?

Partners at AN&P can use many other workflows and features to streamline their communications. They may want to prepare the files for distribution and commenting. If so, either each document in a PDF Package has to be enabled separately for users working with Adobe Reader, or they have to create merged PDF files, like those produced in the Doggone It! package described in Chapter 2.

Extracting hidden data and other structures not necessary to the use of the document means Janet can produce the most compact and accepted PDF files that meet court standards.

Some other PDF features that Janet might want to add to future demonstrations include:

- Producing tagged documents that meet government accessibility requirements (described in Chapter 5, "Making Accessible Documents in Acrobat" and also in the Chapter 5 bonus material).

- Enabling documents for Adobe Reader users to view and mark up (described in Chapter 3, "Communicating with Comments" and Chapter 4, "Collaborating in a Shared Review").

- Applying a range of security options from usage restriction to self-certifying documents (described in Chapter 12).

- Producing documents that comply with new standards as they evolve around PDF, such as PDF/A (described in Chapter 7). The days of associates plowing through boxes of paper documents in a warehouse, meticulously making copies and then hand stamping numbers on each page are becoming extinct, and Janet is doing her part to hasten that extinction.

# Streamlining Form Development and Data Management 10

There are certain inescapable truths in our modern day existence, one being that we rarely go a day without interacting with a form in some way. From contest entries to employment applications, voter ballots to online stores, opportunities to fill in the blanks and "Choose either A or B" abound.

Acrobat 8 Professional offers some fascinating new ways of adding PDF-based forms to the mix. For the first time, enabling a document lets users working in Adobe Reader 7 or 8 save the form data—very handy when you are dealing with long and complicated forms.

In the forms creation realm, a new AI (Artificial Intelligence) feature analyzes a PDF file and places form fields based on its appearance. You won't have a finished form ready for distribution, but you'll certainly have enough for a good start. The Forms tools include some new and simpler ways to select and change the form fields, and a form can be modified in both the Windows and Mac versions of Acrobat 8 Professional.

For those of you who habitually distribute forms to a group of people and then can't remember who you've heard from and who is late getting back to you, the all-new Form Tracker is the answer. One of my favorite new features in Acrobat 8 Professional, the Form Tracker works much like the Review Tracker, helping you keep an eye on the form distribution process. Once the forms are distributed, features help you aggregate the data and archive returned forms.

As in past versions, Acrobat 8 Professional for Windows also includes the Adobe LiveCycle Designer program; you can now use an existing PDF file as artwork for a form background. A LiveCycle version of this chapter's project form is available from the book's Web site at www.donnabaker.ca/downloads.html. You can download the form and interact with it using either Windows or a Mac; the form can be manipulated in LiveCycle.

# The Rocky Road to Success

Pelican Bay Products is a distributor of natural and engineered stone products, and has a number of locations in the Midwest and western Canada. Some of its larger retail customers are ordering more traditionally commercial products, such as stone veneers and sidings. The company's management team sees the sales trends as indicative of new opportunities, but wants more information from the residential consumer before advancing any new sales or marketing strategies.

Where do you find residential consumers looking for unique and different products? At Home and Garden shows, of course.

Enter our champion, Garry Northman: Sales hero, warrior of the cold call, and a legend in his own mind. Garry enjoys his work as a West-Central representative, responsible for overseeing a number of distributorships, but has his sights set higher. He originally brought the product trends (and himself) to the attention of management and is now working on some ideas for collecting information from visitors to the trade shows.

Garry has identified some basic information necessary to plan future forays into residential offerings. He wants to create a form to use for collecting information from consumers; he plans to present the form at the next regional distributors' meeting.

# Steps Involved in This Project

Garry doesn't have to start from scratch. Pelican Bay Products has a form it has used at a few consumer trade shows, but there hasn't been any concerted effort to track and evaluate the feedback.

Garry will start with the existing form and plans to have a working model to demonstrate at the next meeting (**Figure 10.1**).

To achieve his goal, Garry has to:

- Evaluate the existing form and modify it as necessary to focus the questions.

- Use the new features in Acrobat to automatically capture fields from the flat form.

- Decide on the types of form fields necessary to both provide him with the desired feedback and make it easy for the consumer to complete.

- Make adjustments to the form fields and add other fields as necessary.

- Add a background to jazz up the form's appearance.

- Send a few test forms to his staff using the Distribute Forms wizard.

- Track and collect the form data.

- Archive the forms in a PDF Package.

- Collate the form data.

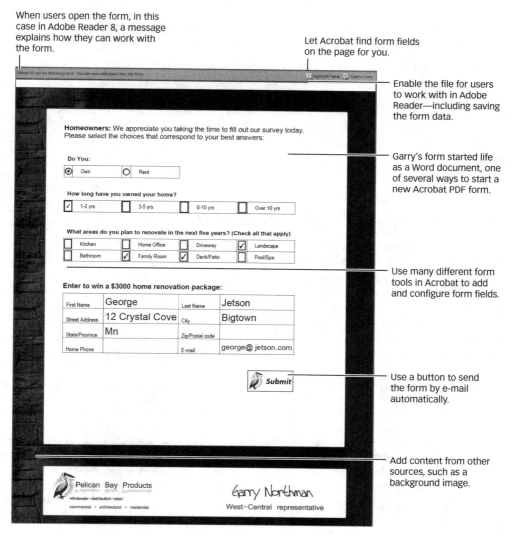

When users open the form, in this case in Adobe Reader 8, a message explains how they can work with the form.

Let Acrobat find form fields on the page for you.

Enable the file for users to work with in Adobe Reader—including saving the form data.

Garry's form started life as a Word document, one of several ways to start a new Acrobat PDF form.

Use many different form tools in Acrobat to add and configure form fields.

Use a button to send the form by e-mail automatically.

Add content from other sources, such as a background image.

**Figure 10.1** Acrobat 8 Professional offers a collection of tools and methods to produce an attractive easy-to-use form.

**CREATING A NEW FORM WITH THE WIZARD**

Adobe LiveCycle Designer is a separate forms development program included as part of Acrobat 8 Professional for Windows. The program includes a wizard for starting new forms from a variety of templates. You can access the wizard in a number of ways, such as choosing Forms > Create New Form, or from the Getting Started window.

A form saved in LiveCycle Designer can be opened and distributed in Acrobat. However, the Forms tools in Acrobat—commonly referred to as the AcroForms tools—won't edit the fields in a LiveCycle Designer form. The form created in this project using the Forms tools in Acrobat is also available in a LiveCycle Designer version from the book's Web site. The file is named Survey2007LC.pdf. Read how the form is constructed in the Chapter 10 bonus material, also available from the book's Web site.

# Working with What You Have

First things first: Garry has to check out the existing form. Every form drawn on paper isn't necessarily going to make a good PDF form, nor is every form especially user friendly. Garry opens a Word copy of the form used in the past to see what the previous attempt at collecting customer data looks like (**Figure 10.2**).

 **DOWNLOAD** To see what Garry has to work from, download **customer form.doc** from the book's Web site. Download **survey2007.doc** to see the form after it is simplified and modified.

Garry isn't particularly worried. The form is quite basic, some of the information asked for is rather pointless, and he's not crazy about the captions. On the upside, the page is well laid out, and it's easy to read the questions on the page.

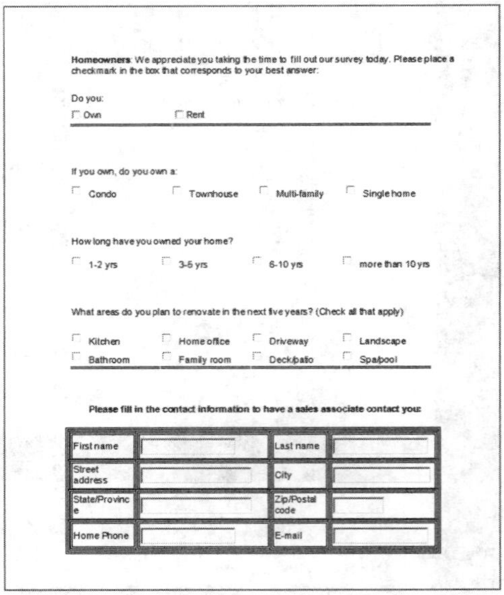

**Figure 10.2** The original form is very basic and not very attractive.

## Changing the Form's Content

Garry decides to simplify the form's content by deleting the question about the type of home owned by the person filling out the form. It's extra data to track that isn't especially relevant. The key information is that the respondent actually owns the property, since renters aren't as likely to be interested in custom stone installations.

Next, he turns to the labels for the segments of the form. Most are usable, with the exception of the last section on the page. Garry's figured out why the forms haven't been very successful in the past: The label for the contact section at the bottom of the form reads, "Please fill in the contact information to have a sales associate contact you."

Rather than drive a prospective customer away, Garry decides on a strategy to bring them in. He changes the label by typing `Enter to win a $3000 home renovation package.` He'll have to get approval for the contest, but he thinks he can convince management of the value of a real incentive in collecting usable customer leads.

## Simplifying the Fields

Next, Garry decides to simplify the appearance of the form fields. The existing fields are too fussy and overly decorated. In his experience, Garry knows that Acrobat interprets each line in a table included in a document as a separate object. He thinks that using the form recognition process in Acrobat would likely be more successful without superfluous lines and frames. He's right, of course.

Garry simplifies the form's appearance by:

- Deleting the shaded boxes used to identify check boxes and text fields
- Removing the borders around fields
- Removing extra borders on the layout to show just the captions for fields and their user response area

When he's finished with the form, he checks it for errors and saves it as survey2007.doc (**Figure 10.3**).

So far, so good. Next, Garry produces the PDF version of the form.

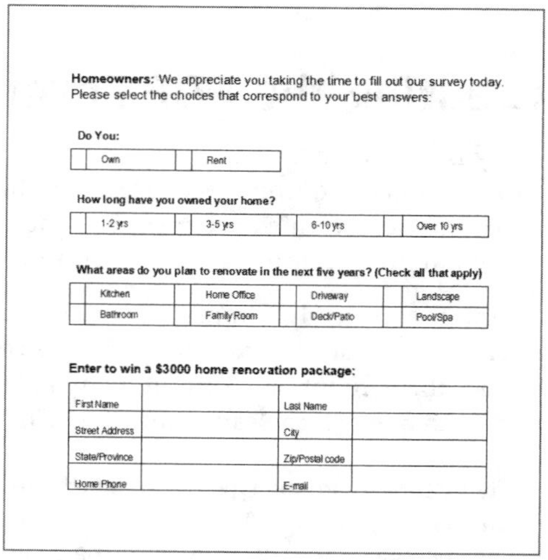

**Homeowners:** We appreciate you taking the time to fill out our survey today. Please select the choices that correspond to your best answers:

**Do You:**

| | |
|---|---|
| Own | Rent |

**How long have you owned your home?**

| | | | |
|---|---|---|---|
| 1-2 yrs | 3-5 yrs | 6-10 yrs | Over 10 yrs |

**What areas do you plan to renovate in the next five years? (Check all that apply)**

| | | | |
|---|---|---|---|
| Kitchen | Home Office | Driveway | Landscape |
| Bathroom | Family Room | Deck/Patio | Pool/Spa |

**Enter to win a $3000 home renovation package:**

| | | | |
|---|---|---|---|
| First Name | | Last Name | |
| Street Address | | City | |
| State/Province | | Zip/Postal code | |
| Home Phone | | E-mail | |

**Figure 10.3** The modified form is much simpler for both Acrobat and the user to understand.

### LINES AND MORE LINES

An example of what Garry is pondering is shown in **Figure 10.4**. The original form has multiple lines to define each field. Converting the original form to PDF and then selecting the form with the TouchUp Object tool 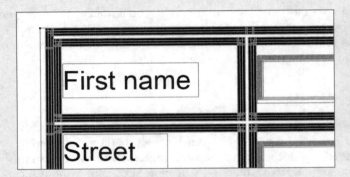 identifies each object.

There are so many lines identifying each field that it looks like a piece of plaid fabric rather than a form. The extreme number of objects is difficult for the program to interpret. Garry simplifies his form, and rightly so.

**Figure 10.4**
Although the multiple lines make an interesting pattern, they are far too numerous to use as form fields that Acrobat can readily interpret.

# Creating the PDF Form

Garry is creating his form from a source Word file. Alternatively, he could use a form structure imported from Excel, InDesign, Illustrator, or any of scores of other programs. He could use a scanned paper copy of the form, an existing PDF file, or create one from scratch in Acrobat using a blank page and the Forms tools in Acrobat.

A form that is overly complex or ornate is difficult for the user to interact with accurately, which leads to incorrect data. The complexity of a form lies beneath. Acrobat defines the content of a form in many more ways than the obvious text and images. In this chapter, Garry learns how the fields in a form are constructed and used.

**NOTE** If you are the type of person who likes to look under the hood, check out the information in Chapter 5, "Making Accessible Documents in Acrobat," on using tags. You can read about other structures, including content, order, and articles in the Chapter 5 bonus material, available from the book's Web site.

# Converting the Form

Before converting the file, Garry checks the conversion settings. He doesn't need anything fancy for the PDF version of the form. Quite the opposite. The default settings option for Standard PDF documents is fine for his form. Since Garry has been working in Word, he converts the file from Word using the PDFMaker.

To convert the file, Garry follows these steps:

**1.** Choose Adobe PDF > Change Conversion Settings to open the Acrobat PDFMaker dialog.

**2.** On the Settings tab, check that the Conversion Settings choice is Standard (**Figure 10.5**).

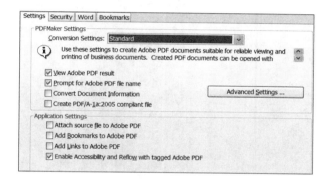

**Figure 10.5** Use a minimum of features in the conversion to keep the document simple.

**3.** In the PDFMaker Settings portion of the dialog, deselect the "Convert Document Information" check box. Garry won't be doing anything else with the document and doesn't need extra information to create the form.

He decides to leave the "View Adobe PDF result" option selected since he intends to move to Acrobat next, and that saves him a couple of mouse clicks. Always thinking is our Garry!

**4.** Deselect the Application Settings options except for "Enable Accessibility and Reflow with tagged Adobe PDF." Garry doesn't need bookmarks or links for his form.

**5.** Click Convert to Adobe PDF on the PDFMaker toolbar to open the Save Adobe PDF File As dialog. Garry uses the Word document's name and saves the form as survey2007.pdf.

## Recognizing Form Fields

When the document opens in Acrobat 8 Professional, Garry chooses Forms > Run Form Field Recognition to start up the Acrobat AI engine. The program scans the file, searching for what looks like form fields and draws them on the document (**Figure 10.6**). At the same time, the Recognition Report displays in the Navigation panels area, which Garry will check out shortly. Cool. Extremely cool.

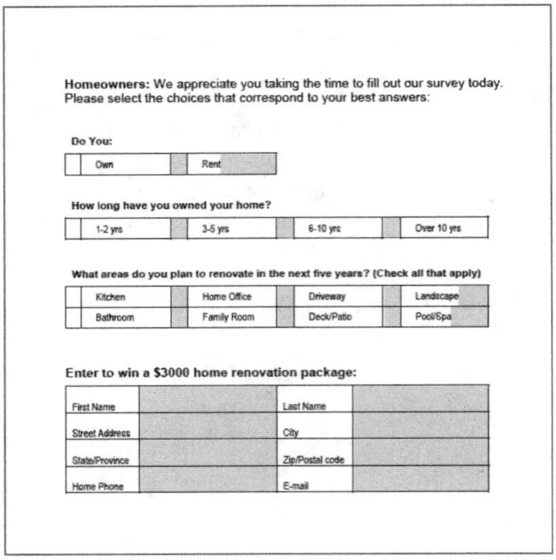

**Homeowners:** We appreciate you taking the time to fill out our survey today. Please select the choices that correspond to your best answers:

**Do You:**

| | |
|---|---|
| Own | Rent |

**How long have you owned your home?**

| | | | |
|---|---|---|---|
| 1-2 yrs | 3-5 yrs | 6-10 yrs | Over 10 yrs |

**What areas do you plan to renovate in the next five years? (Check all that apply)**

| | | | |
|---|---|---|---|
| Kitchen | Home Office | Driveway | Landscape |
| Bathroom | Family Room | Deck/Patio | Pool/Spa |

**Enter to win a $3000 home renovation package:**

| | | | |
|---|---|---|---|
| First Name | | Last Name | |
| Street Address | | City | |
| State/Province | | Zip/Postal code | |
| Home Phone | | E-mail | |

**Figure 10.6** Acrobat reads the page and attempts to place form fields where they might belong. The places where fields are placed are highlighted on the document page.

### STARTING FROM SCRATCH

It's a rainy Saturday. The kids are away for the day. Your chores are finished. Your golf game or tennis match is cancelled. Now what?

Instead of flaking out on the couch in front of the TV, get thee to yon computer and try making a form from scratch. Start a new blank document in Acrobat 8 Professional and use the PDF Editor tools to add text (check out how to use and edit a blank page in Chapter 4, "Collaborating in a Shared Review"). Next, use the Forms tools to add form fields.

If the rain drags on, go all out and add a programmed field or two like an e-mail button or a button to load form data automatically.

Ta Da!

# Checking the Results

Moving right along...Garry needs to see the results of the form recognition process and make some modifications to the fields. Before he starts, he needs to add a few tools to the visible toolbars to make working with the form simpler.

## Organizing the Toolshed

Acrobat shows different types of information after it has run the form recognition process.

The program window shows the following:

- The Document Message Bar, which displays the standard form message. Click Highlight Fields ▦ on the bar to color the fields on the form.
- The form in the Document pane with all detected form fields highlighted.
- The Recognition Report, displayed in the Navigation panels area.

In addition to the features shown automatically, Garry needs to show more tools and features. He needs the Forms toolbar to make it simpler to choose and use the Forms tools. He also intends to use the Fields panel, which lets him see a list of the fields in the form. (**Figure 10.7**).

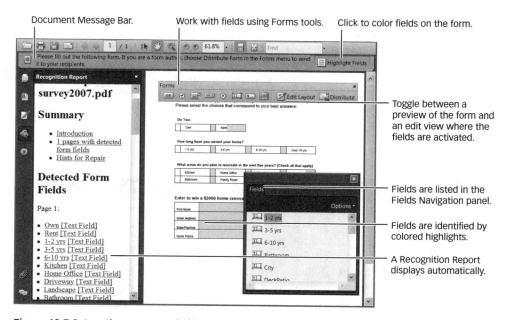

Figure 10.7 Set up the program window to make tools and information easy to find.

Garry follows these steps:

1. Right-click/Control-click the Navigation panel area to open a list of available panels and choose Fields ▤.

   The Fields panel probably won't open in the usual Navigation panels area unless it has been used before. The default arrangement combines a number of the panels including Fields, Tags, and Content as a separate floating window, with a tab displayed for each panel.

2. Drag the Fields tab to the Navigation panels area. The panel locks into place with the other panels, and the Fields icon displays in the list of icons.

   Garry isn't going to use the Fields tab until he's finished evaluating the Recognition Report, but prefers to set up all the program features he needs for a task before he starts.

3. Right-click/Control-click the toolbar well and choose Forms. Garry knows he can save several mouse clicks by opening the toolbar rather than repeatedly selecting individual tools from the menu.

Some of the form fields need changing, some are fine as they are, and some aren't included at all. Garry checks the fields added to the form next.

## Evaluating the Report Results

Acrobat 8 Professional obligingly generates and displays a Recognition Report on the examined document. The report, named Detect Form Fields Report for [filename], contains several sections that are linked together in the report's Navigation panel for ease of access. Be sure to work through the report as soon as you generate the fields. Unlike some reports, like the Accessibility Report, the Detect Form Fields Report and the Recognition Report panel that displays the report are temporary. The report can't be saved or reused, and the Recognition Report panel isn't included in the Navigation panels' list. If the file is saved with a different name, the report is discarded.

Garry decides to postpone lunch and check out the report's contents.

### Summary and Introduction

The Summary section of the Recognition Report explains what fields were found and how they are identified, and provides suggestions for modifying the contents if necessary. The Summary area includes useful links (**Figure 10.8**). Click a link to show the corresponding section of the report.

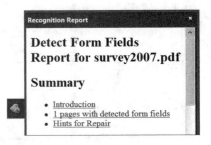

**Figure 10.8** The basic components of the report are listed in the Summary as links.

The Introduction explains how the report works, what it shows, and how it is used. The Introduction to the report also describes the temporary nature of the report in detail.

The fields on the form are placed with default form field settings. This means Garry has to define any necessary custom settings, such as making the content visible or invisible. He also has to manually add programmed actions as required, such as sending an e-mail or opening a file.

## Reviewing the Detected Form Fields list

The Detected Form Fields are listed by name and by type of field (**Figure 10.9**).

When Garry clicks the name of a field in the Recognition Report, it is difficult to see which field is active on the form itself. By default, a new form opens with automatic field highlighting. All the fields are identified in color, but it's difficult to differentiate the selected field on the form page.

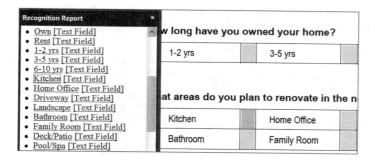

**Figure 10.9** The Recognition Report lists the fields Acrobat identifies by name and type. The Kitchen field is active in the figure.

Garry clicks Highlight Fields 🔲 on the Document Message Bar to toggle off the colored backgrounds from all the fields. Then he clicks the name of a field to identify the field with the highlight color (**Figure 10.10**).

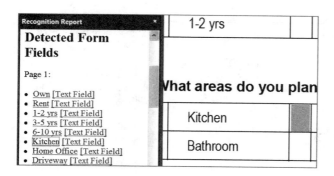

**Figure 10.10** Toggle off the Highlight Fields command to see just a selected field.

## Reading the helpful hints

Another section of the report includes hints for repairing the form fields. All the fields in Garry's form are defined as text fields, although he won't leave all of them in that format.

To review the hints, click the [Text Field] listing following the name of a form field to display the "How to Fix Text Field Form Fields" section of the Recognition Report.

The report explains how a text field is defined and that the settings applied are the defaults. It's easier for Garry to start from a batch of fields using the program default settings since all the fields are the same and won't have special attributes included such as spell check or text appearance.

Garry thinks he has the situation under control—he's checked out the form and has seen which form fields Acrobat has generated for him; he knows which form fields he can maintain and which he has to modify. He saves the form with the recognized fields as survey2007A.pdf.

 **DOWNLOAD** If you'd like to see the form as described in this section, download the file survey2007A.pdf from the book's Web site.

# Planning the Form Modifications

The contact information at the bottom of the form is fine as is. Each is a text field, and Garry isn't planning to make any changes to that part of the form.

Garry does need to change the form fields for the questions at the top of the form (**Figure 10.11**).

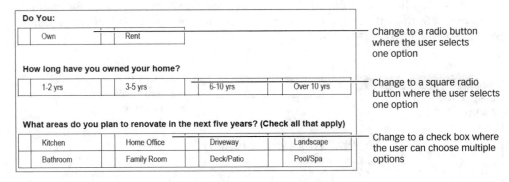

**Figure 10.11** Garry intends to change the types of some of the options for responses on the survey form.

He plans to:

- Change the Own/Rent question to radio buttons where only one choice is accepted.

- Change the second question on length of ownership to a set of square or check radio buttons, where again only one choice is accepted.

- Change the third question on planned improvements to a set of check boxes where the user can select as many choices as desired.

Of course, Garry could use other types of fields in the form as well. Since the form contains a simple, easy to read layout, he decides against using a type of field that uses a list, such as a listbox. Read about the different field types and tools available in Acrobat 8 Professional in **Table 10.1**.

**Table 10.1** Types of Form Elements

| TOOL | FORM ELEMENT | LOOKS LIKE... | USED FOR... |
|------|--------------|---------------|-------------|
| | Barcodes | 2 3 4 7 8   8 9 6 6 1   9 9 9 9-7 7 | Encoding content from selected fields that is displayed as a visual pattern. Barcodes need separate decoding software or hardware to be interpreted. |
| | Buttons | *Website* | User commands such as e-mailing or printing a form. Buttons can be customized to coordinate with the appearance of the form using color, images, and so on. |
| | Check boxes | ☑ True ☐ False | Offering choices for items. When there are two check boxes, the choice is yes/no. A check box form element can also have multiple choices and be configured to allow either one or more than one choice. |
| | Combo boxes | plums ⌄ <br> citron <br> lemon <br> orange <br> peach | Giving the user several standard options and allowing user input if none of the standard options apply. |
| | Digital Signature field | donna baker | Signing a document with a digital signature. |

**Table 10.1** *continued*

| TOOL | FORM ELEMENT | LOOKS LIKE... | USED FOR... |
|------|-------------|---------------|-------------|
| | Document Message Bar | | Displaying information to the user about what the form contains, such as fields, or what rights have been enabled, in the case of Adobe Reader enabled forms. When designing a form, the Document Message Bar toggles off in the Preview mode and toggles on when using the Edit Layout mode. |
| | Listboxes | chalk<br>charcoal<br>pen<br>pencil | Offering the user a list of selections. A listbox can allow one choice or multiple choices using Shift-click (contiguous selection) or Ctrl/Control-click (noncontiguous selections). |
| | Radio buttons | ⊙ True ○ False | Allowing the user to make a choice between two options. |
| | Text boxes | First Name [＿＿＿＿＿] | Inputting data such as name and address. |

# Creating the Radio Buttons

Radio buttons are a type of form field named after an old-fashioned radio that had a number of buttons to choose stations. Press one button in, and the previously selected button pops out. Regardless of the number of buttons, only one is active at a time. The same applies to Radio button fields. One choice is correct, the rest are not—I apologize if that sentence produced flashbacks to multiple-choice exams in college!

Garry will start from the existing fields that Acrobat placed on the form and then change their positions, type, and value. He doesn't need to add any actions such as opening another file or playing a sound in response to the buttons, nor does he have to modify the appearance of the buttons since the defaults look good on his form.

## Adding the First Button

Garry will add one button, configure its appearance and values, and then reproduce it for the second button.

Follow these steps to produce the first radio button:

1. Click Edit Layout 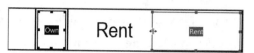 on the Forms toolbar to activate all the fields on the form. The Edit mode is the working view where you modify and adjust the fields on the form.

   The fields are outlined with a bounding box, have resize handles around their edges, and have a label corresponding to the captions Acrobat interpreted as belonging to a specific field (**Figure 10.12**).

**Figure 10.12** The existing fields are identified with a bounding box and a name, and can be resized.

2. Select the field named Own and press Delete to remove it from the form. It is a text field, and Garry wants to change it to a radio button.

3. Select the field named Rent and press Delete to remove it from the form as well.

4. Click the Radio Button tool 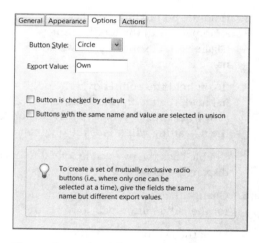 on the Forms toolbar and drag a small marquee to identify the size of the form field.

5. Release the mouse to open the Radio Button Properties dialog. The General tab displays by default. Garry types Ownership in the Name field.

6. Click the Options tab. The default value for the Button Style is Circle, which Garry uses.

7. Click the Export Value field and type own (**Figure 10.13**).

**Figure 10.13** Using different export values means duplicates of the same button can send different values to the spreadsheet where the form data is stored.

8. Click Close to close the dialog and finish the button's settings.

   On the form, the radio button's shape is within the bounding box and the name "ownership" overlays the button (**Figure 10.14**).

**Figure 10.14** The active field shows the new name.

The first part of the button pair is finished. Now for the second one.

## Adding the Second Radio Button

Garry doesn't have to start from scratch to build the second button. Instead, he can merely copy and paste a duplicate and then slightly change its properties.

Garry follows these steps to add the second copy of the button:

1. Click to select the radio button. Its bounding box and name appear red rather than the default black, meaning it's the active button on the page.

2. Ctrl-Shift-Alt-drag/Control-Shift-Command-drag away from the button to add a duplicate button on the page. Move it into the correct position in the small square preceding the "Rent" caption.

3. Hold the pointer over the field for a moment until the tooltip displays (**Figure 10.15**). Notice the new field's name is "ownership.1."

**Figure 10.15** The names of the fields are changed automatically to distinguish duplicates.

   If you hold the pointer over the original field, the tooltip shows its name as "ownership.0." When you create duplicate fields, Acrobat automatically numbers them, starting with .0 for the original.

4. Double-click the ownership.1 field to open the Radio Button Properties dialog and display the General tab.

5. Change the name of the duplicate field from ownership.1 to ownership.0. In order for the radio button pair to work, the two fields need the same name.

6. Click the Options tab. In the Export Value field, type rent.

7. Click Close to close the dialog and configure the field.

Do the radio buttons work like a—well, like a radio? It's time for the test.

## Testing the Radio Buttons

To test the radio buttons, Garry follows these steps:

1. Click Preview ![icon] on the Forms toolbar to toggle the view from the working view to an active view.

2. Click the Own radio button, which fills with a solid dot indicating it is selected.

**3.** Click the Rent radio button, which fills with a solid dot. At the same time, the dot is removed from the Own radio button (**Figure 10.16**).

Success! Next it's on to the check boxes.

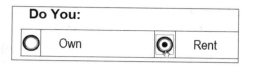

**Figure 10.16** The radio buttons toggle on and off depending on which is selected.

# Placing Multiple Form Fields

The second question on the form identifies how long the respondent has lived in his or her home. This question has only one appropriate response, just as the radio buttons did. Garry will use a radio button again, but this time will change its appearance to look like a check box.

## Drawing the First Field

Like the radio buttons, the check boxes can be configured by adding and customizing the first field, and then applying duplicates.

Follow these steps to add the first field:

**1.** Click Preview 🖼 on the Forms toolbar to toggle the view back to the Edit Layout view, showing the form fields on the page.

**2.** Select and delete the four fields added to the second question on the form by the Form Field Recognition process. The fields are text fields named 1–2 yrs, 3–5 yrs, 6–10 yrs, and over 10 yrs.

**3.** Select the Radio Button tool 🔘 on the Forms toolbar and drag a marquee where the field will be placed. Release the mouse to finish the field's marquee and open the Radio Button Properties dialog.

**4.** On the General tab, shown by default, Garry types time for the field's name (**Figure 10.17**).

**5.** Click Options to open the Options tab and click the Button Style down arrow to display the menu. Garry chooses Check.

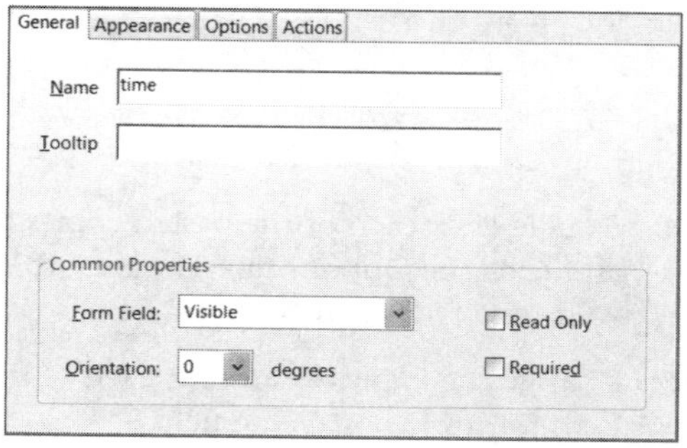

**Figure 10.17** Type a custom name for the field in the General tab.

6. Select the default text in the Export Value field and type 1-2, indicating the export value for the first button, which is 1–2 yrs.

7. Click Close to close the dialog and return to the form.

## Configuring the Remaining Choices

It's simple for Garry to add three additional copies of the same field to the form using another field duplication method.

1. Select the existing time field and press Ctrl/Control-C to copy the field.

2. To add the other copies, press Ctrl/Control-V three times to add three copies to the page (**Figure 10.18**).

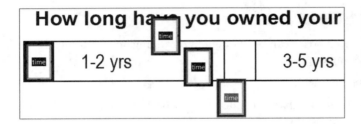

**Figure 10.18** Copy and paste is a simple way to add copies of the same field using the same name.

3. One by one, drag the three additional fields to the proper locations that correspond with rectangles before each choice caption in the question (**Figure 10.19**).

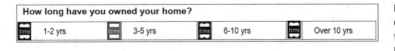

**Figure 10.19** Position each of the fields in the small rectangles before each caption on the question.

4. Double-click each of the pasted copies to open the Radio Button Properties dialog and click the Options tab. The Export Value is shown as 1–2, corresponding to the value entered for the original field.

5. Change the Export values for each of the fields by typing the following values in each form's Export Value field:

   ■ Type 3–5 for the field with the caption 3–5 yrs.

- Type 6–10 for the field with the caption 6–10 yrs.

- Type >10 for the field with the caption over 10 yrs.

6. Click Preview 📄 on the Forms toolbar to toggle the view and deselect the fields on the page.

7. One by one, click the fields on the form (**Figure 10.20**). The checkmark is shown in the field you click, and any previous checkmark is removed.

**Figure 10.20** Test the fields. As one field is selected, the previously selected field is deselected.

There's one more question to take care of.

# Offering Multiple Choices

Garry has to add fields for the third question to find out which areas respondents intend to renovate. For this question, he'll use a check box that allows for multiple selections.

## Placing the First Check Box

To add the first check box, Garry follows these steps:

1. Click Preview 📄 on the Forms toolbar to toggle the view back to the Edit Layout view, showing the form fields on the page.

2. Drag a marquee around the eight fields added to the third question on the form by the Form Field Recognition process (**Figure 10.21**). Press Delete to remove the fields from the form.

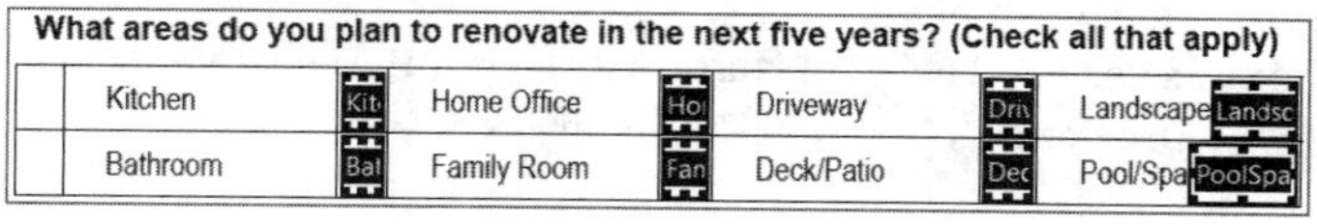

| What areas do you plan to renovate in the next five years? (Check all that apply) | | | |
|---|---|---|---|
| Kitchen | Home Office | Driveway | Landscape |
| Bathroom | Family Room | Deck/Patio | Pool/Spa |

**Figure 10.21** Select all the fields for deletion at the same time.

3. Select the Check Box tool ☑ on the Forms toolbar and drag a marquee where the field will be placed. Release the mouse to finish the field's marquee and open the Radio Button Properties dialog.

4. On the General tab, shown by default, Garry types reno for the field's name.

5. Click the Options tab. Select the default text in the Export Value field and type 1. The eight fields for the question's choices will be numbered 1 through 8 for convenience.

6. Click Close to return to the form. The first field is added to the page.

**TIP** The default appearance for a form field is without a border or fill color. If you see the field on the form has a border or fill, double-click the field to reopen the Radio Button Properties dialog and click the Appearance tab. Choose No Color from the Border Color drop-down menu, and No Color from the Fill Color drop-down menu.

Garry's finished the first check box, and he'll use a dialog to specify the rest of the fields.

## Automatically Duplicating Fields

Garry could reuse either of the methods he used for the fields in the first two questions. But instead he'll use a field duplication method by following these steps:

1. Right-click/Control-click the "reno" field and choose Place Multiple Fields. The Create Multiple Copies of Fields dialog opens.

2. In the Number of Fields area, enter 4 for "Copy selected fields across" (**Figure 10.22**). Leave the default "Copy selected fields down" field set at 2.

3. In the Overall Size (All Fields) click the up arrow for the Change Width field until each field fits within its surrounding rectangle (**Figure 10.23**). You can see the fields expand across the page. If you can't see the preview of the fields on the page, make sure the Preview check box is selected. The default option is to show the preview.

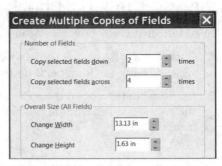

**Figure 10.22** Specify the duplicates to add horizontally and vertically.

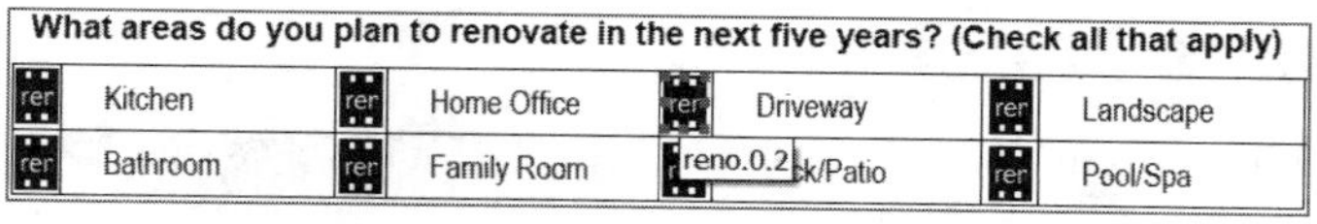

| What areas do you plan to renovate in the next five years? (Check all that apply) | | | | |
|---|---|---|---|---|
| Kitchen | Home Office | Driveway | Landscape |
| Bathroom | Family Room | reno.0.2 k/Patio | Pool/Spa |

**Figure 10.23** The dialog lets you space the duplicate fields evenly.

**TIP** You can also make adjustments by dragging the check boxes to the appropriate locations on the page after closing the dialog.

4.  Click OK to close the dialog. The set of eight check boxes are added to the page. The top row of fields is numbered reno.0.0 through reno.0.3; the second row is numbered reno.1.0 through reno.1.3.

5.  One by one, double-click the different check box fields to open the Check Box Properties dialog and change the number in the Export Value field on the Options tab.

6.  Garry's form is numbered 1 through 4 in the first row and 5 through 8 in the second row.

7.  Click Preview 📇 on the Forms toolbar to toggle the view and deselect the fields on the page.

8.  One by one, click the fields on the form. The checkmark is shown in the field you click (**Figure 10.24**). Select as many check boxes as you wish; click again to deselect the check box.

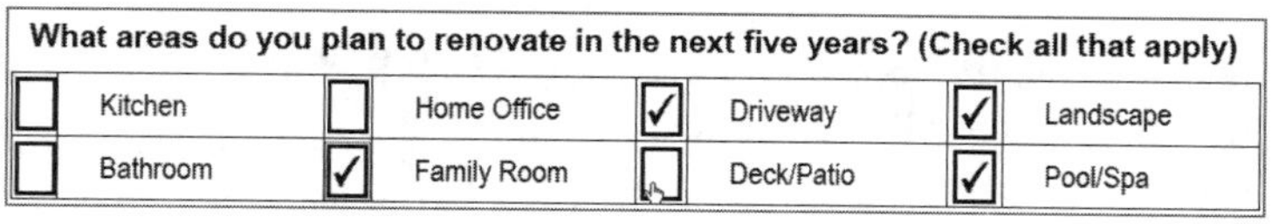

| What areas do you plan to renovate in the next five years? (Check all that apply) | | | | |
|---|---|---|---|---|
| ☐ Kitchen | ☐ Home Office | ☑ Driveway | ☑ Landscape |
| ☐ Bathroom | ☑ Family Room | ☐ Deck/Patio | ☑ Pool/Spa |

**Figure 10.24** The finished question lets you select and deselect any number of checkmarks.

9.  Save the form. Garry continues to save the form as survey2007A.pdf.

Garry has finished the form field changes. He decides to check out the Fields panel to see what's left in his form document.

# Reading the Fields Panel

Originally, the form fields were all identified as Text fields using the field's caption as a name . The fields were listed in the Fields panel in alphabetical order.

Now that the form's content is complete, the look of the Fields panel is considerably different than when Garry first opened the panel (**Figure 10.25**):

- The form fields are listed in alphabetical order and then by the order in which the new fields were added.

- The first question's radio button, named "ownership" shows the pair of radio buttons as nested elements. Each copy of the button is named similarly: "ownership.0#0" identifies the button corresponding to the Own choice and "ownership.0#1" corresponds to the Rent choice.

- The multiple-choice check box responses for question three are divided into two groups based on how Acrobat added the duplicate fields. Garry recalls the duplicates were added in two rows, the first row named "reno.0," the second named "reno.1." Each row's listing has the check box options nested within it.

- Since they appear alphabetically, the second question follows the third in the Fields panel's list. Each field shows its icon and is numbered.

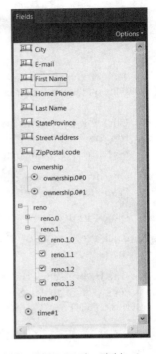

**Figure 10.25** The Fields panel shows the form's contents arranged by type and in alphabetical order.

Now the form is easy for a participant to fill in and will provide the information Garry needs. All that's left to do is some final tweaking and cosmetic work.

# Making Final Adjustments to the Form

Garry has a few more details to take care of to make the form better to look at and simpler for users to interact with.

**DOWNLOAD** the file **survey2007B.pdf** to see how Garry's form looks with the final touches. If you want to produce the finished form yourself, start with the **survey2007A.pdf** form—either your own or downloaded from the Web site. You'll also need the **bkgd.jpg** file for this section.

# Adding a Background Image

Garry thinks the actual form looks tidy and is well laid out, but the entire presentation lacks appeal and doesn't identify the company in any way (**Figure 10.26**). He decides to jazz up its appearance and reuse a background image from a notice document he sometimes sends out to clients and staff.

Follow these steps to add a background image to the form:

**1.** Choose Document > Background > Add/Replace to open the Add Background dialog.

**2.** Click File in the Source area of the dialog and then click Browse to display the Open dialog.

**3.** Locate the file to use for the background. Garry chooses the bkgd.jpg file and clicks Open; the dialog closes.

Acrobat can insert PDF files created from several image file types automatically, including BMP, PDF, and JPG formats.

**4.** The file is converted to PDF automatically and added as the form's background. The Preview shows the image placed on the form (**Figure 10.27**).

**5.** Click OK to close the dialog; save the file with the background image. Garry saves his file as survey2007B.pdf.

Now that the form looks better, Garry checks to see how it works.

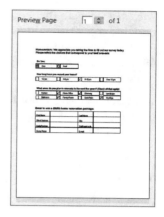

**Figure 10.26** The form looks functional—but boring.

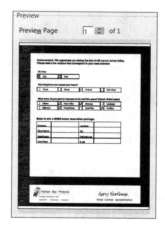

**Figure 10.27** The background image adds a professional finishing touch to the document.

## Setting Navigation Order

*Tab order* refers to the sequence in which the program moves focus from field to field in response to pressing the Tab key. The standard order is for fields to be activated from left to right, top to bottom. Having a predictable path makes it simpler for those of us who tab through forms on a regular basis and is imperative for those working with screen readers and other assistive devices to understand how the form is laid out.

You can check the tab order by clicking the first radio button on the form, and then pressing the Tab key repeatedly. As Garry presses the Tab key, the focus jumps all over the page, but not in the orderly way he had expected.

Follow these steps to change the tab order:

1. Select the Pages icon 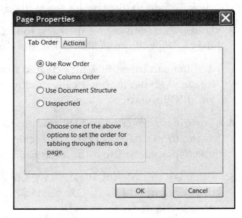 in the Navigation panels area to display the Pages panel.

2. Select the page thumbnail.

3. Select Options > Page Properties to open the Page Properties dialog and click Tab Order (**Figure 10.28**).

4. Choose an option from the list. Garry chooses Use Row Order since his form is structured in rows.

5. Click OK to close the dialog. Now when Garry tests the form, each time the Tab key is pressed the focus moves to the next selection in order.

The last task before sending the form is to make it usable for those working in Adobe Reader.

**Figure 10.28** Specify how users tab through the form using Tab Order.

## Enabling the Form

In the past, users working with Adobe Reader could fill out a form and print the form, but they couldn't save the form data.

To enable the form for users working with Adobe Reader 7 or 8, Garry chooses Advanced > Enable Usage Rights in Adobe Reader.

The Enable Usage Rights in Adobe Reader dialog opens explaining the outcome of enabling the usage rights, which includes:

- Allowing the saving of form data

- Allowing the use of commenting and drawing markup tools (described and used in various chapters, including Chapters 3, 4, and 12)

- Signing existing signature fields (described in Chapter 12, "Secure Reviewing and Reporting")

- Digitally signing anywhere on the page if used in Adobe Reader 8

- Restricting some editing features

Garry clicks Save Now to open a Save As dialog and saves the file as survey2007E.pdf.

The form is done! It looks great! It's ready to go!

Or is it? (Isn't the suspense killing you?)

# Distributing the Form

Acrobat 8 Professional conveniently offers a wizard to distribute the form via e-mail.

To send the form on its way, Garry follows these steps:

**1.** Click Distribute  on the Forms toolbar. An information dialog opens explaining there isn't a Submit button in the form for returning the data from the form.

**2.** Click Cancel to close the dialog and return to the form.

False start: But no big deal. Garry can easily add a button to the form, if he had the time.

## Adding the Submit Button

Like the dialog indicates, in order for the Distribute Form wizard to do its thing, Garry needs to include a Submit button on the form.

> **DOWNLOAD** the button file named **submit.pdf** from the book's Web site. The finished form is saved as **survey.pdf** and is also available from the Web site.

Unfortunately, he doesn't have time to script buttons. He has a meeting, but his assistant Gloria volunteers to configure a button for him and send it to him in a PDF file. By the way, for the lowdown on building and configuring buttons, including using different actions, check out Chapter 11, "Building a Powerful Interactive Document." The project in Chapter 12 also describes adding actions. To see how buttons are added to a form in Adobe LiveCycle Designer, refer to the Chapter 10 bonus material on the book's Web site.

> *… In a movie, you'd now see the screen morph into a blurry mess as harp music plays, and then gradually sharpen again to show Garry back from his meeting and ready to carry on…*

A button is an object, like any other. Garry can simply copy it from one document and move it to another by following these steps:

1. Open the button file submit.pdf in Acrobat. The entire document is the size of the button.

2. To select the button, click Edit Layout 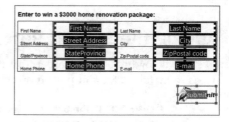 on the Forms toolbar to activate the field. The form field's bounding box and name overlay the button's appearance on the document (**Figure 10.29**).

**Figure 10.29** The button field shows its name and bounding box when selected.

**NOTE** For the curious among you, double-click the button to open the Button Properties dialog. Click the Action tab, and you see the Submit Form action is listed as part of the button's properties.

3. Choose Edit > Copy or press Ctrl/Control-C to copy the button object to the clipboard and close the submit.pdf file.

4. Open the form document, survey2007E.pdf.

5. Choose Edit > Paste or press Ctrl/Control-V to paste the button to the form. The button is pasted to the center of the page by default.

6. To select the button, click Edit Layout on the Forms toolbar to activate the fields on the form.

7. Drag the button to position it on the form in the space below the third question (**Figure 10.30**).

8. Save the file. Garry saves the form as survey.pdf.

Now for the Distribute Form wizard— part deux.

**Figure 10.30** Place the button on the form in a location convenient for the form users.

# Running the Wizard

With the Submit button in place, Garry reruns the Distribute Form wizard. The dialogs that display depend on the characteristics of the file.

Follow these steps to see one scenario:

1. Click Distribute on the Forms toolbar.

2. A dialog opens explaining that some fields already contain data and asks if Acrobat should clear the fields. Click Yes to reset the form and continue.

3. The next dialog states that the form needs to be saved before sending. Click Save and rename the file if desired in the Save As dialog. Garry saves the file using the survey.pdf name again.

4. The Form Distribution Options dialog displays (**Figure 10.31**). Choose either "Send now via email" or "Save and send later." The fundamental difference is that the e-mail application must be active on the computer on which Garry is working: It is. He clicks OK.

**NOTE** The Form Distribution Options dialog contains a link to information about the EULA (End Users' License Agreement), which describes limits placed on the number of copies of the form that can be distributed and aggregated. Be sure to read the EULA.

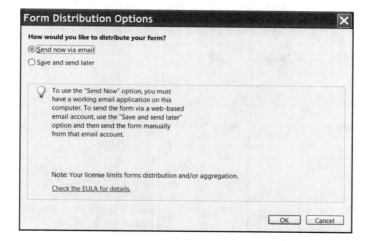

**Figure 10.31** Choose when to send the form by e-mail.

5. The Distribute Form wizard opens. The wizard has four panes to follow that include:

   ■ **Delivery Options.** Type the e-mail address where the forms are to be returned. Click Next.

   ■ **Data Collection File.** Click Browse to locate and specify a file where you want to store the data. The wizard creates a file automatically and defines the location of the form as its default location. The file is named using the form's name and two suffixes. The project file is named survey_dataset_0001.pdf, identifying it as the first dataset file for the survey form. Click Next.

   ■ **Recipients.** Type the e-mail addresses for the recipient(s), or click Address Book and select names from your e-mail address book. Garry adds a couple of names of colleagues who have volunteered to test the project. Click Next.

- **E-mail Invitation.** The final pane adds a subject line for the e-mail, as well as boilerplate text asking the recipient to complete the form and click the Submit Form button to return it. Click Done.

6. Depending on your computer's configuration you may have to grant permission for the e-mail client to send the e-mail. Proceed through the dialogs as necessary.

7. In Acrobat, the Distribute Form dialog shows information about the e-mail. To add the form to the lists in the Form Tracker (coming up later in the chapter), click "Add to my form library" (**Figure 10.32**).

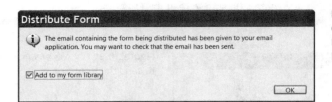

**Figure 10.32** Any form you distribute can be added to the Forms Tracker from the Distribute Form wizard.

8. Click OK to close the dialog.

Garry checks out the information stored in the Forms Tracker.

# Tracking Forms

The challenge of handling items like forms is how to manage them and remember where you are in any particular workflow. Acrobat 8 and Adobe Reader 8 offer the Forms Tracker, a form workflow dialog that works very much like the Review Tracker used for managing commenting and review cycles.

Garry can keep an eye on the forms he's working with in the Forms Tracker by following these steps:

1. Choose Forms > Track Forms from the menu or click the Forms Task button and select Track Forms to open the Forms Tracker dialog (**Figure 10.33**).

   The Review Tracker, Forms Tracker, and RSS Feed icons are arranged at the left of the dialog. Click any button to display its respective tracking information.

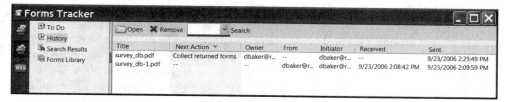

**Figure 10.33** Keep an eye on forms you are working with in the Forms Tracker.

2. Choose an option from the menu in the left pane of the dialog:

- **To Do.** Click the To Do command to show any forms that are in a partially completed state. For example, if you have created a form but not sent it, it'll be included on the To Do list.

- **History.** The History listing shows forms you have in progress. You can see who's responsible for the forms, important dates like receiving/sending, and what actions are outstanding. The form in Figure 10.33 shows the History list. You can see returned forms that have been collected and their data processed, or those that haven't been sent.

- **Search Results.** Type a search term in the Search field at the top of the dialog and click Search. Returns are shown in the Search Results view.

- **Forms Library.** Forms are added to the library as the last step in the distribution process, shown in Figure 10.31, and list the form's title and date.

3. Select the appropriate form in the list at the right side of the dialog. Click Open to view the file in Acrobat 8 Professional.

When you have finished working with a form, collected its data, and processed its results, take a minute and click Remove to delete the form from the tracker. That way, only the forms that are currently in progress are listed and it's easier to keep track of your workflows.

4. Close the dialog.

**NOTE** Anyone working with a form can check what he or she has to do in the Forms Tracker. If you are participating in a review, for example, the To Do list might include "Fill and return" as an action you have to complete.

Garry checks his e-mail. It's been two or three minutes since he sent the form, after all. Eventually, the returned forms show up.

# Collecting the Data

Each of Garry's e-mail recipients open the form in either Acrobat or Adobe Reader and follow the instructions described in the Document Message Bar (**Figure 10.34**). When the form is complete, they click the Submit button Garry added to the bottom of the form or the Submit Form button on the Document Message Bar. Their forms are returned automatically.

**Figure 10.34**
The Document Message Bar explains what can be done with the document's form.

# Receiving Returned Forms

E-mailed returns are listed in Garry's e-mail client's Inbox (**Figure 10.35**). Notice that the return e-mails show slightly different names, depending on the location in which the e-mail is opened and the form completed.

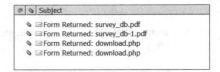

**Figure 10.35** E-mail messages are generated automatically and the completed forms are returned to Garry.

For example, the two copies of the form with the Subject line "Form Returned: download. php" were completed via Web mail clients rather than on a desktop, whereas the first two, named survey_db.pdf and survey_db-1.pdf were completed on the desktop with a resident e-mail client.

# Aggregating and Viewing the Data

Garry saves the returned surveys as they come in. When he has his returned files, he assembles them in Acrobat 8 Professional. How often and when you assemble files depends on your workflow. You might want to aggregate them every day, on a weekly basis, or at the end of the return period.

# Choosing the Dataset File

Follow these steps to add the form data to a selected dataset file:

1.  Double-click a returned form to open it in Acrobat 8 Professional. The Add Completed Form to Data Set dialog opens.

2.  The "Add to an Existing Data Set" option is selected by default, and the dataset file associated with the form is shown in the field (**Figure 10.36**). Garry can click Browse and choose an alternate dataset file or use the default file associated with the form. He leaves the default choices.

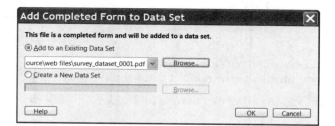

**Figure 10.36** Specify the dataset file to use for collecting the form returns.

3.  Click OK to close the dialog. The survey_dataset_0001.pdf file opens in Acrobat. As described previously in the section "Running the Wizard," the dataset file is created automatically, and Acrobat uses it as part of the distribution process.

Garry notes that the dataset file is a PDF Package that is created automatically as part of the Distribute Form wizard's function (**Figure 10.37**). The original survey_datasheet_0001.pdf file is used as the cover sheet for the package.

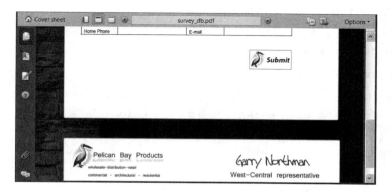

**Figure 10.37** The dataset file is a PDF Package and includes special commands for adding form data.

## Adding More Form Returns

Add more returned forms to the PDF Package by following these steps:

**1.** Click Import Data  on the Document Message Bar in the PDF Package to open the Add Returned Forms dialog (**Figure 10.38**).

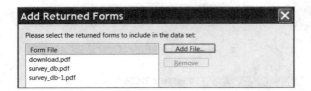

**Figure 10.38** Locate and select the rest of the returned forms to add to the PDF Package.

**2.** Click Add File to open a dialog. Locate and select the returned form files stored on the hard drive. Click Open to add the files to the Add Returned Forms dialog.

**3.** Click OK to close the dialog and add the other files to the PDF Package.

**4.** Save the PDF Package file.

> **DOWNLOAD** If you want to see the finished PDF Package that Garry assembles, download **survey_dataset_0001.pdf** from the book's Web site. The complete package includes four copies of the form returns. You can also find the **survey_dataset_0001. csv** and **survey_dataset_0001.xls** files in the chapter's folder on the Web site.

Now what? For the grand finale, Garry needs to see how the information gathered in the survey can be viewed and used for planning sales and marketing efforts.

## Exporting the Data

Garry can aggregate the returned data into a CSV (comma-separated value) file that he can then use in a spreadsheet or database.

Follow these steps to view the form results in an Excel spreadsheet:

**1.** On the Document Message Bar of the PDF, click Export Data ▣ to open the Select Folder to Save File dialog. The file is named according to the PDF Package by default and is saved as a CSV file by default. Exported data can also be saved as XML.

**2.** Specify the storage location and name, and click Save. The dialog closes and the file is saved.

**3.** Open Excel, or your favorite spreadsheet or database program.

**4.** Choose File > Open and locate the survey_dataset_0001.csv file. Click Open to load the file into the spreadsheet.

At the top of the spreadsheet file, notice that the field names are transferred from the forms (**Figure 10.39**). Each row on the spreadsheet represents one form return.

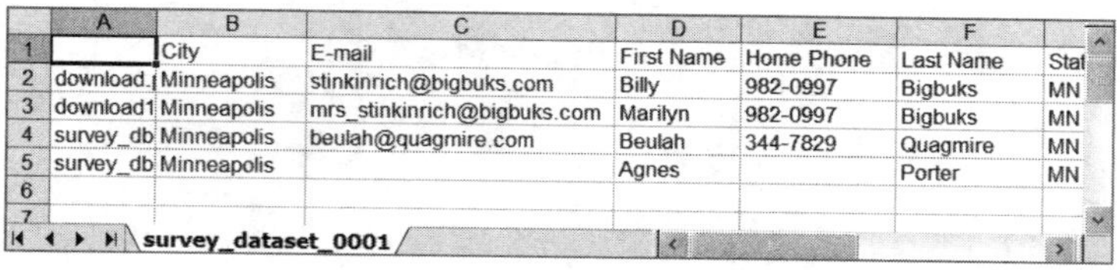

| | A | B | C | D | E | F | |
|---|---|---|---|---|---|---|---|
| 1 | | City | E-mail | First Name | Home Phone | Last Name | Stat |
| 2 | download.| Minneapolis | stinkinrich@bigbuks.com | Billy | 982-0997 | Bigbuks | MN |
| 3 | download1 | Minneapolis | mrs_stinkinrich@bigbuks.com | Marilyn | 982-0997 | Bigbuks | MN |
| 4 | survey_db | Minneapolis | beulah@quagmire.com | Beulah | 344-7829 | Quagmire | MN |
| 5 | survey_db | Minneapolis | | Agnes | | Porter | MN |
| 6 | | | | | | | |
| 7 | | | | | | | |

survey_dataset_0001

**Figure 10.39**
The fields are shown as column heads and each form returned is a separate row on the spreadsheet.

Garry is suitably impressed. It took a bit of time to design the form, and there are still some changes he'd like to make, but he is sure it will provide useful information for the company.

# What Else Can Garry Do?

Forms can be as intricate or as simple as you like. In some cases, such as Garry's form, the goal is to gather a small amount of highly targeted information. In other circumstances, such as insurance or medical forms, the scope of required information is much more extensive; therefore, the design of the form must be more sophisticated and incorporate more types of form fields and even secondary forms.

Garry notices at the end of his trial that there are still some changes he'd like to make. For instance, he'd like to make it easier to read the results in the spreadsheet. To do this, Garry has to revise the tabbing order of the fields in the form because the sequence of spreadsheet column headings is the same as the sequence of fields in the form.

He didn't really pay attention to the size or contents within the form. If he were planning a big distribution, it would be worth his while to look into condensing the size of the file somewhat, either by using the Examine Document process, described in Chapter 9, "Packaging and Preparing Legal Documents" or by using the PDF Optimizer used in Chapter 11.

Many more actions could also be added to the form. He might like to program a message to thank the recipient for filling out the form, for example. If he were feeling especially cheesy one day, he could add some theme music to serenade users as they filled out the form (Heaven forbid!).

He added a Submit button to the form that his assistant created for him. You can read much more about actions attached to form fields and navigation items like links in Chapters 11 and 12.

If Garry needed to protect the content of the form, he could enclose it in a Secure Envelope, as described in Chapter 6, "Managing and Organizing E-mail Using Acrobat."

# Building a Powerful Interactive Document

What do you think when you hear the phrase "PDF file?" Do you associate PDF files with flat, printed documents? Or do you associate PDF files with those viewed or downloaded from an online source, again as flat, two-dimensional files? That, amigos, is just the beginning.

Acrobat's functions and objects can be controlled by Acrobat JavaScript, a version of the powerful and highly configurable language that is behind many of the interactive objects and elements you see every day online. It may come as a surprise that much of the interactivity you see online, such as video, forms, and buttons is also available in a PDF document.

Using a PDF file as a vehicle for multimedia and interactive content is a wise choice. You don't have to worry about a user's Internet connection or speed; the PDF file can be downloaded page by page, it is self-contained, and there's no waiting for content to load each time you view the file. You don't have to worry about missing parts either, since images and scripts are embedded within the document.

You're curious now, aren't you? Different types of media are usable in Acrobat, and you'll learn how to work with images and movie formats in this project. Media can be attached to different actions, such as clicking a button. In this project, you'll see how an action can be attached to a document function, such as closing a page, in addition to the usual button or link actions we are all accustomed to using.

Building an interactive document, especially one that is part of a collection of similar documents, requires careful planning. You'll pick up some valuable workflow design tips in this project.

And now, the story of the samurai realtor.

# The Way of the Samurai

This is the tale of Jack Taggart, ex-Navy SEAL, martial arts expert, ponytail-wearing, soft-spoken adherent of Eastern philosophies, and owner of upstart Samurai Realty.

His company has landed a plum listing—exclusive sales representation for an exciting new waterfront development in the region's choicest vacation and resort area.

In Jack's business, appearances are important. He knows that sometimes a client will discover a listing on his site and then print the page for reference. He has seen and worked with PDF documents, and has for some time offered listings as PDF files to provide printable information about his listings in a way that maintains the look of the document.

Jack decides he wants to embellish the way he presents information about his listings. He's prepared a PowerPoint presentation for trade shows and the like, and plans to use its content as a starting point for some interactive material.

Starting from an interface page, the user can choose image viewing options, view maps, and follow links to local information sources and to Jack's Web site. And, because presentation is important in his business, Jack wants to add little touches like a slideshow or two (**Figure 11.1**).

Specify a magnified view of an image as a link or button action.

Make changes to an image in Photoshop directly from Acrobat.

Add labels, links, and buttons to navigate through a document.

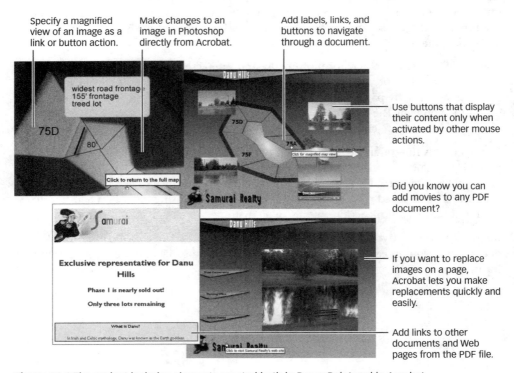

Use buttons that display their content only when activated by other mouse actions.

Did you know you can add movies to any PDF document?

If you want to replace images on a page, Acrobat lets you make replacements quickly and easily.

Add links to other documents and Web pages from the PDF file.

**Figure 11.1** The project includes elements created both in PowerPoint and in Acrobat.

# Steps Involved in This Project

Jack is selling upscale properties for the vacation home market. The market is active, but there are other developments vying for the attention (and pocketbooks) of the buyers. Jack is confident that although his properties could sell themselves, his engaging sales materials are sure to give sales a boost.

After exploring several options, Jack and his staff decide to use Acrobat to manage a workflow that includes the following:

- Producing a PDF interface file from a PowerPoint slideshow that displays the property Jack is marketing.

- Reconfiguring one of the pages in the slideshow to remove existing content and add another map image.

- Revising the map image from within Acrobat 8 Professional.

- Adding a set of buttons to hold images of the properties for sale.

- Programming a set of buttons on the interface page to display images of the properties in pop-ups.

- Creating more actions for the buttons to display a magnified view of the development's map.

- Adding buttons from the magnified map view to return users to the default map page.

- Adding a slideshow movie in Acrobat.

- Creating Web links from the interface page to sites of interest for prospective buyers, including the company's Web site.

- Inserting one more image.

- Optimizing the PDF document to make the file size as efficient as possible for online viewing.

- Setting up an online meeting using Acrobat Connect.

The first stage in the project is to create the PDF document from PowerPoint slides to use as a starting point.

 **DOWNLOAD** The final two tasks on Jack's list are included in the Chapter 11 bonus material, available from the book's Web site at www.donnabaker.ca/downloads.html.

# Building the Interface Document

The first step of the project is to build a document to use as the interface. The interface document begins as PowerPoint slides that include a background, some text, and an overview map of the property development.

Jack converts the document using the PDFMaker in PowerPoint. Because Jack wants the pages to be as compact as possible, he needs to change the conversion settings (for more information, see the sidebar "Why the Smallest File Size Works for the Web"). Jack plans to include two links—one to his Web site and one to his listing service. The links can be added either in PowerPoint or in Acrobat. In this project, he'll add them in Acrobat.

 **DOWNLOAD** You can download the original PowerPoint file, **DanuHills.ppt** file from the book's Web site if you'd like to start the project from scratch; download **DanuHills. pdf** file to see the converted interface document.

Follow these steps to create the PDF document from the PowerPoint document:

1. Choose Adobe PDF > Change Conversion Settings to open the Acrobat PDFMaker dialog.

2. On the Settings tab, click the Conversion Settings down arrow and choose Smallest File Size from the list (**Figure 11.2**). The Smallest File Size option is ideal for Web and online use because it is the most compact conversion format.

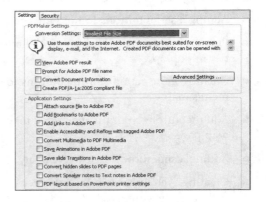

**Figure 11.2** Choose the conversion settings appropriate for online use of the document.

3. Clear all the PDFMaker Settings at the top of the dialog except for "View Adobe PDF result."

Jack will move to Acrobat as soon as he's converted the file, so leaving the option selected will open the program, saving him a couple of mouse clicks.

4. Clear all the Application Settings options except "Enable Accessibility and Reflow with tagged Adobe PDF."

Document tags provide a structure for the document by defining each of the file's elements, such as headings, paragraphs, images, table rows and cells, and so on.

5. Click OK to close the dialog.

**6.** Click the Convert to Adobe PDF icon on the PDFMaker toolbar. The PDF document is created and saved with the name DanuHills.pdf.

It's time for Jack to take a look at the file in Acrobat 8 Professional.

---

### WHY THE SMALLEST FILE SIZE WORKS FOR THE WEB

Jack intends for the documents to be used online. The default Smallest File Size conversion option is tailor-made for this purpose:

- The PDF file is compressed.

- Any images on the page are downsampled (the number of pixels in the image is decreased, producing a smaller file) and the resolution (the number of pixels per inch) is decreased.

- The colors of all images are converted to a color system called sRGB, which is designed for onscreen viewing.

- The files are optimized for *byte serving* automatically, which means the document is downloaded to a user's Web browser on a page-by-page basis, resulting in faster page displays.

- Fonts are not embedded to reduce file size.

---

# Getting Organized

Before he starts working with the file, Jack wants to organize his work environment by opening and docking the toolbars. For much of the work in the project, Jack needs to use the Advanced Editing tools.

To make these tools simpler to find and easier to access, Jack follows these steps:

**1.** Right-click/Control-click the toolbar well and choose Reset Toolbars. Any toolbars other than the default set of tools and toolbars are hidden.

**2.** Choose Tools > Advanced Editing > Show Advanced Editing Toolbar to open the toolbar, or right-click/Control-click the toolbar well and select the Advanced Editing Toolbar.

**3.** To keep your screen space clear for working, drag the toolbar to dock it with the others in the toolbar area.

**4.** Right-click/Control-click the toolbar well again and choose Forms to open the Forms toolbar; drag it to dock it with the other toolbars.

The original PowerPoint presentation has three pages, which Jack has converted to PDF format. He'll use the first slide later in the project, but as the third page.

To reorder the pages, Jack follows these steps:

**1.** Click the Pages icon  in the Navigation panel to display the Pages panel.

**2.** Select the thumbnail image for page 1, the cover slide for the original presentation.

**3.** Drag the thumbnail to the right to follow the second slide and release the mouse— the cover slide is now shown as page 3

**4.** Drag the thumbnail showing the map to the page 1 position (**Figure 11.3**).

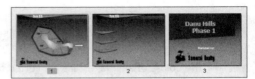

The page Jack starts with has a simple design—a caption at the top of the page identifying the property development, a map of the area, and his Samurai Realty logo.

**Figure 11.3** Rearrange the order of the slides in the Pages panel.

Jack edits the repositioned page and includes another map image next.

# Modifying Content on a Page

Jack now removes most of the content from the page and adds another image.

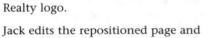 **DOWNLOAD** the image file **DanuHills2.png** to use for the replacement map.

## Removing and Replacing Objects

Follow these steps to remove existing objects from the page:

**1.** Click page 3 in the Pages panel to display it in the Document pane.

**2.** Select the TouchUp Object tool  on the Advanced Editing toolbar.

**3.** Remove these objects from the page:

- "Danu Hills Phase 1" heading and its two underlying red shapes
- "Marketed by:" heading
- Samurai Realty logo

The page is blank except for its gradient background.

Follow these steps to add a new object to the page:

1. Right-click/Control-click the page with the TouchUp Object tool and choose Place Image.

2. In the Open dialog, locate the DanuHills2.png image file and click Open. The dialog closes and the map is placed on the PDF page (**Figure 11.4**).

   The image is automatically centered on the page and doesn't need adjusting.

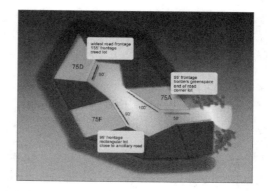

**Figure 11.4** The new map is added to the document once the other objects are removed.

3. Save the document. Jack saves the file as DanuHills01.pdf.

Egads! Jack checks out his new map image and realizes it is missing content.

# Round-trip Editing of an Image

Jack's map should include lines indicating the properties' borderlines in the water since each lot also includes a portion of the channel.

 **DOWNLOAD** the replacement PDF project named **DanuHills_edited.pdf** if you don't want to do the image editing yourself.

Jack can do one of the following:

- Remove the incomplete image and replace it with a correct version that includes the water borderlines.

- Open the image in an image editing program from within Acrobat 8 Professional.

# Setting Image Editing Preferences

Jack decides to take the latter route and will try to edit the image directly from Acrobat 8 Professional. He first has to specify an image editor for Acrobat to use. You specify the image editing program in the program preferences by following these steps:

1. Choose Edit > Preferences/Acrobat > Preferences to open the Preferences dialog and choose TouchUp from the left column.

**2.** Click Choose Image Editor to open a dialog. Locate and select the program you want to use for editing images. Jack uses Photoshop CS2.

**3.** Click Open to select the program and close the dialog. The chosen program is listed in the Preferences dialog (**Figure 11.5**).

**4.** Click OK to close the Preferences dialog.

**Figure 11.5** The selected image editing program is shown in the Preferences dialog.

With the program chosen, Jack can now edit the image. The file containing the image remains open in Acrobat while Jack edits the image.

## Editing the Map

Follow these steps to edit an image from within an open document in Acrobat 8 Professional:

**1.** Select the image using the TouchUp Object tool located on the Advanced Editing toolbar.

**2.** Right-click/Control-click and choose Edit Image.

**3.** The TouchUp dialog opens and states that the image contains transparency and might look different after editing. Click Yes to close the dialog and continue.

The TouchUp dialog will usually appear, and you may see different messages depending on the characteristics of the image you are editing.

**4.** The image editor—Photoshop CS2 in this case—opens, and then an Adobe Photoshop dialog opens to explain in what circumstances the file must be flattened (**Figure 11.6**).

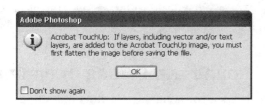

**Figure 11.6** Photoshop advises you on how to make Acrobat edits.

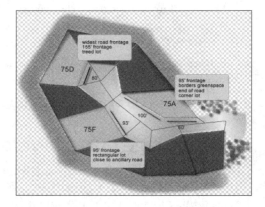

**Figure 11.7** Make the edits to the copy of the image open in Photoshop.

**5.** Click OK to close the dialog and show the image in Photoshop. Acrobat assigns a name to the image automatically. Jack adds lines indicating the approximate areas of the properties' water borderlines (**Figure 11.7**).

**6.** Close the image window in Photoshop. A dialog opens asking whether or not to save the changes. Click Yes; the Save Adobe PDF dialog opens.

**7.** Choose file options in the Save Adobe PDF dialog if necessary. By default, the image uses the same settings as those of the parent file.

Jack chose the Smallest File Size preset before he converted the PowerPoint presentation to PDF, so the default is fine for his edited image.

**8.** Click Save PDF to close the dialog and save the file. Close Photoshop.

**9.** Return to Acrobat 8 Professional. The image is replaced on the page (**Figure 11.8**).

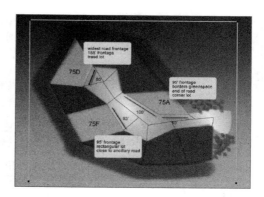

**Figure 11.8** The modified image is automatically transferred to the PDF file.

## CHOOSING THE BEST WORKFLOW

In the project, Jack prepared the map image, and will then add buttons linking from the first page to the third page. He'll add other button actions later to trigger changes to the visibility of more buttons.

Instead of adding buttons with several functions, Jack could use different buttons, links, and labels as separate objects. The scenario in the chapter is realistic, though: As you work with one type of object, you often figure out new ways to enhance the project further. It may not be the most efficient method, but it will be effective and achieve the desired outcome.

Whether you choose the same workflow as Jack is a matter of circumstance and your preferred work habits. Some people like to have all the project parts in place, such as inserting images, movies, and so on before adding elements like links—the way Jack is working. Others prefer to do the project one step at a time: Still others prefer to do one task from start to finish.

Now that Jack has the new map image in place, he needs to go back to the first page. He wants the user to see a photo of the property when the mouse pointer moves over a lot number. He first needs to insert the photos on the page somehow, but he doesn't want the photos to display all the time.

Jack pauses to meditate on the best way to achieve this worthy goal.

# Buttoning Up Some Images

Jack sees the way clear before him: The simplest way to display an image in response to a mouse action is to use a button field. Buttons aren't just for forms, nor do they necessarily have to be used to initiate an action. As Jack learns, a button can be the target of an action. He wants the image to display in a pop-up fashion when the user mouses over the lot's label.

By the way, if talk of objects and actions is a bit confusing, be sure to check out the sidebar "About Triggers and Events," later in this chapter.

**DOWNLOAD** the three image files to use for the buttons: **lot75A.jpg**, **lot75D.jpg**, and **lot75F.jpg**.

# Adding the First Image Button

Other projects in the book use buttons in the more traditional sense. For example, Chapter 10, "Streamlining Form Development and Data Management," explains in detail how to use a button to trigger an e-mail window. The project in Chapter 12, "Secure Reviewing and Reporting," uses links for the same purpose, although buttons could perform the same function.

Jack will use a button as a field. One feature of a field is that you can specify its visibility as either visible or—wait for it—hidden. It's the state of visibility that does the trick in this project.

To add the first button, Jack follows these steps:

**1.** Select the Button tool  on the Forms toolbar and double-click the page with the tool to open the Button Properties dialog.

A default button is drawn on the page automatically in the area clicked; if you prefer, drag a marquee with the Button tool and release the mouse to open the Button Properties dialog.

**2.** On the General tab, Jack clicks the Name field and types 75A_pop to identify the button.

**3.** Click the Form Field down arrow and choose Hidden. The button won't be shown by default on the project's page (**Figure 11.9**).

**4.** Click the Appearance tab. Click the Fill Color swatch to open a Color Picker and choose No Color (**Figure 11.10**). By default, the button has a gray fill and no border.

**5.** Click the Options tab: Here's where the magic happens! Make these selections:

- Click the Layout down arrow and choose Icon only. The Icon is an image and doesn't need a label.

- Leave the Behavior and State defaults of Invert and Up, respectively.

Notice that the Choose Icon button is active in the dialog (**Figure 11.11**).

**6.** Click Choose Icon to open the Select Icon dialog and then click Browse to open another dialog. Click the Files of type down arrow and choose JPEG.

**7.** Locate and select the image to use for the button. Jack selects the lot75A.jpg image file and clicks Select to convert and load the image into the Select Icon dialog. Click OK to close the Select Icon dialog and return to the Button Properties dialog.

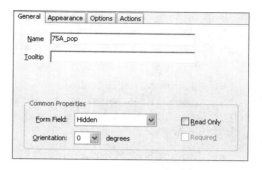

**Figure 11.9** Change the default state of the button to hide it.

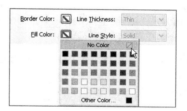

**Figure 11.10** Make sure the button doesn't have a default colored fill or background.

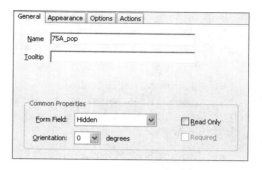

**Figure 11.11** Specify settings for the button's options to configure how it will display on the page.

**8.** Back on the Options tab, click Advanced to open the Icon Placement dialog (**Figure 11.12**). Jack chooses these settings to specify how the image is scaled within the button's shape:

- Click the When to Scale down arrow and choose Always. The provided images are different sizes, and Jack wants their appearance on the page to be uniform.

- Click the Scale down arrow and choose Proportionally.

- Select Fit to bounds.

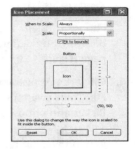

**Figure 11.12** Make sure the image used in the button is scaled to fit the project page.

**9.** Click OK to close the Icon Placement dialog and return to the Button Properties dialog. Click Close to return to the project.

**10.** Position the button shape above the map, and drag one of the corner resize handles to resize it to a size that's easy to see without dominating the page (**Figure 11.13**).

One button down and two more to go.

**Figure 11.13** Move and size the button so the image is easy to view.

## Replacing Pop-up Button Images

Copy and paste the existing button two times for a total of three buttons. Drag the copies to the left of the 75D and 75F labels on the map (**Figure 11.14**).

**NOTE** Read more detail on creating duplicate fields in Chapters 10 and 12.

 **DOWNLOAD** The project file **DanuHills02.pdf** complete with the buttons is available from the book's Web site.

Double-click each button to open the Button Properties dialog, and make these changes to each button copy:

- On the General tab, rename the buttons to 75D_pop and 75F_pop.

- On the Options tab, click Choose Icon and replace the image. Use lot75D.jpg for lot 75D, and use lot75F.jpg for lot 75F.

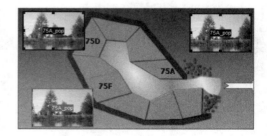

**Figure 11.14** Paste two copies of the button to the page and position them.

- Close the Button Properties dialog. The three buttons display individual images (**Figure 11.15**).

- To test the buttons, click the Preview tool 🖳 on the Forms toolbar. The buttons are now hidden, as you specified.

- Save the file.

Next Jack plans to add some buttons using the lot's labels to make the images (buttons) appear and disappear.

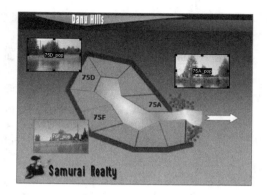

**Figure 11.15** Replace the original image with those of the other properties in the button copies.

# Making the Buttons Appear—and Disappear

The page 1 map contains three labels identifying the lots for sale. Jack will place buttons over the labels that will be used for two different purposes: He'll use a rollover effect to show and hide the image buttons, and later he'll use the buttons to show a magnified view of the lot on another map.

Follow these steps to add the new button and action over the 75A label:

1. Select the Button tool 🔘 on the Forms toolbar and drag a marquee over the 75A label. Release the mouse to open the Button Properties dialog.

2. On the General tab, type 75A in the Name field and Click for magnified map view in the Tooltip field.

   The button will be used later for another action, and Jack may as well add the tooltip while he's changing the name.

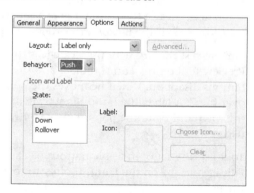

**Figure 11.16** Specify how the new buttons will behave on the page.

3. Click the Appearance tab and set the Fill Color to No Color.

4. Click the Options tab; click the Behavior down arrow and choose Push. The three button states—Up, Down, and Rollover—are shown in the State list. (**Figure 11.16**)

**5.** Click the Actions tab and choose Mouse Enter from the Select Trigger list.

**6.** Choose Show/hide a field from the Select Action list.

**7.** Click Add to open the Show/Hide Field dialog (**Figure 11.17**). The three button fields showing the property images are listed along with the new button Jack is configuring, which is hidden by default.

**8.** Click the 75A_pop field and select Show. Click OK to close the dialog and return to the Button Properties dialog.

**9.** Click the Select Trigger down arrow and choose Mouse Exit.

**10.** Click the Select Action down arrow and choose Show/hide a field.

**11.** Click Add to reopen the Show/Hide Field dialog. Select the 75A_pop field and click Hide; click OK to close the dialog and return to the Button Properties dialog.

**12.** You'll see the two actions listed in the Actions area of the dialog (**Figure 11.18**). Click Close to exit the Button Properties dialog.

Time to test the first actions: Jack clicks the Preview tool on the Forms toolbar and the buttons disappear. When he moves the pointer over the 75A label, the button is activated, showing the tooltip and the pop-up image button (**Figure 11.19**).

To finish the set of invisible buttons, Jack clicks Edit Layout ☑ on the Forms toolbar to toggle the fields to active. He copies and pastes two copies of the 75A field.

Jack repeats the steps for configuring the buttons' settings, using the values listed in **Table 11.1**. All buttons share the same appearance, tooltip, and actions. The names and field selections vary.

**Figure 11.17** Select the field to show or hide from the list in the dialog.

**Figure 11.18** The buttons' actions are listed in the dialog in the order they are added.

**Figure 11.19** Move the pointer over the link and button area to show the image pop-up and the tooltip.

**NOTE** For easy reference, the values used for the first button, described in the preceding steps, are included in Table 11.1.

To edit the actions on the Actions tab of the Button Properties dialog, Jack must do the following:

- Click the Show/hide a field action to activate the Edit button.

- Click the Edit button to reopen the Show/Hide Field dialog.

- Select the 75A field, selected in the original button.

- Click Hide to hide the 75A field, set in the original button.

Once the original action is removed, he can apply the actions specific to the 75D or 75F buttons and test the buttons. Finally, he saves the file.

Next, Jack adds another action to the set of buttons over the property labels on the map.

**Table 11.1**   Values for Invisible Buttons

| BUTTON NAME | MOUSE ENTER ACTION | MOUSE EXIT ACTION |
| --- | --- | --- |
| 75A | Show field 75A_pop | Hide field 75A_pop |
| 75D | Show field 75D_pop | Hide field 75D_pop |
| 75F | Show field 75F_pop | Hide field 75F_pop |

**TIP** To make sure the pop-up image buttons' appearances stay as programmed, click Locked on the lower left of the Button Properties dialog. It isn't always necessary, but in some cases when the buttons don't seem to behave, locking the field can prevent great quantities of irritation, gnashing of teeth, and pulling of hair.

# Linking to a Specified View

Remember those tooltips that Jack added to the buttons, instructing the user to "Click for magnified map view"? Well, it's time to add button actions linking to a view of the map image on page 3.

## Adding the Action

Follow these steps to add the action:

**1.** Click Edit Layout on the Forms toolbar to toggle the button fields to visible again on the page.

2. Double-click the 75A button to open the Button Properties dialog, and click the Actions tab.

   The Select Trigger default choice is Mouse Up, which is used for the new action.

3. Click the Select Action down arrow and choose Go to a page view from the list (**Figure 11.20**). Click Add.

4. Don't be alarmed when the dialog disappears! You'll next see the Create Go to View instruction dialog (**Figure 11.21**).

   The Create Go to View dialog floats, letting you specify any view, location, or magnification you want to use for the action.

5. Display page 3 in the Document pane. Click the Marquee Zoom tool 🔍 on the Select & Zoom toolbar, which is one of the default toolbars.

6. Drag a marquee around the area of the map showing the information about lot 75A (**Figure 11.22**). Release the mouse to display the magnified view. Jack's map is magnified 150 percent.

7. Click Set Link in the Create Go to View dialog. The dialog closes and returns you to page 1 of the PDF file.

**Figure 11.20** Use the default trigger and select its action.

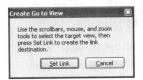

**Figure 11.21** Follow the instructions in the dialog carefully.

**Figure 11.22** Display the area of the image you'd like to show when the button is clicked.

8. The Button Properties dialog is grayed out since the page is automatically viewed in Preview mode. Click Close to exit the Button Properties dialog.

9.  Click Edit Layout again on the Forms toolbar to toggle the button fields to visible, and double-click the 75A button to reopen the Button Properties dialog.

10. Click the Actions tab to check the new action. The Mouse Up trigger lists its action as going to a page in the document using a custom Zoom level (**Figure 11.23**).

11. Click Close to exit the dialog again.

Jack needs to add the same action to the other two buttons, but before he does that he'll check to see if the first button works.

**Figure 11.23** The new action is added to the button's list of actions.

## Testing and Duplicating the Action

Jack checks out the button's action next. To test the button, follow these steps:

1.  Click Preview on the Forms toolbar to toggle the fields to invisible.

2.  Select the Hand tool 🖐 on the Select & Zoom toolbar.

3.  Move the pointer over the 75A button and click when you see the pointer change to a hand (**Figure 11.24**).

    The area of the map Jack specified in the previous set of steps is shown in the Document pane.

**Figure 11.24** Test the new button action on the page to be sure it works.

The first button works well. Jack gets back to page 1 to add the actions to the other buttons.

Repeat the steps to add links from the 75D and 75F labels to the corresponding areas of the detailed map on page 3. It's simpler to add the remaining actions because the Button Properties dialog automatically opens on the Actions tab with the correct trigger and action already selected. All he has to do is click Add and then configure the view as he did for the first button's action.

When Jack tests the button, the document's view is magnified. He has to manually return to the original map page, and then manually adjust the magnification.

All that is shown is a bit of the heading on the page (**Figure 11.25**). In order to view the original image, click the Zoom Out tool 🔍 on the Select & Zoom toolbar several times.

It's good design etiquette to offer users a way to return to a previous view when they have followed a link in your PDF file. For the buttons on the first page, adding a return link or button from the magnified view is a requirement, not merely polite.

**Figure 11.25** When returning to the original page after seeing a magnified view, the page doesn't display at the original magnification unless the document is configured with other actions.

## Configuring the Return Buttons

To add navigation that returns the user to the proper view, Jack needs to add one button on the third page and then create two copies by following these steps:

1. On page 1, click the 75A button to display its magnified view in the Document pane.

2. Select the Button tool on the Forms toolbar and draw a marquee at the lower right of the Document pane. Release the mouse to open the Button Properties dialog.

3. Choose these settings in the Button Properties dialog:

   - On the General tab, name the button back; and type `Click to return to the full map` in the Tooltip field.

   - On the Appearance tab, click the Border Color swatch to open a Color Picker and choose a dark blue; select white from the Fill Color's Color Picker. In the Text area, click the Font Size down arrow and choose Auto.

   - On the Options tab, type `Click to return to the full map` as the button's label.

   - On the Actions tab, click the Select Action down arrow, choose Go to a page view, and click Add. Follow the Create Go to View dialog's instructions as explained in the section "Linking to a Specified View," specifying the view of page 1 at a convenient size, such as the project's view, which is set at 66.7%. Click Set Link.

4. Click Close to exit the dialog and return to the magnified view on page 3. You see the new button on the page—make adjustments to its size and location as desired (**Figure 11.26**).

5. Select Preview on the Forms toolbar and click the new button. You see the full map view on page 1. Much better!

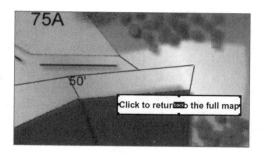

**Figure 11.26** The new button serves as a return to the original page at its original magnification.

To add the other buttons, Jack follows these steps:

1. Click Edit Layout on the Forms toolbar. Select and copy the new button in the magnified view.

2. Click Preview on the Forms toolbar to toggle off the Button tool and activate the Hand tool.

3. Click the new button to return to the page 1 view.

4. Click the link for the next lot label to display its magnified view and paste the copied button.

5. Repeat steps 1–4 to paste one more copy of the button on the third magnified view.

Now test the links from the labels on the page 1 map to the magnified views and back to the original map. In Jack's opinion, the return navigation path is far more professional. Wouldn't you agree?

Jack wants more action. In the next section, he adds a movie to the project.

# Adding Zing with a Movie

To add some pizzazz, Jack decides to show a little slideshow to draw attention to the beautiful scenery of the area.

There are two steps to placing a movie in a PDF document. First, the movie is inserted into the document using the Movie tool. Second, the settings are adjusted and customized according to how you plan to use the movie.

 **DOWNLOAD** the two variations of the movie named **channel.mov** and **channel.wmv**. If you like, you can download the **DanuHills03.pdf** project file, which is complete with the movie and its renditions.

## Placing the Movie File

In this project, the movie runs when the viewer clicks a link placed over the arrow labeled "Channel to Lake." Follow these steps to add the movie:

**1.** Click the Movie tool ▣ on the Advanced Editing toolbar.

**2.** Double-click the page where you want the upper left of the movie to be placed, or drag a marquee. Don't worry about the size of the marquee or its precise location because you can adjust the movie on the page. The Add Movie dialog opens (**Figure 11.27**).

**3.** Click Acrobat 6 (and Later) Compatible Media to access all the available options, including embedding, adding posters, and using Flash files.

**Figure 11.27** Select the movie file to use in the PDF document.

**4.** Click Browse to locate the movie and select it. Jack decides to start with the QuickTime movie, channel.mov. The file's location is shown in the dialog in Figure 11.27.

Acrobat assigns a content type automatically when you select a file and determines the player needed to view the movie. You can select a different format from the Content Type pull-down menu, but you may have difficulties playing the movie.

**5.** Leave the two additional options selected (they are selected by default). "Snap to content proportions" maintains the movie's size in the document; "Embed content in document" stores the movie file within the PDF file.

**6.** Choose a poster option: A *poster* is a still image that displays on the page when the movie isn't running.

- "Use no poster" shows the movie's background document and is the option used in this project. In Jack's project, an action will be attached to the movie to make it play in response to a mouse click.

- "Retrieve poster from movie" uses the first frame of the movie as a static image.

- "Create poster from file" lets you choose and use a different image for the poster.

**7.** Click OK to close the dialog and insert the movie. Acrobat draws a box the size of the movie on the page. If you had chosen either "Retrieve poster from movie" or "Create poster from file," that content would appear in the box; but because you chose the "Use no poster" option for this project, you don't see any content in the box.

**8.** Position the movie's box on the document page as necessary by dragging it with the Movie tool's cursor (**Figure 11.28**). Since the "Snap to content proportions" option was selected in the Add Movie dialog, the box is sized correctly for the movie.

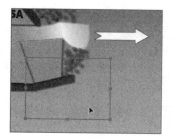

**Figure 11.28** Drag the movie's box to the correct position on the page.

## ADDING A MOVIE TO A DOCUMENT

It's usually best to embed the movie in the document unless you know for certain that both the PDF file and the movie file can be accessed uniformly. For example, you may want to deselect the embedding option if you are using the document on a company intranet because you can make sure the PDF and movie files remain in the same folder location. For online use, however, it's much simpler and less likely to produce errors if you embed the movie.

# Testing the Movie

Before he adjusts the movie's details, Jack decides to check it out. Follow these steps to test the movie:

**1.** Click the Hand tool on the Select & Zoom toolbar. The movie's area on the page is surrounded by a black border.

**2.** Click within the border on the page. Rather than showing the movie, the Manage Trust for Multimedia Content dialog opens (**Figure 11.29**).

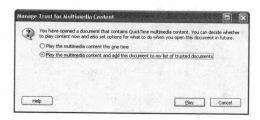

**Figure 11.29** Specify how Acrobat should treat the document in the future.

3.  As the dialog describes, specify whether to play the movie once or to play the movie and add the document to a list of trusted documents.

4.  Select "Play the multimedia content and add this document to my list of trusted documents," and then click Play.

 **DOWNLOAD** Read the Chapter 11 bonus material section "Setting Trust Preferences" for information on how to control the way media of different types is handled in Acrobat 8.

5.  The dialog closes, and the movie starts. The movie plays through once and stops. When it is finished, it disappears again (**Figure 11.30**).

6.  To run the movie again, click within the movie's frame on the page. Acrobat uses a Mouse Up action as the default trigger or event (see the sidebar, "About Triggers and Events" for more information) that starts the movie playback.

**Figure 11.30** The movie opens in the designated area of the page and plays.

Not too bad. Jack wants to get rid of the black border surrounding the movie's area on the page and find some playback controls, but first he'll add a separate link to start the movie playback.

## Starting the Movie from a Link

The movie playback is triggered by a mouse click, but Jack decides to add one more button to use to trigger the movie playback instead.

To insert a button and attach a trigger, follow these steps:

1.  Select the Button tool on the Forms toolbar and drag a marquee around the arrow on page 1 of the document. Release the mouse to open the Button Properties dialog.

2.  Choose these settings for the button:

    ■  On the General tab, type `movie` for the button's name and type `Click to see the lake channel in early summer` in the Tooltip field.

    ■  On the Appearance tab, set the Border and Fill Color to No Color.

    ■  On the Options tab, use the default Label only layout, and type `View the lake channel` in the Label field.

**3.** Click the Actions tab. In the Add an Action section, leave the default Mouse Up trigger selected. Click the Select Action down arrow, choose Play Media (Acrobat 6 and Later Compatible), and then click Add.

**4.** In the Play Media dialog, leave the two default settings (**Figure 11.31**). Click the Associated Annotation listing for the "Annotation from channel.mov" on Page 1 to activate the OK button. Annotations are names assigned to objects by Acrobat.

**5.** Click OK to close the dialog and return to the Button Properties dialog. The Play Media action is added to the Actions tab in the Button Properties dialog (**Figure 11.32**). Click Close to exit the dialog.

**6.** Adjust the button's size and location on the page as necessary so the text and the arrow make up the hot area on the page (**Figure 11.33**).

**7.** To test the link, click Preview on the Forms toolbar and click over the button. The movie plays through.

Acrobat uses some default settings when it adds a movie to a document, including a black border around the movie and an action that plays the movie triggered by a mouse click. Jack wants to customize the appearance and function of the movie next.

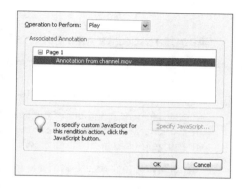

**Figure 11.31** The new button will play the movie embedded into page 1.

**Figure 11.32** The button now has an action attached to play the media file.

**Figure 11.33** Adjust the button's size and location on the page.

# Customizing the Movie

You can modify a movie inserted into a PDF document in Acrobat through the Multimedia Properties dialog by adding multiple versions of the movie, adding actions, and customizing the movie's appearance on the page.

## ABOUT TRIGGERS AND EVENTS

A trigger is a user interaction or document activity that produces an event in a PDF document. For example, clicking a button is a trigger, and what happens when the button is clicked—such as opening another document or an e-mail window—is the event.

Acrobat includes a number of triggers that vary depending on the type of object you are working with. Media clips can be triggered by page events, such as the Page Enter trigger used in this project, whereas links and bookmarks can't.

The following triggers are available for buttons and media clips:

- **Page Visible.** Trigger occurs when the page containing the media clip is visible in the Document pane.

- **Page Invisible.** Trigger occurs when the page containing the media clip is not visible in the Document pane.

- **Page Enter.** Trigger occurs when the page containing the media clip is the current page.

- **Page Exit.** Trigger occurs when a user goes to a page other than the page containing the media clip.

- **Mouse Up.** Trigger occurs when the mouse button is released after a click.

- **Mouse Down.** Trigger occurs when the mouse button is clicked and held down.

- **Mouse Enter.** Trigger occurs when the pointer enters the movie's play area.

- **Mouse Exit.** Trigger occurs when the pointer leaves the movie's play area.

- **On Receive Focus.** Trigger occurs when a form field receives focus (becomes active), either through a mouse click or tabbing to a different field.

- **On Lose Focus.** Trigger occurs when a form field becomes inactive, either through a mouse click or tabbing to a different field.

In addition, you can create a number of versions, or *renditions,* of the movie. Renditions are used when you want to distribute the movie to as wide an audience as possible, want to use both high- and low-quality versions, or want to use different renditions for different actions. The sample project uses two renditions.

Follow these steps to make changes to the movie's settings:

**1.** Select the Movie tool on the Advanced Editing toolbar, and then double-click the movie on the page to open the Multimedia Properties dialog. Click the Settings tab (**Figure 11.34**).

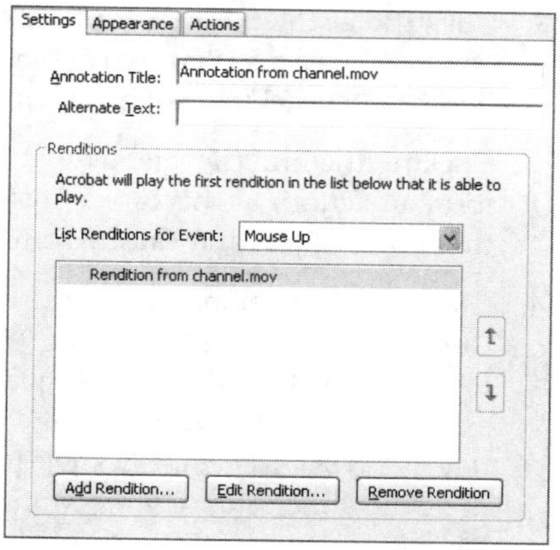

The Annotation Title is the name assigned by Acrobat to identify the object and is shown at the top of the Settings tab. Leave the default title.

**Figure 11.34** Change the default movie settings in the dialog.

**NOTE** You can type a description for an alternate text tag if you are creating an accessible document. In an accessible document, all visual content needs a text tag that describes what the image or movie contains so viewers using assistive devices like screen readers can understand the page's content.

**2.** Select the default "Rendition from channel.mov" shown in the Renditions list and click Remove Rendition.

The List Renditions for Event default is Mouse Up, and the Rendition from channel. mov is shown as the rendition that plays in response to the Mouse Up trigger. Jack doesn't want the movie to play if the user clicks the movie's area on the page.

**3.** Click the List Renditions for Event down arrow and choose On Receive Focus. The On Receive Focus event refers to the program action that occurs in response to clicking the Channel to Lake/arrow link created in the previous section.

Clicking the link triggers Acrobat to perform an action, in this case focusing on the movie object and causing it to play.

**4.** Click Add Rendition and choose By Copying an Existing Rendition. The Copy Rendition dialog opens and displays the existing channel.mov file as the Rendition to Copy (**Figure 11.35**). Click OK to close the dialog and return to the Multimedia Properties dialog.

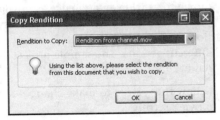

**Figure 11.35** Choose the movie you want to specify as a rendition.

**TIP** The action can be changed from either the Settings tabs or the Actions tab. If you take a look at the Actions tab, you'll see the same triggers and events as those adjusted on the Settings tab.

**5.** Select Edit Rendition to open a five-tab dialog. Jack chooses these settings from the dialog and then clicks OK to close the dialog and return to the Multimedia Properties dialog:

- On the Media Settings tab, leave the default options.

- On the Playback Settings tab, select "Show player controls" and Repeat; click Continuously to define the repeat method (**Figure 11.36**).

- On the Playback Location tab, leave the default options to play the movie in the document rather than full screen in a floating window or hidden.

- Leave the default options for both the System Requirements and Playback Requirements tabs.

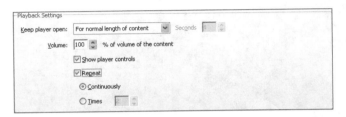

**Figure 11.36** Specify how the movie should appear in the document as it plays.

**6.** Select the Appearance tab. On this tab, you can specify whether to use a border for the movie as well as any border characteristics such as color and line type. Jack chooses Invisible Rectangle from the Border Type list (**Figure 11.37**).

**7.** Click the Settings tab again, and start all over with the second rendition: This time, click Add Rendition, and choose Using a File. In the Select Multimedia File dialog that opens, locate the channel.wmv movie file and click Select to close the dialog.

**8.** The selected file and its content type are shown in the Add New Renditions Using a File dialog (**Figure 11.38**). The "Embed content in document" setting is active by default.

**9.** Click OK to close the dialog and load the second rendition into the Multimedia Properties dialog (**Figure 11.39**).

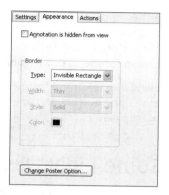

**Figure 11.37** Define the appearance of the movie's border on the page.

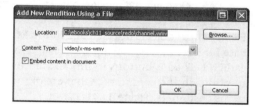

**Figure 11.38** Acrobat defines the annotation for the new movie rendition.

**NOTE** Click the up and down arrows on the Multimedia Properties dialog to the right of the Renditions list to reorder the files. Acrobat tries to play the first rendition in the list; if unsuccessful, it tries the second, and so on until the movie and player versions are compatible.

**10.** Select the Rendition from channel. wmv file in the Renditions list, and click Edit Rendition to reopen the Rendition Settings dialog. Use the same settings as those chosen for the first rendition, channel.mov. Click OK to close the dialog and return to the Multimedia Properties dialog.

**11.** Click Close to exit the dialog and return to the document.

**Figure 11.39** The second type of movie is listed as a rendition for the On Receive Focus event.

Save the file and then click the Channel to Lake link with the Hand tool to start playing the movie. It plays through once and then shows the controls at the bottom of the screen (**Figure 11.40**)

The fancy image and movie control features are finished. Jack hasn't done much with page 2, so he turns to that page next.

**Figure 11.40**
The movie displays controls for the user to manipulate the playback.

# Adding Some Final Navigation

Jack's final task is to add some Web links from the second page of the document.

 **DOWNLOAD** You can download Jack's Web site files from the book's Web site. Look for **samurai.html, web_bkgd.jpg**, and **samurai.swf**.You'll also find the extra image **bkgd.jpg** and the final project file named **DanuHills04.pdf**.

He has three objects on the page to use as the base for his links. Following the steps described earlier, Jack adds buttons to link to various organizations in the community that are of interest to his customers (**Figure 11.41**).

The buttons use labels specified in the Button Properties dialog: Please review the instructions earlier in this chapter to see how he uses labels. By the way, although the buttons have different labels, they all link to http://www.adobe.com, which must be typed in full in the Actions dialog (**Figure 11.42**).

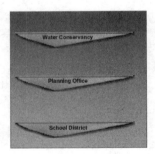

**Figure 11.41** Jack adds links to a number of community resources.

**Figure 11.42** The buttons provide labels and links to Web pages—well, one Web page in the sample project.

Jack also includes another invisible button over his logo to link to his Web site. In the Button Properties dialog, Jack would select the Open a Web page button action in real life—in order to see the project files. But he instead chooses "Open a file in the Select Action list" of the dialog, choosing samurai.html as the file to open (**Figure 11.43**).

> **TIP** In your project, you won't be able to select the same file as the one used in the sample project because your file will be stored on your hard drive, which uses a different path.

Finally, Jack decides that page 2 of the document is rather sparse in appearance. Following the steps described in the section "Modifying Content on a Page," he decides to drop in another image file named bkgd.jpg, which is available from the book's Web site (**Figure 11.44**).

And on it goes…as Jack sells out the properties available in the first phase of the development, a second phase gets underway.

**Figure 11.43** Since Jack's Web site isn't a live site, you can't link to the Web page, but you can link to the actual file.

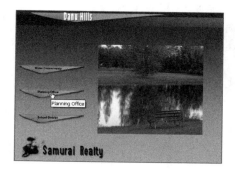

**Figure 11.44** Jack adds one more image for good measure.

## UPDATING THE DOCUMENT

A key task in any project is designing an efficient workflow, which Jack has done. Another key task is designing a workflow that can be readily reused when necessary. In Jack's document, for example, as the development's properties are sold, he'll remove links to current listings and add links to new listings.

The pages can be started from scratch, or Jack can reuse what he has. For example, he can:

- Save a map showing the new lots.

- Exchange the original maps for the Phase 2 maps on pages 1 and 3.

- Swap out images in the pop-up views.

- Adjust other content on the page.

- Reset the magnified views to show the new property.

# What Else Could He Do?

Jack's system for creating the PDF property listing documents is complete. His goal was to devise a method for building a compact and functional interactive PDF file for his new development.

Jack can add other content to the PDF documents as well, depending on how he would like to use the document. For example, he can add a button that opens a form a customer can fill in and e-mail to him to request more information about a property or to arrange a meeting, like the form designed in the project in Chapter 10, or the form in the Chapter 10 bonus project available from the book's Web site.

Instead of using a set of buttons to show and hide the image pop-ups, he could have the images on separate layers and use links to show/hide the layers. Read about using layered documents in Chapter 4, "Collaborating in a Shared Review."

To prevent changes, Jack can secure the files using a document password, like the sample project in Chapter 6, "Managing and Organizing E-mail Using Acrobat," and restrict the actions a user is allowed to perform with the file.

If Jack wants to set up a meeting online with his customers, he can use Acrobat Connect, which is described in the Chapter 11 bonus material on the book's Web site.

# Secure Reviewing and Reporting 12

Many aspects of modern business require that the exchange of information is secured in some way, whether it's a package the receptionist signs for on delivery or a briefcase cuffed to a courier's wrist. PDF documents are no different.

Several chapters in the book have included review cycles and options as part of the project or as additional steps the project participants could take. This chapter focuses on collecting, collating, and exchanging information where each level of interaction is secured using digital signatures.

Rather than a standard review cycle initiated by Acrobat, you can use PDF Packages and a custom cover sheet to control the signing and routing processes.

# Sign Here, Please

Erin Crowley is the document manager for Barber Black & Co., a financial management company. In her role, Erin is responsible for coordinating incoming information from regional offices. To ensure compliance with government and regulatory requirements, the sales reports sent from regional offices are usually signed by hand and sent by courier to the head office on a weekly basis.

The courier fees are accepted as a cost of doing business, but the transportation of the signed documents is only one part of the equation. When the reports reach Erin and her staff, they are compared line-by-line against the reports' source files. Multiple copies are distributed for signing by in-house signatures; the copies are collected, processed, and stored.

Erin thinks—and rightly so—that the system is far too complex, labor-intensive, and expensive. She thinks she can streamline the job substantially using Acrobat 8 Professional.

Key staff at regional offices and head office staff have recently upgraded to Acrobat 8 Professional. Those with Acrobat 8 Professional produce and distribute reviews and documents enabled for use in Adobe Reader 8, which is used by the remainder of the Barber Black staff.

> **NOTE** See how to manage e-mail using Acrobat in Chapter 6, "Managing and Organizing E-mail Using Acrobat."

# Steps Involved in This Project

Erin plans to have the regional reps use digital signatures to identify their submitted material and forward the data by e-mail to her department. The sales sheets are combined in a PDF Package, a cover sheet containing signature fields is added, and the document is certified and routed for signatures (**Figure 12.1**).

Erin is looking forward to getting the project underway. To complete the project, Erin and her staff need to:

- Show regional staff how to create PDF versions of the sales reports that include the source file as an attachment.

- Sign and e-mail the document.

- Create a custom cover sheet for the PDF Package that acts as a control document for the approval process.

- Add signature fields, instructions, and e-mail links to the control document.

- Create a PDF Package from submitted sales reports without violating the signatures on the original files.

- Certify the package as to its integrity.

- Set up and initiate the approval process.

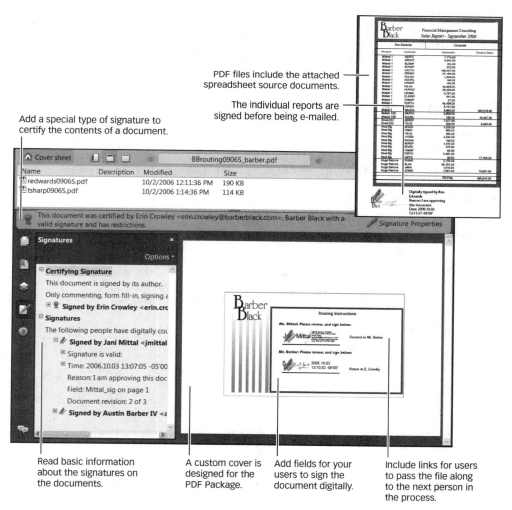

PDF files include the attached spreadsheet source documents.

The individual reports are signed before being e-mailed.

Add a special type of signature to certify the contents of a document.

Read basic information about the signatures on the documents.

A custom cover is designed for the PDF Package.

Add fields for your users to sign the document digitally.

Include links for users to pass the file along to the next person in the process.

**Figure 12.1** Use Acrobat's features to manage content in your documents, such as signatures.

# Preparing the PDF Reports

All regional offices of Barber Black use Excel spreadsheets to manage sales information and other data. Erin has learned from the in-house training officer that regional sales staff have received some training in Acrobat 8 Professional and that more is ongoing. She is quite sure the area sales managers will be able to produce the PDF version of the sales figures in the format she needs for controlling the content.

 **DOWNLOAD** If you would like to start with the original Excel spreadsheets, download them from the book's Web site at www.donnabaker.ca/downloads. The files are named **tsharp0906.xls** and **redwards0906.xls**. A copy of the converted spreadsheets is also available—download **tsharp0906.pdf** and **redwards0906.pdf**.

## Choosing Conversion Settings

Erin has two area managers ready and willing to serve as experimental subjects for her project—Tanis Sharp in Salt Lake City and Ron Edwards in Cincinnati.

To convert the files from spreadsheets to PDF, follow these steps:

1. Open the spreadsheet file in Excel.

2. Choose Adobe PDF > Change Conversion Settings to open the Acrobat PDFMaker dialog (**Figure 12.2**).

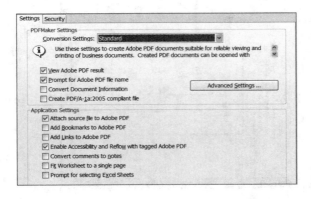

**Figure 12.2** You can specify file conversion settings from within Acrobat.

3. Choose Standard from the Conversion Settings menu. If you haven't previously used the PDFMaker in Excel, the Standard settings are shown by default.

4. Clear the Prompt for Adobe PDF file name check box, since the PDF uses the spreadsheet file's name.

5. Clear the default options from the Application Settings area in the dialog.

6. Select these choices in the Application Settings area:

   ■ Attach source file to Adobe PDF

   ■ Enable Accessibility and Reflow with tagged Adobe PDF

7. Click OK to close the dialog.

8. Choose Convert to Adobe PDF 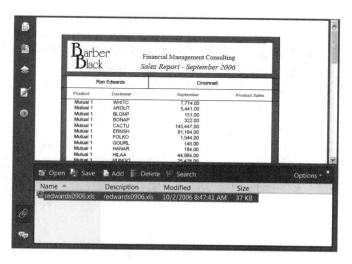 on the PDFMaker toolbar.

   If you see a message saying the file can't be converted with tags when the Print Area is set, click No to close the dialog. Then choose File > Print Area > Clear Print Area, save the file, and try again.

9. The file is converted to PDF and opens in Acrobat 8 Professional.

## Checking the File

After the file is converted, Tanis and Ron check out their results in Acrobat. The conversion settings included the option to open the PDF file in Acrobat automatically, saving them a couple of mouse clicks.

In Acrobat, click the Attachments 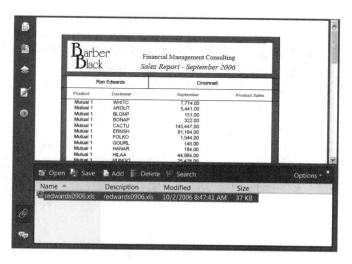 icon in the Navigation panel to display the Attachments panel across the bottom of the program window (**Figure 12.3**). You see the name of the attached spreadsheet as well as a description, modification date, and size. Next, it's time to add a signature to verify the contents.

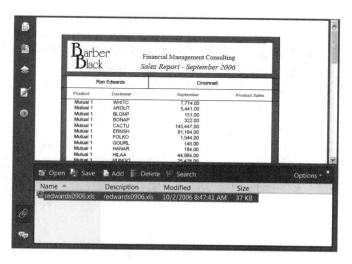

**Figure 12.3** Check the Attachments panel for the source file.

**NOTE** Read about using and working with attachments in Chapter 6.

# Signing the PDF Report

The terms digital signature, digital ID, and digital profile all refer to the same digital identification used to certify or sign a document, and they can all be used interchangeably. Digital ID is the term used in the book and bonus materials for convenience.

Regardless of the term you use, the information about a digital ID is contained in a certificate that can be shared and exchanged like any other type of file.

Ron and Tanis have converted their respective sales reports and have checked that the file includes the source spreadsheet as an attachment. They'll sign the PDF files after reviewing the content of the document for accuracy.

 **DOWNLOAD** Copies of the signed documents are available from the book's Web site. The files are named **redwards0906S.pdf** and **tsharp0906S.pdf**.

## Applying the Signature

Ron and Tanis follow these steps to sign the file (Ron's document is shown in the example):

**1.** Click the Sign Task button 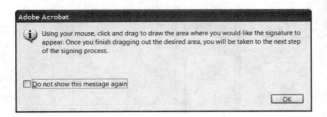 and choose Place Signature.

**2.** A dialog opens explaining how to define the signing area on the document page (**Figure 12.4**). Click OK to close the dialog.

When you have added a few signatures to a document, select "Do not show this message again" since you'll be familiar with drawing a marquee to designate where the signature is placed.

**Adobe Acrobat**

(i) Using your mouse, click and drag to draw the area where you would like the signature to appear. Once you finish dragging out the desired area, you will be taken to the next step of the signing process.

☐ Do not show this message again

[ OK ]

**Figure 12.4** Read how to define the area for the signature in the dialog.

3. Move the pointer over the page. It changes to crosshairs ⊡. Drag the area on the page where you want to place the signature (**Figure 12.5**). Release the mouse, and the Sign Document dialog opens.

4. Click the Digital ID down arrow and choose the signature to use. Ron chooses his default digital ID. The image of the digital ID is displayed in the preview area.

5. Type the password in the Password field. Ron types password.

6. Click the Appearance down arrow and choose an option (**Figure 12.6**). Any custom appearances you have created for the selected digital ID are listed; Ron chooses the appearance named "redwards". The contents on your computer will vary from those in the figure.

7. Click the Reason down arrow and choose why the document is being signed. There are a number of options ranging from defining yourself as the author, approving the document, and agreeing to terms (**Figure 12.7**). Adding a reason for signing isn't mandatory.

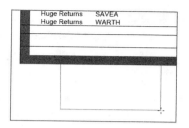

**Figure 12.5** Drag a marquee on the page to use for inserting the signature.

**Figure 12.6** If you have created custom signature appearances, you can choose them from the dialog.

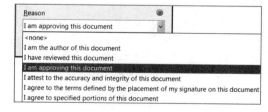

**Figure 12.7** In some workflows, choose a reason for signing as part of the signature.

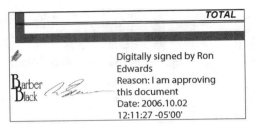

Figure 12.8 The completed signature is shown on the page.

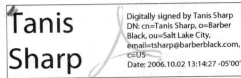

Figure 12.9 Tanis uses the program defaults for her signature.

8.  Click Sign. The Sign Document dialog closes and is replaced by the Save As dialog. Ron attaches an "S" to the file's name—the signed version is named redwards0906S.pdf—and clicks Save.

9.  The signature is added to the page in the area specified (**Figure 12.8**). The details and the image Ron selected are included in the signature block.

Tanis uses the default signature appearance and the default settings to sign her document. She then saves the file as tsharp0906S.pdf (**Figure 12.9**).

> **NOTE** For more information on configuring and applying signatures, read the section "Specifying Digital ID Characteristics" and "Customizing the Signature Appearance" in the Chapter 12 bonus material available from the book's Web site.

## Viewing Basic Signature Information

After Tanis and Ron have finished signing their respective documents, they can check the signature's information in the Signatures panel. Adding a signature opens the panel automatically. If the panel is closed, right-click/Control-click the column of Navigation panel icons and choose Signatures. Toggle the Signatures icon ▨ to open or close the panel.

The Signatures panel in Tanis's document is shown in **Figure 12.10**. It contains the following:

- Nested items that can be toggled open or closed by clicking the (-) or (+) prefacing the list item.

- Validity of the signature as well as whether or not the current user is also the signer.

- The time the document was signed.

- A reason for signing.

- Which signature field contains the digital ID.

- The number of existing document revisions.

Most of the entries are straightforward, with the possible exception of the field numbers. The list item specifies that the document is signed in "Field: Signature2 on page 1." Obviously, Tanis added and deleted a signature field at some time prior to signing the document, which has no bearing on its security.

Finally, Ron and Tanis send their reports to Erin via e-mail. Erin stores them for future use. She'll include the reports in a PDF Package but needs to build the cover document first.

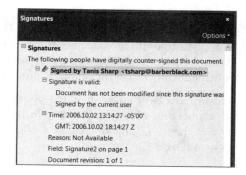

**Figure 12.10** The Signatures panel shows basic information about the signature.

## HOW A DIGITAL ID WORKS

Digital IDs use a key encryption process. For you to share secure documents with others, and for others to share secure documents with you, you need to use digital IDs.

A digital ID is composed of two parts: a public key and a private key, which are both created automatically by Acrobat when you create the digital ID. A signature contains two keys. The private key is yours alone, and Acrobat uses it for signing and certifying your documents; you share the public key with others. In the same way, another person's digital ID contains a pair of keys; the private key is maintained by his or her system, and the public key can be shared with you.

If a coworker has your public key listed in a document, that coworker can share the information with you; if you have that coworker's public key listed in a document, you can share with him or her. You can share a document and keys with a group because Acrobat lets you use a number of keys for the same document. You don't have to figure out which part of the signature is private and which is public—Acrobat takes care of the details for you.

Read more about working with signatures and certificates in this chapter's bonus material on the book's Web site.

# Producing the Custom Cover

Erin plans to route the documents for signature by the vice president of sales and the chief financial officer. She needs a custom cover sheet for the PDF Package to serve as a control document for the approval process.

Creating the basic cover sheet is a simple matter of modifying the company's fax cover page and converting it to PDF (**Figure 12.11**). Read about converting files to PDF in several chapters, such as Chapter 2, "Building a Cohesive Document" and Chapter 7, "Assembling a Library."

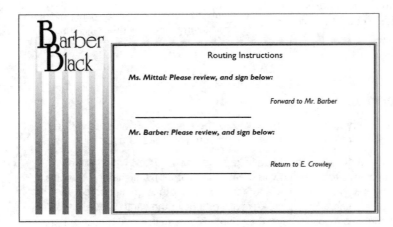

**Figure 12.11**
Erin starts with a modified version of the company's fax cover page.

 **DOWNLOAD** To view the original PDF file Erin works with, download **routing.pdf**.

On the cover page, Erin needs to do the following:

- Add and configure two signature fields.
- Add and configure two e-mail links.

Erin first adds the signature fields.

# Adding the Signature Fields

The PDF document already displays underlines that Erin will use as the location for the signatures.

## Configuring the first field

To add the first signature field to the document, Erin follows these steps:

1. Right-click/Control-click the toolbar well and choose Forms to open the Forms toolbar.

2. Click the Digital Signature tool 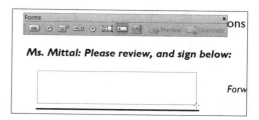 and drag a marquee on the page above the uppermost underline (**Figure 12.12**). Release the mouse to complete the marquee and open the Digital Signature Properties dialog.

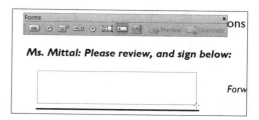

**Figure 12.12** Specify the location for the first signature field on the page.

3. On the General tab, name the field and include a tooltip (**Figure 12.13**). Erin types Mittal_sig for the Name and Please sign here as the tooltip.

4. Click Close to add the field to the page and close the Digital Signature Properties dialog.

5. Position and resize the field if necessary. Erin's finished signature field is slightly above and the same size as the underline on the document (**Figure 12.14**).

Erin adds another signature field to use for the CFO's signature.

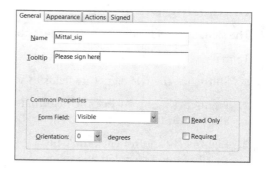

**Figure 12.13** Configure the properties for the first signature field.

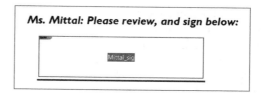

**Figure 12.14** Position and resize the signature field to suit the page's layout.

## Placing the second field

Follow these steps to create the second signature field:

1. Drag a marquee for the second signature on the page above the lower horizontal underline. Release the mouse to place the marquee and open the Digital Signature Properties dialog.

2. On the General tab, type `Barber_sig` in the Name field, and type `Please sign here` in the Tooltip field.

3. Click Close to close the dialog and complete the field (**Figure 12.15**).

Next, Erin resizes and aligns the two fields.

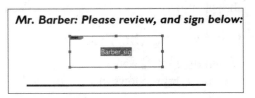

**Figure 12.15** Add the second signature to the page—don't worry about its size or location.

## Organizing the fields

The signature fields don't have borders or backgrounds but will contain visible signatures.

To make sure the two fields are visually the same after signing, Erin follows these steps:

1. Shift-click the two signature fields to select them both.

2. Right-click/Control-click the field that is the size you want for both fields and choose Size > Both from the shortcut menu. Both fields are now the same dimensions.

3. Right-click/Control-click the field that has the correct left alignment and choose Align > Left from the shortcut menu. Both fields now align at the same location (**Figure 12.16**).

4. Click Edit Layout ![icon] on the Forms toolbar to toggle to the Preview mode to check out the final appearance of the signature fields on the page.

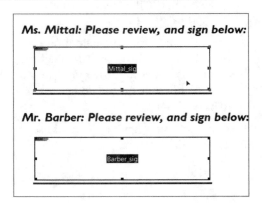

**Figure 12.16** The two fields are the same dimensions and are aligned at their left margin.

**5.** Move the pointer over one of the signature areas on the page. The pointer changes to a pointing hand and the tooltip displays (**Figure 12.17**).

You don't have to add the tooltip in the Digital Signature Properties dialog, by the way—it is added as part of the default content for the field type.

**6.** Click Preview 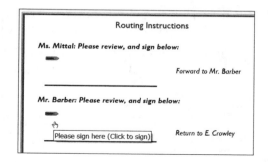 on the Forms toolbar to toggle to the Edit Layout mode and continue editing the page.

**Figure 12.17** Check out the signature field's appearance in the Preview mode.

> **NOTE** Read more about working with form fields, including copying form fields—in Chapter 10, "Streamlining Form Development and Data Management." Read more about forms in the Chapter 10 bonus material available from the book's Web site.

Looking good! Next, Erin will add link actions to the document.

# Adding an E-mail Link

A link in a PDF file uses an action, such as a mouse click, to initiate a response. In the project, Erin will apply an e-mail link to the phrases "Forward to Mr. Barber" and "Return to E. Crowley."

## Applying the first link

Follow these steps to add the first e-mail link:

**1.** Right-click/Control-click the toolbar well and choose Advanced Editing to open the Advanced Editing toolbar.

**2.** Click the Link tool 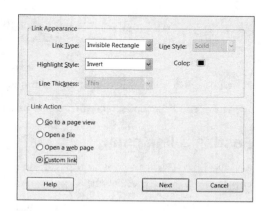 and drag a marquee on the page to surround the text that reads "Forward to Mr. Barber."

**3.** Release the mouse to complete the marquee and open the Link Properties dialog (**Figure 12.18**). In the Create Link section of the dialog, click the Link Type down arrow and choose Invisible Rectangle. The text on the page is used for the link and doesn't need to be framed by a border.

**Figure 12.18** A link can be a visible rectangle with custom color or invisible, as in the project.

**4.** In the Link Action section, choose Custom link and click Next. A new tab is added to the Link Properties dialog. Click the Actions tab.

**5.** Click the Select Action down arrow and choose "Open a web link" (**Figure 12.19**); click Add to open the Edit URL dialog.

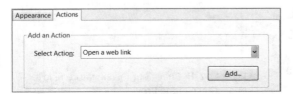

**Figure 12.19** Select from one of many actions that can be used in a PDF file.

**6.** In the field in the Edit URL dialog, Erin types `mailto:abarber@barberblack.com` and clicks OK. The text she typed is displayed with the selected action at the lower part of the Actions tab (**Figure 12.20**).

**Figure 12.20** The details of the action are listed in the dialog.

**7.** Click OK to close the dialog and complete the link.

Leave the link tool selected to create and configure the copy of the link.

## Pasting a link copy

To save time, Erin can copy and paste the link and change the settings for the pasted copy by following these steps:

**1.** Click the existing link to select it, and press Ctrl/Control-C to copy it.

**2.** Press Ctrl/Control-V to paste the link to the center of the document.

**3.** Drag the pasted link to the correct location (**Figure 12.21**). Erin moves the link over the phrase "Return to E. Crowley" on the page.

**4.** Double-click the link with the Link tool to open the Link Properties dialog and click the Actions tab.

**5.** Click the "Open a web link" action and then click Edit to reopen the Edit URL dialog, which shows the original URL that Erin typed (**Figure 12.22**).

**6.** Delete the existing text and type `mailto:ecrowley@barberblack.com`. Erin wants the contents to return to her automatically after the CFO reviews the reports.

**7.** Click OK to close the Edit URL dialog and return to the Form Properties dialog; click OK again to return to the program window.

**8.** To check the links, select the Hand tool on the Select & Zoom toolbar. Move the pointer over the link area (**Figure 12.23**). The pointer changes to a hand with a "W," indicating a Web link, and the URL is shown in a tooltip.

**9.** Save the file. Erin saves the file as BBrouting.pdf.

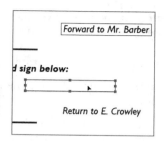

**Figure 12.21** Drag the pasted link to its new position over the second link's text.

**Figure 12.22** Reopen the action's dialog to change the URL for the link.

**Figure 12.23** An active link shows its destination and a special pointer.

 **DOWNLOAD** Erin's **BBrouting.pdf** file from the book's Web site.

The parts are ready, but before Erin can continue building and checking the PDF Package, she has to import the certificates for the signature process.

# Collecting Certificates

Suppose Erin has sent and received certificates, and has exchanged File Data Format (FDF) files with several people. Before they can be used in her project, she has to import them into her list of trusted identities. Like other features in Acrobat, there are several ways to do this.

**DOWNLOAD** For more information on exchanging certificate files see "Exchanging Data Files" in the Chapter 12 bonus file on the book's Web site.

Follow these steps to use one method for importing contacts:

1. Choose Advanced > Manage Trusted Identities to open the Manage Trusted Identities dialog.

2. Choose either the Contacts or Certificates option from the Display pull-down menu—these steps use the Contacts option. You can assign an identity either way, and in practical terms, there's no difference between them.

3. Click Add Contacts to open the Choose Contacts to Import dialog.

4. Click Browse to open the Locate Certificate File dialog, where you can browse for the file you'd like to import.

5. Select the file, and click Open to close the dialog and load the certificate into the Choose Contacts to Import dialog (**Figure 12.24**).

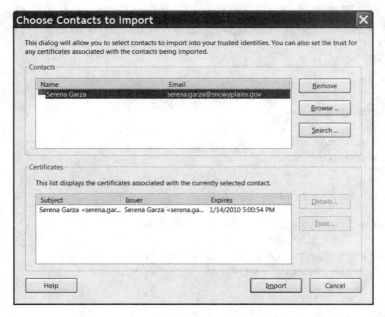

**Figure 12.24**
The selected certificate is displayed in the dialog.

6. Click the name in the Contacts window to display the basic certificate information associated with the contact in the Certificates window.

**7.** Click Import; the dialog closes, and the Import Complete dialog opens, stating you've successfully imported the certificate.

**8.** Click OK to close the dialog.

**9.** Your new certificate is now listed in the Manage Trusted Identities dialog. Continue adding other certificates as necessary, or click Close to exit the Manage Trusted Identities dialog and return to the program window.

 **DOWNLOAD** Download the set of digital certificates from the Chapter 12 material on the book's Web site. The files are named **ErinCrowley.pfx**, **RonEdwards.pfx**, **TanisSharp.pfx**, **JaniMittal.pfx**, and **AustinBarberIV.pfx**.

Before proceeding with the next part of the project—creating the PDF Package—Erin checks the available digital IDs one more time.

Choose Advanced > Security Settings to open the Security Settings dialog. Click Digital ID Files in the left column to display the list of imported digital ID files (**Figure 12.25**).

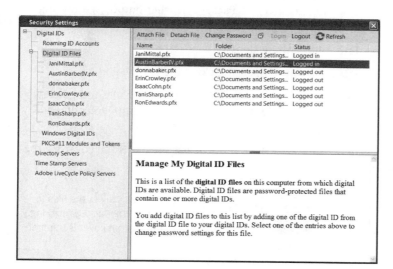

Figure 12.25 Review the digital ID files in your collection in the dialog.

**NOTE** By the way, all passwords for the digital IDs available for this project are the word "password," probably the most obvious password in existence. For the sake of security, please be more creative in real life!

**ROAMING IDS FOR DIGITAL SIGNATURES**

Acrobat 8 and Adobe Reader 8 offer the ability to enroll in a signing service where the private key for the user is stored on the service's server. If you are using the service, Acrobat can authenticate your signature to the server, and the document can be signed by the server. No certificates are necessary.

## Combining Signed Documents

One new feature in Acrobat 8 Professional is the ability to combine PDF files into a single package and retain the identities of each component of the package. The separate identity extends to digital signatures as well, as Erin discovers. For a complete discussion on PDF Packages, refer to the projects in Chapters 2, 7, and 9. In Erin's package, she's planning to have just the cover page signed by the signing authorities. A single signature can't be applied to multiple documents in a PDF Package. For her purposes, a routing document works fine.

To build the PDF Package, Erin follows these steps:

**1.** Click the Combine Files Task button to open the Combine Files dialog.

**2.** Click Add Files ![icon] to open a browse dialog. Locate and select the files to include in the PDF Package. Erin chooses the files BBrouting.pdf, redwards0906S.pdf, and tsharp0906S.pdf.

   Ensure that the BBrouting.pdf file is at the top of the list since it is the cover for the package (**Figure 12.26**). Click Next.

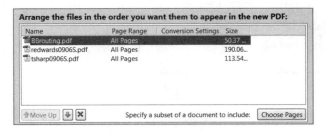

**Figure 12.26** Collect the files to use for the PDF Package, making sure the custom cover is the first file in the list.

**3.** Choose Assemble files into a PDF Package.

**4.** Select "Use first document" in the Select Cover Sheet area at the bottom right of the dialog (**Figure 12.27**).

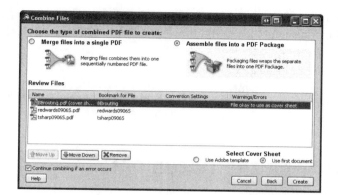

**Figure 12.27** Specify if the files are merged or combined in the dialog.

5. Click Create to show the final pane of the dialog. You see progress bars as the files are processed and a notification of successful processing.

6. Click Save to close the Combine Files dialog and open a Save As dialog. Save the file. Erin saves the file as BBrouting0906.pdf.

When the file is opened in Acrobat 8 Professional, you'll see the features added to the custom cover sheet (**Figure 12.28**).

The files added to the PDF Package are listed.

Information about the PDF Package and navigation and layout controls display above the document pane.

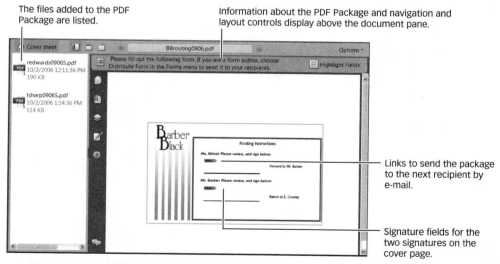

Links to send the package to the next recipient by e-mail.

Signature fields for the two signatures on the cover page.

**Figure 12.28** The new PDF Package contains the features Erin has defined so far in the project.

Because the file is a combined PDF document, the component PDF files aren't affected and are combined in the package without affecting their signatures (**Figure 12.29**).

**Figure 12.29** A signed document isn't affected by combining it with other files in a PDF Package.

Speaking of signatures, Erin needs to add hers as well, although in her case she's certifying the document. She'll work in the new Preview Document mode, which is available for the first time in Acrobat 8 Professional.

# Viewing and Certifying the Document

Acrobat 8 Professional includes a new feature that lets Erin check out the document using the Preview Document mode. The new view option describes how the document complies with document signing specifications, following the method first introduced as the Document Integrity Checker in Acrobat 7 Professional.

Previewing can be done as a routine inspection of every document or on a file-by-file basis by specifying an Acrobat program preference.

## Changing the Preview Preference

The program preferences include an option for defining whether or not all files are previewed prior to signing. To enable the preview process, Erin follows these steps:

1. Choose Edit > Preferences/Acrobat > Preferences to open the Preferences dialog.

2. Choose Security in the Categories list to display the preferences.

3. Choose "View documents in preview document mode when signing" in the Digital Signatures section of the dialog (**Figure 12.30**).

4. Click OK to close the dialog and set the preference.

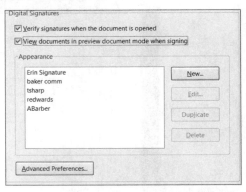

Rather than working with one file at a time, Erin changed the program preference to automatically preview documents before signing. This way, the preview is initiated automatically when she starts the certification process, as you'll see next.

**Figure 12.30** You can specify that all documents be previewed before being signed if it fits with your workflow.

**NOTE** Enter the Preview mode one document at a time by choosing Advanced > Sign & Certify > Preview Document to display the Document Message Bar. Click View Report to read details of any issues in the file, and close the report.

# Previewing the Document

A document may contain elements such as transparency, JavaScript, and fonts that Acrobat defines as dynamic, or subject to change. Before signing, Erin can use the Preview Document mode to view the document content as it would appear without its dynamic elements. It isn't necessary for Erin to remove any of the identified content, but it's good to see where a problem could arise and also to see if there are any hidden elements she may not be aware of.

 **DOWNLOAD** The PDF Package Erin uses in this part of the project is available from the book's Web site. Download **BBrouting0906.pdf**. The version containing her signature is also available and is named **BBrouting0906S.pdf**.

To preview the BBrouting0906.pdf document—the cover sheet for the PDF Package—follow these steps:

**Figure 12.31** The first signature in a document is a certifying signature, which can be visible or invisible.

1. Click the Sign Task button and choose Certify without Visible Signature (**Figure 12.31**).

2. The Document Message Bar displays over the Document pane and explains the status of the file (**Figure 12.32**).

**Figure 12.32** The Document Message Bar provides tools for certifying the file and information about its status.

3. Click View Report to open the PDF/SigQ Conformance Report dialog (**Figure 12.33**). Read about the reports in the sidebar "It's *Not* a Problem". The list includes:

   - "Comment or form field may silently change" in reference to having the Digital Signature form fields on the page.

   - "Document contains hidden behavior" in reference to the `mailto:` HTML tag added to the document to define the executive's routing path added in the section, "Adding an E-mail Link."

- "Document contains hidden behavior" for a second time, in reference to the actions applied to the links on the document for the executives to route the PDF Package for signature.

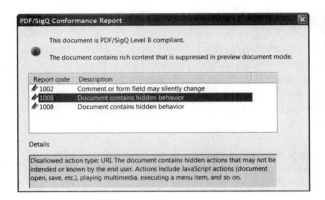

**Figure 12.33** Read how the file's content may produce signing issues in the future.

4. Click Close to return to the program window.

Erin doesn't see anything unusual in the file and decides to carry on with the signature process.

### IT'S *NOT* A PROBLEM

As part of the preview process, Acrobat evaluates the file according to PDF/SIGQ (Qualified Signatures) conformance checks and assigns one of three outcomes. The options include:

- **PDF/SigQ Level A.** Level A conformance means that the document contains no dynamic content that can alter its appearance.

- **PDF/SigQ Level B.** Level B conformance means that the document contains dynamic content that can be suppressed during signing.

- **Unknown.** If a document doesn't comply with Level A or B qualifications, you can sign the document or contact the author about the problem.

# Certifying the PDF Package

As a result of changing the program preference to examine all files intended for signature, the Document Message Bar for the PDF Package is open in Acrobat. Erin plans on certifying the document since hers is the first signature applied to the PDF Package. A certifying signature means she vouches for the document's contents.

Follow these steps to certify the document:

1.  Click Sign Document ✎ on the Document Message Bar to open the Save as Certified Document dialog (**Figure 12.34**).

    The dialog offers Erin the choice of obtaining a digital ID from a third-party source, which would be used to control signatures in very large reviews and other secure processes (such as online distribution of content) where each user is granted rights to a document. The third-party company controls the keys for the digital IDs rather than the user and recipient having a private and public key, respectively.

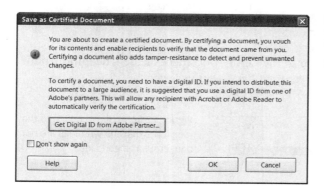

**Figure 12.34** Erin can use a digital ID from an external source by following the instructions in the dialog if she wishes.

2.  Select Don't show again to prevent displaying the dialog in the future, and then click OK to close the Save as Certified Document dialog. The Certify Document dialog opens.

3.  Specify the signature's characteristics in the Certify Document dialog (**Figure 12.35**). Erin:

    ■ Chooses her digital ID from the Digital ID drop-down menu.

    ■ Types password in the Password field.

    ■ Chooses "I attest to the accuracy and integrity of this document" from the Reason drop-down menu.

■ Chooses "Annotations, form fill-in, and digital signatures" from the Permitted Changes after Certifying drop-down menu. She needs to enable form-fill in to allow the others to sign the document, and she wants to give them a choice to add more comments if they wish.

**Figure 12.35** Specify the characteristics for the digital ID in the dialog.

4. Click Review to open the same PDF/SigQ Conformance Report as the one shown in Figure 12.32 but with one addition (**Figure 12.36**).

Since the recipients also see the warnings, the comment "I have included this content to make the document more interactive" accompanies the file so Erin's recipients won't be hesitant to interact with the file. Click OK to close the dialog and return to the Certify Document dialog. The information message now reads "Document warnings have been reviewed."

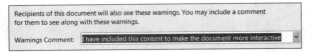

**Figure 12.36** Adding a notice to the recipients that the warnings are not dangerous is a good idea.

5. Click Sign. The Certify Document dialog closes and the Save As dialog opens. Name the file and specify its storage location. Erin names the file BBrouting0906S.pdf. Click Save to save the file and close the dialog.

After Erin has signed the document, the Certification icon 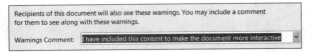 displays at the left side of the Document Message Bar. The only place her signature is visible is in the Signatures panel (**Figure 12.37**). In the Signatures panel you can see the choices Erin made as she worked through the certification dialogs, such as the actions allowed and the reason for signing.

**DOWNLOAD** To read more about certificates, download the Chapter 12 bonus file from the book's Web site and read the section "Extracting Certificates." Read about the contents of a certificate in the section "Customizing the Signature Appearance."

Drum roll please—it's finally time to get the show on the road and route the reports for approval signatures.

Icon identifies a certifying signature

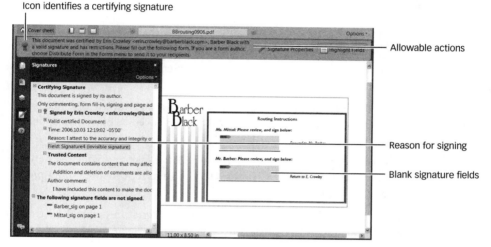

**Figure 12.37** The certification is described in the Document Message Bar, and information about Erin's signature is shown in the Signatures panel.

## WHY ERIN SIGNS THE PACKAGE

Erin decides to sign the document before routing it for these reasons:

- She wants to preview the files to see if there will be any conflict issues when recipients sign the documents.

- The first signer of a document is given the choice of signing or certifying the document. Erin's grasp of Acrobat is extensive, and she's afraid the choice between signing and certifying might be confusing to her colleagues.

- She wants to have a signed copy of the document that shows how it existed at the time she completed it and to identify any changes other signers may make.

We now return you to your regularly scheduled project.

# Routing and Signing the Document

Erin has done a lot of work to complete the document. She instructed two of the area managers on how to produce a PDF report and apply their signatures. She created a custom routing slip to use as a cover for a PDF Package, which she then created to combine the content to be reviewed without jeopardizing its signature status. Now that she's added her certifying signature, she's ready to send it.

The workflow includes these steps:

1. Erin e-mails the PDF Package to Jani Mittal, the company's VP of sales.

2. Jani adds her signature to the document by clicking the field specified in the document and follows the process described in the earlier section "Applying the Signature."

3. Jani clicks the link "Forward to Mr. Barber" to open an e-mail window. She needs to insert the message and attach the document, which she's saved as BBrouting0906S_mittal.pdf.

4. When Mr. Barber receives the e-mail, he opens the PDF Package and adds his signature, saving the file as BBrouting0906S_barber.pdf, and then repeats the e-mail process to return the file to Erin.

5. Finally, Erin opens the file to view the end results. In the Signatures panel, she can see the valid signatures added by the two routing recipients (**Figure 12.38**).

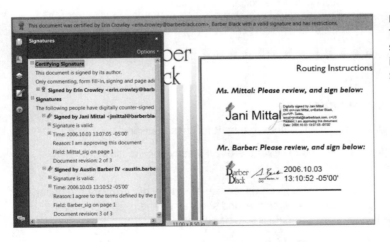

**Figure 12.38**
The two new signatures are included in the Signatures panel.

**6.** Opening the contents of the PDF Package,
she can see that the sales reports still maintain the valid signatures of the area managers
(**Figure 12.39**).

It's been a long day. Erin has set up a small document approval route to make it easy for her recipients to figure out where the file should go next.
Erin's approval system works well since there are
only two people involved in the process.

**Figure 12.39** The original signatures
are unaffected by the routing and
signing process.

## What Else Can She Do?

If Erin was involved in a review rather than a simple signature routing process, it would
make sense to use one of Acrobat's Comment and Review features. She could use either
the shared review or e-mail review, depending on the locations of the participants and
company or organizational protocols and requirements. Read about using an e-mail review
in Chapter 3, "Communicating with Comments" and a shared review in Chapter 4,
"Collaborating in a Shared Review."

If the situation required it, Erin could use a set of duplicated fields to copy the signa-
ture fields to each page to accept initials, which are required in some types of reviews.
You can read more about duplicating fields in Chapter 11, "Building a Powerful
Interactive Document."

To provide security during the e-mail process, Erin could apply a Secure Envelope, like the
one used in the project in Chapter 6. Speaking of security, rather than using signatures
or envelope security, Erin could use certificate encryption, where only those participants
whose signatures are part of the document's information are allowed to access the file.

# Managing Print Jobs

# 13

There's no question that PDF files have greatly impacted the way we do business. And there is no doubt that they will continue to do so. Perhaps the area where the greatest and most obvious improvements have been made is printing.

In the not-so-distant past, it could be very difficult to produce a professional product—such as an advertisement—without involving a third party, who would typeset it for you in the format required by the publication. It would be simply too time consuming to learn all the various programs and too expensive to own them all, especially for a small business.

Recently, a number of standards have been developed that define specific characteristics and features to ensure that electronic content in a PDF document prints exactly as you intended, using all the correct fonts and colors, for example.

Published standards have given companies and individuals the ability to do their own layout and printing, saving them a lot of money and time. If you are a print designer, using standards helps to save time in the production process, although it takes time to make sure the copy coming from your clients is ready to use.

Using Preflight, a process for examining a file in Acrobat 8 Professional, you can create a file that complies with any number of print standards, and even make corrections and changes to files that often make them standards-compliant. Now that's a timesaver!

# Randy's Design Dilemma

Randy Weber is a print designer contracted by a community newspaper association. He frequently receives material from customers for different sorts of print jobs. Randy knows his workload could be decreased and his billings increased dramatically if customers could figure out how to submit files.

Randy has just completed a rigorous week. Every month, before the color inserts are printed by the newspapers that make up his customers load, Randy spends days on the phone answering questions and exchanging e-mails with customers preparing advertising. Randy works long into the night preparing ads and layouts that are usable and comply with the print shop's requirements.

One of his regular clients is Samurai Realty, featured in Chapter 11 "Building a Powerful Interactive Document." Jack Taggart, retired martial arts champion and owner of Samurai Realty, purchases a substantial amount of print advertising, as well as colored circulars and inserts.

Randy decides the best way to handle the issue is to produce checklists and instructions for the client to use when generating print material, and for him to use his own automated features for processing the documents (**Figure 13.1**).

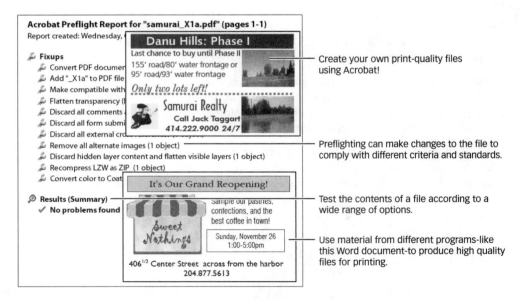

**Figure 13.1** Acrobat 8 Professional can evaluate, examine, and modify files according to a diverse range of print requirements and other criteria.

# Steps Involved in This Project

Due to the wide variety of programs used, level of user expertise, and familiarity with terminology, Randy has decided to make things as easy for the customers submitting ad copy as he possibly can. He knows how he needs the files submitted in order to save everyone time and effort. To get everyone on the same page (no pun intended) he needs to do the following:

- Create client instructions for submitting newspaper ad quality files, both as black-and-white and color.

- Construct a set of instructions for customers to use for developing high quality material for printing.

- Design a set of PDF settings he can send to a customer when they want to produce high-quality print output.

- Build a Droplet program that will open and evaluate files submitted by customers.

- Develop a batch conversion script to process groups of files simultaneously.

# Understanding Client Requirements

In a perfect world, every print client would create standards-compliant PDF files from InDesign or Illustrator documents according to predefined standards. The files would flow into Randy's e-mail inbox; he'd leisurely open them, check them out, and drop them into the circular or paper's layout.

Sadly, Randy's world isn't perfect. He was pondering the idea one morning over coffee when he realized his customers fall into three coffee-shop related groups:

- **The Plain Coffee (PC) type.** These are the folks that send him the facts, such as sales information, contacts, dates, and so on, and want him to "do it up right". He generally gets Word or e-mail files from the PC customers these days, but occasionally content still comes scribbled on paper and dropped in his mailbox (**Figure 13.2**).

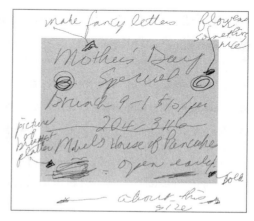

**Figure 13.2** It wasn't easy in the "old days" either, when ad copy arrived as suggestions scribbled on paper.

- **The Basic Latte/Cappuccino (BLC) type.** This group of customers have experience and know what they want, but don't share Randy's background or level of technical expertise. They've done a considerable amount of advertising and marketing material development over the years, and aren't afraid to try. Some BLC-level customers ask in advance what Randy needs to work with their files, and he can generally explain it in terms that they understand.

- **The Half-Caf/Skim Soy with Foam (HCSS-F) type.** These customers are in the groove. Some are designers themselves, are highly computer-literate, and may be involved in other technical design like 3D modeling or animation. The HCSS-F customer needs a minimal amount of input from him to get the output he needs.

Randy realizes that his customers fall into similar categories, just as the coffee shop crowd separates into different levels of understanding, passion, and interest.

## Meeting the Basic Customers' Needs

Randy knows that his customers who aren't comfortable with computers require much more time for coaching than it takes him to evaluate a document and make the changes himself. He also knows that he's not going to do all the work for them!

For the Plain Coffee (PC) group, Randy decides the safest way is to have them create the minimal amount of information and provide directives for him. Randy develops a checklist including answers to the questions customers ask over and over, and it takes the form of an FAQ file.

## FAQ: Preparing Advertising Materials for Weber Design

You want your advertising ready in the simplest way possible, and so do we. We have put together the questions that customers ask when they are preparing files for ads.

Here are some pointers and things to look for before sending your files to us.

**Q**   **How do I know what sorts of ads I need? Do you figure that out for me?**

**A**   No. That is something to determine with the ad representatives from your newspaper. We keep lists of ad sizes, and the ad representative will give you code numbers to include with the ad information for us.

**Q**   **How do I know where to start? What do I need? How do I get it to you? I don't have a clue.**

**A** We need all the elements that are used in your ads. You'll send us everything in an e-mail, described later in these questions. The place to start is to make a folder where you can store all the contents for the ad. Add a new folder somewhere on your hard drive and name it using your company's name and something to indicate it is for your ads (**Figure 13.3**). Some people like to put a folder on their desktop, others like to use the My Documents folder—it depends on what you are comfortable using. Don't name any of the files "Weber Design"—we won't know who sent us the file when it is using our name!

**Figure 13.3** Start with a folder dedicated to the ad content.

**Q** Do I need to have the layout for the ad drawn in a special program?

**A** No. If you use an illustration program like Corel Draw or Expressions Graphic Designer, send us that file in an image format like JPEG or TIF (common file formats for saving images). If you have the details in a Word file, send us that file with some instructions. What we want to see is how you think the finished ad should look. If you prefer, draw the ad on a piece of paper and show us where pictures, text, graphics, and other elements should go. Be sure to add labels to all the content on the ad so we can figure out what you want to include.

**Q** My ads have a lot of text. How do I send that?

**A** Put your text in a Word file. If your company uses a particular font (letter appearance), be sure to use it in the file.

**Q** I have the font that my company uses for the business name. Can't I send that to you to keep for my ads? How do I do that?

**A** Yes, some customers who have us do their layout send font files. Follow these steps:

1. On your computer, click the Start button on the desktop to open the menu, and click Control Panel. Double-click Fonts to open the Fonts folder (**Figure 13.4**).

2. Scroll through the list and select the font name that you use. Be careful—many fonts have many different versions for bold or italics.

**Figure 13.4** Fonts are stored on your hard drive in a system folder.

3. Double-click the font listing to open a dialog that shows its appearance. (**Figure 13.5**).

4. Click Done to close the dialog when you are sure the one you selected is the one you use for the business name.

5. With the name of the font still selected, choose Edit > Copy from the Fonts dialog's menu; close the Fonts folder.

6. Open your ad storage folder, and from the menu, choose Edit > Paste. You see your font file is added to the folder (**Figure 13.6**).

**Q** I don't know the name of the font used for my business and it doesn't really matter as long as it looks OK. What do I send to you?

**A** You don't need to send us a font in that case. If you have something like an existing ad or a business card that shows the sort of font you want to use, send us that. We can find a suitable font to use.

**Q** I have a logo too, which is in some files the person who made business cards sent to me. Do you want those? Or should I send you a business card instead?

**A** We would prefer digital files. Send us copies of the files you have for your business card or other graphic drawings or images that may have been done for your business, such as a sign or a logo (**Figure 13.7**). You might have files in different formats. Look for files such as: TIF, EPS, AI, PS, PDF, and JPG.

**Figure 13.5** Open an example window to be sure the font you've selected is the correct font.

**Figure 13.6** Store the font in the ad folder.

**Figure 13.7** Include any artwork you have from other marketing material such as business cards.

**Q   I don't have any files, but I have a business card. Can I send that instead?**

**A**   Send digital files if you have them. If you don't, please call us to discuss it. The design of a logo is different than preparing an ad. We can certainly recreate the design or design a logo for you, but that's a separate fee and schedule.

**Q   What about pictures? How do I send those to you?**

**A**   Most pictures will work sufficiently for newspaper ads, depending on the size of the ad. Send digital files for your images. We won't be responsible for physical images you bring into the office, nor will we scan images for you free of charge. Please call if you have specific image questions.

**Q   Do I need to do something special to the images?**

**A**   Probably not. Images captured with a digital camera are usually sufficient for newspaper ads. If you intend to use images for colored ads or the monthly circulars, call your newspaper for details. Make sure the files are renamed using your company name and included with the other ad material.

**Q   Can I tell you where the images are on the Internet and let you get them yourself?**

**A**   Absolutely not. We can't use images downloaded from the Internet as there isn't enough detail in the file to make the picture look good when printed.

**Q   How big will my ad be?**

**A**   If you don't know what sizes you want, how big the ad needs to be, be sure to call your newspaper's sales rep. We don't sell the advertising, we just make it happen! Use our checklist to be sure you have done what you need to do.

**Q   What else do I have to do?**

**A**   Be sure to check that all your files are virus free. We scan all material we receive before opening it. Anything that is found to contain a virus will be deleted immediately.

**Q   Do I have to put the files on a disc or a CD or e-mail it?**

**A**   You can send us the files by e-mail. It's easiest for you to send and for us to receive if the files are compressed using a program like WinZip. You could also burn the files to a CD and drop them off at our office or in the mail slot. Be sure to put your contact information on the outside of anything you drop in the mail slot.

Randy needs materials submitted in certain ways, but doesn't want to bog down the customer, nor spend unnecessary time on the phone. I think it works, don't you?

For good measure, Randy creates a simple checklist to go along with the FAQ file, shown in Table 13-1.

**Table 13-1**   Checklist for Sending Ad Material to Weber Graphics

| DID YOU REMEMBER TO: |
| --- |
| ❏   List the size and code number for the ads you receive from the marketing rep at your newspaper |
| ❏   Send the text you want used in the ad |
| ❏   Give us instructions or send a drawing of how you want the ad to look |
| ❏   Tell us the name of any special font that you use for your company name, or send a business card or ad showing the font used in the past if you don't need a special font used |
| ❏   Send us a copy of the font file |
| ❏   Send copies of any files you may have for company logos or printed materials – be sure to change the files' names to include your company name |
| ❏   Phone us to discuss creating a business logo if you don't have any files |
| ❏   Include the digital photos you want to use |
| ❏   Rename the photos to include your company's name |
| ❏   Scan each file for viruses |
| ❏   Burn the files to a CD for drop-off |
| ❏   Combine the files in a zip file to e-mail |
| ❏   Deliver the files |

Next, Randy moves along to the other two groups of customers. They need instruction and assistance, but not much hand-holding.

# Communicating with the Design-Savvy Customer

Since coming to the realization that his customers fall into the same categories as those patronizing coffee shops, Randy has a clear path to simplifying his workload. The Basic Latte/Cappuccino type may drink cappuccino because it's cool; or may be a true connoisseur and drink cappuccino because they find defining levels of caffeine pretentious.

By the same token, Randy can't predict how much each customer understands about modifying content files and testing them according to requirements for different outputs and standards. He comes up with the perfect solution: He's going to prepare another FAQ and checklist.

# FAQ: Technical Specifications for Advertising Content

Many of our customers prefer to prepare their advertising copy and supporting files themselves and then e-mail them to us for processing. We have assembled an FAQ that will assist you in making material submissions as simple as possible.

**Q  What are the basic requirements for ad submissions?**

**A**  We need the copy, images, graphics, fonts, and a sample layout. You can use a number of layout programs, but they should be capable of producing our preferred file formats, indicated below.

**Q  What are the image and graphic requirements?**

**A**  We have different image requirements for newspaper and color circulars. For the simplest reuse of your material, send it to us in the format used for circulars, including:

- Scale photos as close to the reproduction size as possible; we prefer a 20 percent margin more or less.

- Images should have a resolution of 300 dpi.

- Send images in TIF or EPS formats.

- Images downloaded from a Web site are unacceptable.

- Send images as CMYK or grayscale files; we can't use RGB, Lab or Index color files.

- Do not embed ICC or other color profiles.

**Q  How about color issues? Anything to keep in mind?**

**A**  Color issues vary according to the type of ads you are using. Again, it's simpler to send content that complies with color ad layouts. For color, keep in mind that:

- All colors must be CMYK or grayscale; tints and color type in four-color ads must be produced in a CMYK equivalent.

- Black and white images and objects should be grayscale, not the black channel of CMYK.

**Q    What is the best way to handle fonts?**

**A**    The general rule of thumb is that if you are fonts using any other than basic ones, send a copy. Also note that:

- We can use PostScript or TrueType fonts.

- Don't use pseudo-type commands, such as italics or bold. If you need alternate faces, use the appropriate font, and send the font file.

- If you prefer, you can convert the fonts in your ad to outlines to eliminate the need to supply fonts—bear in mind that we can't make any edits to the ad content for you in that case.

**Q    What sort of programs can I use for producing the layout?**

**A**    Virtually any program that can print can be used to create the output, like the ad copy in the image (**Figure 13.8**). Read how to prepare the file in the section "Printing a Document to a File."

**Q    Do I need to buy a program like Adobe InDesign? I don't have that program, but I do have Adobe Acrobat 8.**

**Figure 13.8** The ad copy can be produced in many programs, including Microsoft Word.

**A**    No. You don't need to buy more software. If you have Adobe Acrobat 8, you have all the software you need. You'll see in programs such as Microsoft Word that there are Adobe PDF menus added to the program; these menus offer commands to let you produce content using specific print settings. You will also have access to Acrobat Distiller 8. Read how to use Distiller to prepare the file in the upcoming section "Using Acrobat Distiller."

**Q    Isn't there a simpler way to do this? Can't you just send me the .joboptions file?**

**A**    Absolutely. If you are familiar with Acrobat Distiller, Adobe Acrobat, and PDF, you can use the .joboptions file that we use in-house. We use the standard conversion settings for PDF/X-3:2002, available in any program that employs the Adobe PDF print driver. Please refer to the section "Using Acrobat Distiller" for information and instruction on choosing the settings file.

**Q    I'd prefer to convert and preflight my files myself before sending them. It would save me time, and both of us effort. What do you need?**

**A**    By all means, please convert and preflight your files before sending. Read the section "Preflighting the File" on choosing the appropriate settings for an example ad that complies with the PDF/X-1a:2001 standard; read the section "Interpreting the Preflight Results" to see how the sample file is evaluated. You don't have to send any additional report files—we'll run the Preflight check here as part of our batch file system.

**Q   Any more details I should know before sending?**

**A**   When you have finished prepping the files, run through the Submission Checklist, shown in Table 13-2. Taking the time to check the details before sending files to us saves everyone time.

**Q   How do you want to receive the files?**

**A**   Zip the files and e-mail them to us. If it's more convenient, burn the files to a CD and drop them off. We have an after-hours mail slot available. Be sure all content is labeled with your company name and contact information.

**Table 13-2**   Submission Checklist

| PLEASE ENSURE YOUR FILE SUBMISSION: |
| --- |
| ❑   Includes a layout file that indicate areas for text, graphic, images, callouts |
| ❑   Includes all support files including images and graphics in an accepted file format and resolution |
| ❑   Has all support files named using the company name |
| ❑   Includes the screen and printer fonts used in the layout file and any support files |
| ❑   Is virus free; all files are scanned for viruses |
| ❑   Is compressed in a zip file using your company name as its file name; alternatively, burn to a CD using company name as label |

# Printing a Document to a File

Printing a document to a file rather than to a printer will process the document just as for printing, but instead of printing a page, it saves the document in a different file format. For example, the default format for a Word document is DOC but when you print a Word document to a file it produces a PRN file. Use this method if you want us to do the PDF conversion and test for standards compliance.

 **DOWNLOAD** the advertisement **sweet_nothings.doc** from the book's Web site at www.donnabaker.ca/downloads.html if you'd like to convert the document yourself using the method described in this section. You can also find a copy of the image used in the advertisement called **sweet_nothings.tif**.

Follow these steps to convert the source file to a PostScript PRN file:

1. Choose File > Print to open the Print dialog (**Figure 13.9**).

2. Click the Name down arrow and choose Adobe PDF.

3. Select the Print to file check box.

4. Click Properties at the top right of the dialog to open the Adobe PDF Document Properties dialog; click the Adobe PDF Settings tab.

5. Clear the "Rely on system fonts only; do not use document fonts" check box (**Figure 13.10**).

6. Click OK to close the dialog and return to the Print dialog; click OK to close the Print dialog and open the Print to file dialog.

7. Name the file and choose a folder location in which to store the printed file.

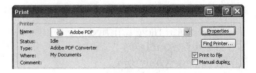

**Figure 13.9** Choose Print settings to print the document to a file instead of a printer.

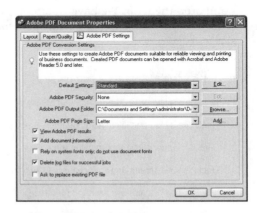

**Figure 13.10** Modify the options to be sure the fonts are sent to the printer.

You see the .prn extension is shown automatically in the Save as type field. The sample project's file is named sweet_nothings.prn.

8. Click OK to close the save dialog and convert the file.

**NOTE** The document is printed using the settings normally used by the selected printer. For a PRN file to function correctly in Acrobat Distiller, you have to choose the Adobe PDF printer option because it applies the PostScript print commands to the file. If you leave your default printer selected, it will create a PRN file, but Distiller won't be able to use it.

Whether you print a document to a file as a PRN file, or are using an EPS or PS file, you can convert to standards-compliant PDF using Acrobat Distiller.

# Using Acrobat Distiller

Acrobat Distiller 8 is a separate program installed as part of the Acrobat 8 installation process, and is listed in the program files. It is also available from within Acrobat 8 by choosing Advanced > Print Production > Acrobat Distiller.

Use Distiller for converting PostScript (PS) and Encapsulated PostScript (EPS) files to PDF. PS and EPS files are produced in a range of programs, including illustration and publishing programs. Distiller can also convert PRN files, the Windows-based version of a PostScript file generated by a specific group of print settings.

 **DOWNLOAD** the document printed to a file, **sweet_nothings.prn**, to practice the Distiller conversion process.

Follow these steps to select and convert a PRN file to PDF:

**1.** If it's not already open, launch Distiller by choosing Advanced > Print Production > Acrobat Distiller. It appears as a small window and has three menus (**Figure 13.11**).

**2.** Click the Default Settings down arrow and choose PDF/X-3:2002 from the list. Information about the conversion option is shown on the dialog.

**3.** Choose File > Open to display the Acrobat Distiller - Open PostScript File dialog. No files are listed in the upper part of the dialog.

**4.** Click the Files of type down arrow and choose All Files (*.*). Now you see the sweet_nothings.prn file is listed (**Figure 13.12**).

**5.** Click the file to select it, and then click Open to dismiss the dialog and return to Distiller.

**Figure 13.11** Acrobat Distiller 8 is a separate program from Acrobat.

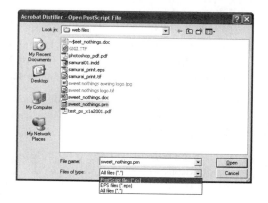

**Figure 13.12** To see the PRN file listed in the dialog, you need to change the default file type.

**6.** The file is processed, and the results are shown at the bottom of the Distiller dialog (**Figure 13.13**).

**7.** Close Distiller.

The file you have created is in compliance with the ISO standards for graphic content exchange, read more about the standards in the sidebar "What is Preflighting?"

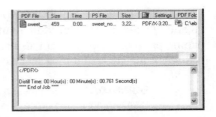

**Figure 13.13** The results of the file's processing are shown on the dialog.

# Preflighting the PDF File

Acrobat 8 Professional provides an extensive range of scans, evaluations, tests, and standards-compliance checks. Randy has an InDesign document he is ready to test to see if it complies with the PDF/X standard.

There are many errors that can occur if the standards aren't met—you'll receive an error if any of the criteria listed in the sidebar "What Is Preflighting?" aren't met, for example.

 **DOWNLOAD** You can download the original advertisement named **samurai.indd** from the book's Web site to convert it in InDesign using that program's PDF Export tools. Download **samurai.pdf** to use the Preflight tool in Acrobat .

## Preflighting the File

Follow these steps to preflight the document:

**1.** In Acrobat, choose Tools > Print Production > Show Print Production Toolbar. The toolbar opens in the program window (**Figure 13.14**).

**2.** Drag the toolbar to dock with the other toolbars in the program, or you can leave it floating in the program window.

**3.** Click the Preflight tool on the Print Production toolbar.

**Figure 13.14** Open the Print Production toolbar to easily access the tools.

## WHAT IS PREFLIGHTING?

Print standards have been developed over the last few years to solve problems related to printing documents and to set criteria for graphic content exchange. The standards, called PDF/X, come in several similar forms, but each is important for ensuring that a document contains only the appropriate features, fonts, and formatting for graphic content exchange. Preflight, or preflighting, is a process that inspects the document's content to ensure that it contains only valid content that complies with the standards.

Acrobat 8 Professional offers the Preflight tool to analyze documents for print production, including drafts of the PDF/X-4 standard, which should be approved in 2007. Preflight can also be used to evaluate other features of a document such as transparency (determining whether there are semitransparent objects in the document) and resolution (detecting the dots per inch—or dpi—of the document).

In addition to analyzing and reporting on a document's adherence to standards, the Preflighting process in Acrobat 8 Professional offers automated fixes and corrections based on preflight rules, and creation of new preflight profiles from imported Acrobat Distiller job option files.

There are criteria that all PDF/X-compliant documents require that Acrobat's Preflight process detects automatically. These criteria specify that:

- All fonts must be embedded in the source application. This means the information about the font is included in the document, ensuring that the fonts used in the output document matches those of the original document.

- Documents must use specific color spaces (methods of producing color). PDF/X-1a can use only CMYK and spot colors, or DeviceN color spaces. CMYK (Cyan-Magenta-Yellow-Black) color is used in four-color processing, like that seen in full-color books and magazines. Spot color refers to specific named colors, such as those found in color systems like PANTONE or FOCOLTONE. For instance, if you specify PANTONE 644C, you are specifying a particularly lovely shade of robin's egg blue. DeviceN color is an Adobe PostScript 3 color space that allows for specifying color components other than CMYK color. PDF/X-3 standards can also use RGB (Red-Green-Blue) color space using specific color profiles.

- Documents must contain information about the intended printing conditions. For instance, the PDF/X-1a:2001 standard defines an output-intent profile named U.S. Web Coated (SWOP).

- Bounding boxes, or coordinates that describe the location of the content in a document, must be specified.

The differences in the actual standards are based on the type of color used, the version of PostScript language each standard is based on, and what version of Acrobat is required to open the files. You can read about the various standards at the ISO Web site, www.iso.org, or at Adobe's Print Resource Center at http://studio.adobe.com/us/print/main.jsp.

4. The Preflight dialog opens, with the Profiles option automatically active; Acrobat loads the profiles from your hard drive, and you see them listed in the dialog. Profiles are created as part of the Acrobat 8 Professional installation process and are stored in the Acrobat installation files in your program files.

5. Scroll through the list of profiles and select the appropriate profile from the PDF/X compliance list—in Randy's project, the PDF/X-1a:2001 profile is required.

6. Read the description in the "Purpose of the selected Preflight profile" area of the dialog. The dialog reads, "Verifies whether the document is compliant with PDF/X-1a:2001" (**Figure 13.15**).

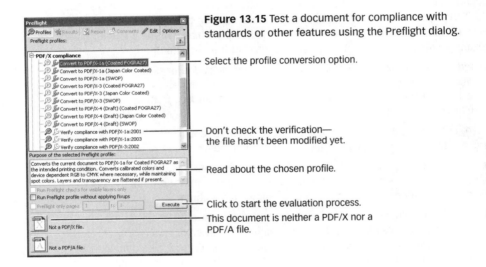

**Figure 13.15** Test a document for compliance with standards or other features using the Preflight dialog.

Select the profile conversion option.

Don't check the verification— the file hasn't been modified yet.

Read about the chosen profile.

Click to start the evaluation process.

This document is neither a PDF/X nor a PDF/A file.

7. Make sure the default setting "Run Preflight profile without applying fixups" is cleared. Acrobat Distiller 8 automatically tries to make your file comply with the standards.

8. Notice that at the lower-left of the dialog, the PDF/X status is shown as "Not a PDF/X file."

9. Click Execute. The Preflight: Profile contains fixups dialog opens, warning you the file may permanently change after the Preflight routine is finished. The only way to revert is to choose Edit > Undo. Click OK to close the warning and start the Preflight process.

Randy's file is processed and saved as samurai_X1a.pdf automatically.

> **NOTE** This section used a new sample advertisement. If you like, follow the steps using the **sweet_nothings.pdf** file to test its standards compliance. Be sure to note the two advertisements are designed to comply with slightly different standards.

# Checking the Results

The Preflight dialog shows the Results next and the Results option is active at the top of the dialog.

Read the results of the evaluation. You can click the (+) to the left of some of the headings to display further information in an expanded view (**Figure 13.16**). In Figure B.16, for example, the Overview information listing is shown expanded, and the (+) has become a (–).

Some of the content can be checked in a special view, following these steps:

1. Select "Show selected page object in Snap view" at the bottom of the Preflight dialog.

2. Scroll through the lists in the Preflight dialog to find the items you want to check, and select them in the dialog.

3. The selected object is shown in the Preflight: Snap View window (**Figure 13.17**).

4. Check out other items, and close the Preflight: Snap View window when you are finished.

**Figure 13.16** View the results in the Preflight dialog; the sections are collapsed into different topic areas.

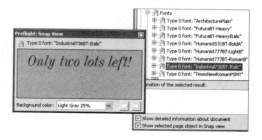

**Figure 13.17** Check out objects in the Snap View.

# Saving a Report

The Preflight results are displayed in the Preflight dialog and can be exported as a PDF document—it's handy to have a full document to read rather than a listing on a dialog, either for reference or if you have errors to correct. Randy decides to create a report document to use as a reference file.

 **DOWNLOAD** the original report named **samurai_X1a_report.pdf** to see Randy's Preflight report results.

Follow these steps to save a Preflight results file:

1. Click the Report icon 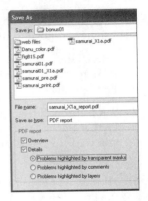 on the Preflight dialog to open a Save As dialog.

2. In the Save As dialog, name the report file. Or you can use the default name, which is the filename with "_report" appended to it. Randy saves his file with the default.

3. Click the Save as type down arrow and choose a format for the report. The default is PDF, which Randy uses. You can also choose a text or XML file.

4. Next, choose a storage location. The default storage location is the folder containing the original PDF document; choose an alternate storage location if you wish. For this project, use the default location because it's simpler to keep track of both the original document and the report if they are in the same folder.

5. Choose the options for information to include in the report at the bottom of the dialog (**Figure 13.18**). You can choose to include an overview as well as details of the report.

   Randy decides on both the overview and the details, which are the dialog's default selections. He also leaves the default display for the details, which is a transparent mask that displays on the document, highlighting any errors. Alternatively, he could choose to have the errors displayed as comments.

6. Click Save; the dialog closes, and the report document is saved and opens automatically in Acrobat.

7. Close the Preflight dialog.

**Figure 13.18** Choose the type of information you want to include in the report document and how you would like it to be displayed.

Randy checks out the file and closes it. The report contains the same list of information he scanned in the Preflight dialog, as well as a copy of the PDF advertisement. Not a bad way to keep track of things as he develops his customer information FAQ and checklists.

Randy is quite pleased with his efforts to streamline his workflow and inform his customers. He's also planning to check out some ways to save himself more time in his own work. His first task is to build a Droplet, a small program he creates through the Preflight dialog.

# Building a Preflight Droplet

A Preflight Droplet is a separate application you build from within Acrobat that is used to perform different Preflight tests. In effect, you create a separate mini program when you create a Droplet. You don't need to open Acrobat to preflight a file if you create a Droplet; instead all you need to do is drag the file to the Droplet's icon to automatically process and test the file using the Preflight settings you chose when you created the Droplet. A Preflight Droplet can be stored on the desktop or added to the Start menu in Windows.

 **DOWNLOAD** You can download Randy's Droplet file, **Weber01.exe** from the book's Web site.

Before creating a Droplet, add folders to your hard drive to use for storing the results of the Preflight Droplet's processing. Randy adds two folders to the desktop named "PDF File Pass" and "PDF File Fail" (**Figure 13.19**).

PDF File Pass    PDF File Fail

**Figure 13.19** Build folders to hold the processed documents before creating the Droplet.

> **TIP** It's simpler to create the folders before configuring the Droplet. When Randy creates the Droplet, he'll assign the PDF File Pass folder as the receiving folder when the Preflight test is correct and specify the PDF File Fail folder to receive a document that contains errors.

Any of the evaluation processes in Acrobat can be used as a Droplet. Randy plans to use the colored newspaper ad that he processes on a regular basis.

Follow these steps to construct the Preflight Droplet in Acrobat:

1. Choose Advanced > Print Production > Preflight from the menu, or click the Preflight tool ![icon] on the Print Production toolbar to open the Preflight dialog.

2. Click Options and choose Create Preflight Droplet from the menu to open the Preflight: Droplet Setup dialog.

3. Choose the profile you want from the "Run Preflight check using:"; if you have selected a profile before opening the dialog, it is automatically selected (**Figure 13.20**).

   Randy is using the Newspaper Ads profile preferred by his newspaper clients.

4. Select the On success check box and specify the options for a successful test. You can move, copy, or create an alias of the document in a specified folder—in this project, Randy chooses Copy PDF file to include a copy of the original file for reference.

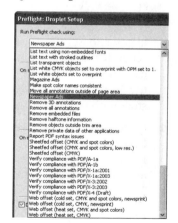

**Figure 13.20** First specify the type of Preflight check to run.

**5.** Click Settings to open the Preflight: Report Settings dialog. Define the format for the report generated by the Preflight process, how it should be structured, and its file format. (**Figure 13.21**).

Randy wants both an Overview and Detailed reports in a PDF file. He prefers to have problems identified using comments.

**6.** Click the Success folder button to open a Browse for Folder dialog and select the folder to store the successfully processed files in—in this case, the "PDF File Pass" folder Randy created earlier.

**7.** Click OK to close the dialog and return to the Preflight: Droplet Setup dialog. The chosen folder's name is now shown on the dialog (**Figure 13.22**).

**8.** Click the On error check box, and choose options for a test that generates errors. Again, you can move, copy, or create an alias, as well as generate reports (shown in Figure B.22).

Randy chooses the option to move the actual PDF folder to his error folder. He uses the same report settings, and selects the "PDF File Fail" folder created earlier to store problem files.

**9.** Click Save, and the Save Droplet as dialog opens. Choose a location to store the Droplet, and click Save to close the dialog and create the Droplet.

In Randy's project, the Droplet is stored on the desktop along with the two folders for convenience (**Figure 13.23**).

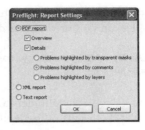

**Figure 13.21** Use the report settings that provide the type of information you need.

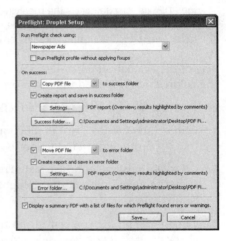

**Figure 13.22** Specify filing and reporting characteristics for evaluated PDF files.

**Figure 13.23** The Preflight Droplet displays its own icon on the desktop.

Now when a PDF document needs Preflight testing against the Newspaper Ads standard, all Randy has to do is drag it to the Preflight Droplet's icon on the desktop. Acrobat starts, the file is tested and then moved to its appropriate folder.

> **NOTE** Because Randy is working on a Windows computer, he could add the Preflight Droplet right to the system's Start menu rather than leaving it on the desktop. To do so, simply right-click the Droplet icon to open the shortcut menu and choose Pin to Start menu.

# Specifying Preflight Batch Sequences

Randy can make more Droplet files to evaluate individual files for compliance. Or, instead of testing one file at a time, he can run a batch sequence against the files.

The decision to use a batch sequence centers around efficiency: Is it worth the time to design and run a batch sequence when a Droplet does the same thing?

The short answer is Yes. In Randy's business files can arrive en masse, particularly close to a publication's deadline. Using a batch process lets multiple files be tested with far less interaction on his part.

> **NOTE** Read about batch sequences in depth in Chapter 7, "Assembling a Library."

## Creating the Batch Sequence

Randy's going to experiment with automating file evaluation and analysis for magazine ads.

Follow these steps to start the batch sequence design:

1. Choose Advanced > Document Processing > Batch Processing to open the Batch Sequences dialog.

2. Click New Sequence to open a field and type the name for the new sequence. Randy types magazine_ads and clicks OK to close the name field; the Edit Batch Sequence – newspaper_ads dialog opens.

3. Click Select Commands to open the Edit Sequence dialog.

4. Scroll down the list at the left of the dialog and select Preflight; click Add to move the command to the list at the right of the dialog (**Figure 13.24**).

**Figure 13.24** Select the commands to include in the batch sequence.

5. Double-click Preflight on the Edit Sequence dialog to open the Preflight: Batch Sequence Setup dialog.

6. The dialog is the same as the one Randy used earlier for the Droplet (**Figure 13.25**). In the batch sequence, Randy follows steps 3 to 8 as outlined in the section "Building a Preflight Droplet" with these changes:

   ■ The Magazine Ads profile is selected.

   ■ The Success folder is named magazine_ad Pass.

   ■ The Error folder is named magazine_ad Fail.

7. Click Save to close the Preflight:Batch Sequence Setup dialog and return to the Edit Sequence dialog.

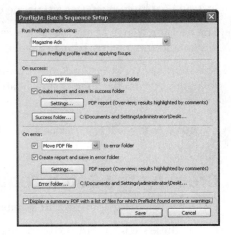

**Figure 13.25** Configure the Preflight settings for a magazine ad analysis.

**NOTE** Be sure the default command "Display a summary PDF with a list of files for which Preflight found errors or warnings" is selected. When the batch sequence is run, a single PDF file shows you the entire range of issues found in the batch of files, which is handy for Randy when he has a number of ads coming from the same customer.

**8.** Check the icon to the left of the Preflight listing on the Edit Sequence dialog. It should appear as a solid gray swatch with a gray border. If it contains a series of dots ▣ the process will stop for confirmations as the sequence is run.

Often confirmations and choosing settings manually are a good idea, but in Randy's case he wants the process as automated as possible. Click the icon to toggle off the interactive mode.

**9.** Click OK on the Edit Sequence dialog to close it, and return to the Edit Batch Sequence – magazine_ads dialog. The Preflight command is listed in the field at the top of the dialog (**Figure 13.26**).

**10.** Click the Run commands on down arrow and choose an option for when the process is run. Randy intends to use a folder to hold the files for processing, and chooses Selected Folder.

**11.** Click Browse to locate and select the folder. Randy selects his folder named magazine_batching.

You can specify that the batch sequence open other file types in addition to PDF files by clicking Source File Options and choosing file formats from the list. Randy intends to use PDF files.

**12.** Click the Select output location down arrow and choose Same Folder as Original(s).

**13.** Click Output Options to open a dialog (**Figure 13.27**). Randy intends to store the edited files in the same folder as the originals and chooses these settings:

- Add to Original Base Name(s).

- In the Insert Before field he types x-.

- Do not overwrite existing files.

- Save File(s) As: Adobe PDF Files.

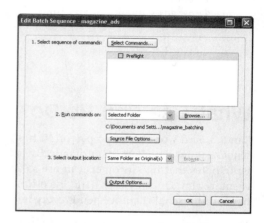

**Figure 13.26** Configure the settings for the batch sequence using the same dialog as that used for the Droplet.

**Figure 13.27** Specify the output options to apply to the files after processing.

**14.** Click OK to close the dialog, returning to the Edit Batch Sequence – magazine_ads dialog.

**15.** Click OK to close the dialog and return to the Batch Sequences dialog (**Figure 13.28**). Randy can select and run the magazine_ads sequence at any time.

Figure 13.28 Existing and new batch sequences are managed in the dialog.

# What Else Can He Do?

Randy's hard work is sure to pay off. It has taken him some time to create the batch sequences and Droplets to automatically process files for him. It's also taken time to write notes that his customers can use to check that their files are correct before sending them to him. On the other hand, he estimates that he's spent less time preparing his new print arsenal than he spends every month getting the customers' files in order.

There are other ideas he can look into in the future. For example, Randy might want to set up watched folders, a collection of folders that are stored on his hard drive or network that automatically check for and process files according to a specified schedule. Watched folders might come in handy if he hires the assistant he would like to have.

Randy may find it useful to develop a set of forms that his customers could access online to streamline their ad submissions. He could experiment with an online checklist developed from the ones created in the project.

Randy can also look at expanding his design service to include custom work for area businesses, such as annual reports and marketing materials. Producing higher end material requires a wider range of customer instruction and assistance, but if more basic printing is handled by his automated features and checklists, Randy may finally find the time.

# Index